# Epiphone
## The Complete History

by Walter Carter

Cover Image by Jimi Stratton

HAL•LEONARD

HAL•LEONARD™
CORPORATION

7777 W. BLUEMOUND RD. P.O. BOX 13819 MILWAUKEE, WI 53213

ISBN 0-7935-4203-0
10 9 8 7 6 5 4 3 2 1
First Edition

# Table of Contents

*Les Paul with his "Bread Wrapper" Epi, a Zephyr that he hot-rodded with his own electronics.*

# Introduction

Epiphone is one of the great names in the history of American guitars, but the Epiphone story—like the Epiphone name today—is global in scope. The roots of the Epiphone tree reach back to the Old World of the nineteenth century; its branches have touched centers of American guitar making in New York and Kalamazoo and stretched onward to the international manufacturing centers of the Pacific Rim; today the fruits of the Epi tree fall into the hands of more guitar players around the world than those of any other brand.

The Epiphone story is really many classic stories: a family story of an old-school patriarch and his modern-day progeny, an American cultural story of an immigrant family building a new life in the New World, an individual achievement story of one man's ability to foresee and capitalize on the twists and turns of American popular music, and a corporate story of survival and triumph in an unforeseen international arena.

History has provided Epiphone a convenient foil, a character that helps define Epiphone and put the company in perspective through most of the twentieth century. That character is the Gibson company. It has been a fascinating relationship, starting with Epi's first glories in the 1920s as one of America's most highly respected banjo makers (a field in which Gibson was an also-ran); followed by Epi's challenge of Gibson on Gibson's own turf in the thirties and forties, when Epi was Gibson's fiercest competitor as a maker of acoustic and electric archtop guitars; then Epi's unexpected decline in the years immediately following World War II, from which Epi was rescued, revived, and then, in the 1970s, almost destroyed by Gibson's parent company; and finally, in a new Gibson family, Epi's emergence in the 1990s as the industry leader in a modern global conception of manufacturing and marketing. e

*In its growth from family to American corporate world to international arena, the Epiphone name—more than any other name—represents the history of the guitar in the twentieth century.*

*G*ood musical instruments do not just happen.—*Epi Stathopoulo, 1928*

I had an old Casino, a Sheraton, a couple of solidbodies. I recently got an Emperor. On my new album I'm playing a Casino reissue. That's the only electric I use. It's a killer. It's a great guitar. If you turn a Casino up to 5 or 6 on a little amp, it feels like it's gonna jump out of your hands.—*Steve Earle, 1995*

Received the new guitar yesterday. It's wonderful. The neck is just the way I wanted it. All I can say is that you did it again.—*George Van Eps, 1940*

Just like there are guitar owners, as opposed to guitar players, there are other guitars, and then there are Epiphones.—*Jeff "Skunk" Baxter, 1995*

It's a beautiful guitar. I've used it for a long time and I think they're wonderful. That's what T-Bone Walker gave me.—*John Lee Hooker, 1995*

I believe that the Epiphone is the finest guitar on the market.—*Tony Mottola, 1934*

# BEGINNINGS

# The Stathopoulo Family

*The Stathopoulo family, circa 1912: Standing in the back, from left, are Alkminie, Epi, Orphie, and Alex. In front are Frixo, Anastasios, Elly, and Marianthe. (Courtesy Diane Cagianese)*

Parents:

**Anastasios Nicolas Stathopoulo** (1863–1915) and

**Marianthe Vomvas Stathopoulo** (1873–1923).

Children:

**Epaminondas "Epi" Anastasios**, 1893–1943.

Epi was named after a Greek military hero from Thebes, a city in central Greece. Epaminondas defeated an army from Sparta (ironically, Anastasios' home town) in 371 B.C., and as a result Thebes became the most powerful of all the Greek city-states.

**Alex (Al Stevens)**, 1895–1971.

With Alex, the Thebean theme continued among the Stathopoulo children. Like many Greeks he was probably named for Alexander the Great, the conqueror from Macedonia (now part of northern Greece) who destroyed the city of Thebes several decades after the death of Epaminondas. Alex Stathopoulo was never involved in the instrument business. Instead he became an actor who worked under the professional name of Al Stevens.

**Alkminie "Minnie" Stathopoulo Malamas**, 1897–1984.

Alcmene was a princess who caught the eye of Zeus, the most powerful of all the Greek gods. Their affair (Zeus had a wife, Hera) produced Heracles, who is better known by his Roman name of Hercules. Minnie Stathopoulo took over the bookkeeping duties for the family business after her mother died.

**Orpheus "Orphie,"** 1899–1973.

Orpheus was one the most talented musicians in mythology. When his wife Eurydice died from a snakebite, he used his music to charm Hades, god of the underworld, into letting him carry Eurydice back to the world of the living—on the condition that Orpheus not look back. He did look back, though, and Eurydice disappeared from his arms. Orphie Stathopoulo ascended to the presidency of Epiphone upon the death of his brother Epi.

**Frixo Nicolas**, 1905–1957.

Phrixus (or Phrixos) and his sister escaped from an abusive father (Athamas, King of Thessaly) and stepmother, riding on the back of a flying ram with golden fleece. The ram of the golden fleece would go on to greater fame with Jason and the Argonauts. Frixo Stathopoulo was treasurer of Epiphone and then vice president after Epi died, but he sold his interest to Orphie shortly thereafter.

**Elly Stathopoulo Retsas**, b. 1908.

Helle was Phrixos' sister. During their escape, Helle fell off the ram into the water at a spot named the Hellespont, which literally means Helle's bridge. Later named the Dardanelles, the Hellespont is the narrow stretch of water that joins the Aegean Sea with the Sea of Marmara, which leads to the Black Sea. In the Stathopoulo family, Elly and Frixo, being the youngest, were very close to each other. Elly's mother died when she was 15, and her older brothers did not want to take care of her, so they found a husband for her. Consequently she was never involved with Epiphone. **E**

*Epi was named after a Greek military hero from Thebes, a city in central Greece.*

# Anastasios Stathopoulos

**Above:**
Anastasios Stathopoulo in his workshop.

**Opposite Page:**
From 1907 to 1912 the Stathopoulo family lived and worked at 121 West 28th Street in Manhattan.
(Walter Carter)

The beginnings of Epiphone lie somewhere back in the second half of the 1800s, in a Greek family named Stathopoulos. Epaminondas "Epi" Stathopoulo, the man who named Epiphone instruments after himself, wrote in Epiphone catalogs of the 1930s that his father began the instrument-making tradition in the year 1873.

Epi also wrote, "For three generations my ancestors have been engaged exclusively in the production of stringed instruments." The third generation Epi mentioned would have been his grandfather Nicolas Stathopoulos. Nicolas grew up in the hills near Sparta in southern Greece. His granddaughter Elly (Epi's sister) recalled that Nicolas was a lumber merchant—a fortuitous profession in light of his son's

interest in building instruments. Whether Nicolas contributed some general knowledge of woodworking or specific knowledge of instrument making is unknown.

Nicolas' son Anastasios Nicolas Stathopoulos was born on February 15, 1863 (according to Anastasios' death certificate). Epi, Anastasios' oldest son, would later write, "My father Anastasios, who was a violin maker and luthier of note, started in business for himself in 1873 as a producer of fine fretted instruments." This was probably an exaggeration, since Anastasios would have been only 10 years old in 1873. Whether Nicolas began making instruments in 1873, whether the young Anastasios made his first attempt at an instrument or began helping his father, or whether the date was simply pulled out of the air by Epi, or by Anastasios for that matter, will probably never be known.

Although Anastasios' death certificate lists his birthplace as Smyrna, he was actually born in Sparta. His father moved the family to Smyrna, across the Aegean Sea in Turkey (Asia Minor), in 1877. Anastasios became quite successful as a maker of lutes, violins, and lioutos (traditional Greek instruments), and he established an instrument factory by 1890. With business booming he married Marianthe Vomvas, a native of Smyrna, and started a family. Their first child was a son, born in 1893, whom they named Epaminondas, after a Greek military hero. By the turn of the century they had three more children: Alex, born in 1895; Minnie, in 1897; and Orpheus, in 1899.

Greeks (and Armenians, too) in Turkey were persecuted by the Turks, and Anastasios decided to emigrate to America. According to Greek custom, the family also took three orphan girls with them, and these girls would work as the family's maids in America.

In 1903 the Stathopoulos family arrived in New York, where the "s" was eliminated from the end of their name. They took up residence in lower Manhattan, on Roosevelt Street (which no longer exists). There, and in a succession of locations in Manhattan, Anastasios set up shop on the ground floor, and the family lived above the shop. Marianthe kept the books for the business (her daughter Minnie would take over the bookkeeping after Marianthe's death on June 13, 1923), and sons Epi and Orphie helped in the shop. The labels on Anastasios' instruments identified him as "A. Stathopoulo, Manufacturer-repairer of all kinds of musical instruments." He held a patent on an "orpheum lyra," an American name for the Greek liouto.

In New York, Anastasios found not only a large Greek community, but also a country caught up in a mandolin craze. He was able to make a good living as a maker of fine fretted instruments. The children were well educated, and Elly recalls private tutors at the house, teaching Greek, French, and piano lessons.

The family moved several times. By 1907 they were at 121 West 28th Street. There, in the family living space above the business, their last child, Elly, was born in 1908. In 1912 the family and business moved to 252 West 42nd Street. Booming business demanded more space, and two years later they leased a warehouse across the street at 247 West 42nd.

Anastasios died on July 22, 1915, at the age of 52. His death certificate listed carcinoma of the breast as the cause. His oldest son had followed him in the trade of lutherie, and Epi would soon need all the luthier's skills of his father, plus a business head and a feel for what was happening in music, if the Stathopoulo name were to survive in the world of musical instruments. ◖

The House of Stathopoulo

**W**ith Anastasios gone, the "A. Stathopoulo" label no longer accurately described the maker of the instruments. To reflect the family involvement in the business, Epi began using the "House of Stathopoulo" brand in 1917.

Although the market for mandolins had remained strong and steady throughout Anastasios' life in America, it changed drastically shortly after his death. The ripples of change had begun as early as 1910 with the arrival of the tango dance craze from Argentina, and the ripples had grown into a wave by the end of World War I in 1918. Before the war, almost everybody played mandolin. After the war, the mandolin crowd turned to a new, louder, more raucous style of music called jazz. The mandolin suddenly seemed like a throwback to the past. Modern musicians set their mandolins aside and picked up the new "tango," or tenor banjo.

It was a tough time for companies that had been entrenched as mandolin makers. Gibson, which had opened its doors one year before Anastasios Stathopoulo arrived in America, was founded on the mandolin, and the change in public taste to banjo almost destroyed Gibson. Martin, the venerable guitar company founded in 1833, had bolstered its moderate guitar sales with mandolin sales and might have had a harder time after World War I had it not snagged another musical craze—Hawaiian music and ukuleles. Lyon & Healy, the biggest instrument maker of the late 1800s (established in Chicago in 1864), lost its clout in the early 1920s and was sold in 1927. The change in musical atmosphere had a crippling effect on these giants of the industry, and it should have destroyed a small family mandolin business in Manhattan, especially one that had just fallen into the lap of a 22-year-old.

Epi Stathopoulo was an accomplished luthier by the age of 22, but he had not spent all of his life cooped up in his father's shop. He had learned to play mandolin, and like other contemporary young musicians, he had kept up with the new music and switched to the tenor banjo when it became popular. He was well educated, having graduated from Columbia University in New York. And he was a man about town. His younger sister Elly recalled him dressing up in tails to go to shows and clubs. "They used to call him 'The Duke,'" Elly said.

........................................................................

*After the war, the mandolin crowd turned to a new, louder, more raucous style of music called jazz.*

Epi's vision was forward-looking, and he didn't think twice about clinging to the family tradition of making mandolins and ethnic Greek instruments. Banjo was the coming thing, and the House of Stathopoulo was in the banjo business from the very beginning. In 1917, the same year the new business name was inaugurated, Epi was granted his first patent. It was *not* related to the mandolin or the lyric orpheum, but to the banjo—for tone ring and rim construction. The course for the future was set.

In 1923 Epi organized the family business more formally, incorporating the House of Stathopoulo. Epi assumed the titles of president and general manager. All of Anastasios' children owned shares of company stock. By that time the business had moved again, to 68 West 39th Street in Manhattan.

*Left:*
*By the 1930s Epi seldom performed publicly, but in the twenties he played mandolin in a small group. (Courtesy Diane Cagianese)*

In the context of the Jazz Age, "House of Stathopoulo" was a stodgy, old-time name. It also had a hard-to-pronounce, ethnic sound. So Epi came up with a better name, combining his own nickname, *Epi*, with *phone*, which not only was derived from the Greek word for sound but also gave the instruments a direct association with the source of much of the new music: the phonograph. He further capitalized on the association with phonograph by naming his new line of banjos the Epiphone Recording series.

The Recording series, introduced in 1924, was a full line of professional-quality banjos. The four models featured names beginning with A, B, C, and D, with D, the De Luxe, the most expensive. Below the De Luxe were the Concert, Bandmaster, and Artist. The House of Stathopoulo also offered a budget-priced banjo, the Wonder, for $50, the Professional banjo-uke at $37.50, and the Wonder banjo-uke at $27.50.

The Recording series was well received, and within a year Epi was looking to expand production. He did it the easy way in 1925, by buying an existing banjo factory, the Favoran banjo company. Favoran was located on Wilbur Avenue (no longer in existence) in Long Island City, just across the river from Manhattan in Queens.

Although the House of Stathopoulo was an upstart in the banjo world, the Epiphone Recording banjos rivaled those of such established makers as Bacon, Lange (Paramount brand), and Vega-Fairbanks, who had been around since the heyday of the "classic" five-string banjo in the late 1800s. The Epiphone line was so successful that the name became better known than House of Stathopoulo. On January 1, 1928, when Epi reincorporated and recapitalized the company, he also renamed it the Epiphone Banjo Company.

1,248,196.

Patented Nov. 27, 1917.

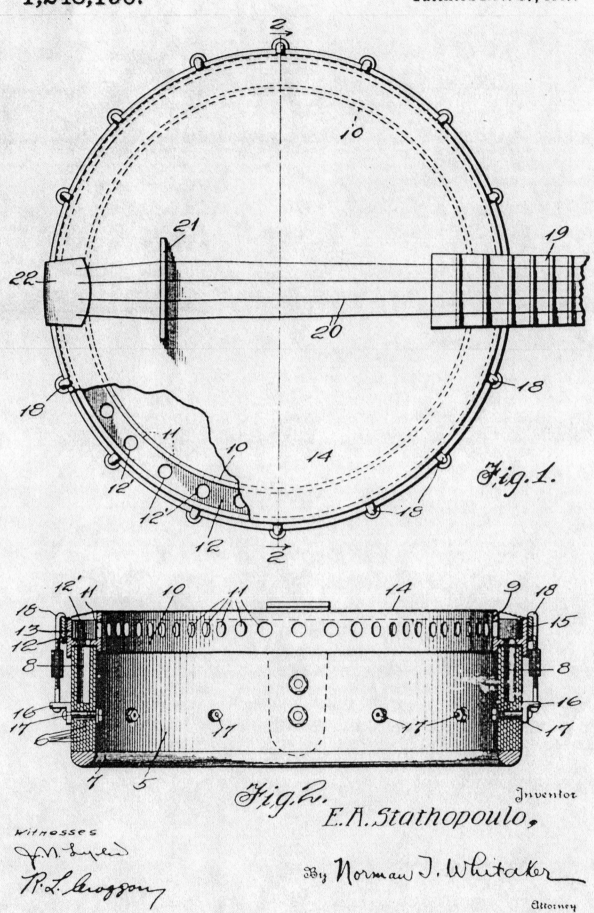

Fig.1.

Fig.2.

Inventor
E. A. Stathopoulo,
By Norman I. Whitaker
Attorney

Witnesses
J. M. Snyder
R. L. Grossory

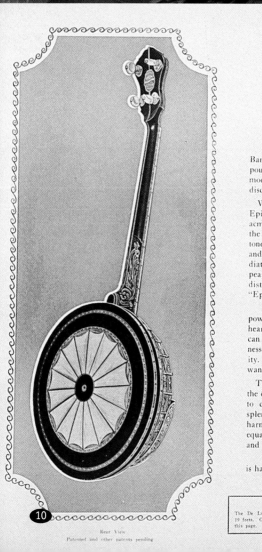

# Epiphone
## De Luxe

Interpreting the new era in Banjos. The House of Stathopoulo, Inc., presents a series of art models designed to appeal to the discriminating artist.

Without doubt the "De Luxe" Epiphone Recording Banjo is the acme of perfection. It embodies the highest type of construction, tone and appearance. Its radiant and flashing beauty attracts immediate attention. Its wondrous appearance and marvelous tone are distinctive and exclusive with the "Epiphone."

The tone is ideal — vibrant, powerful, far reaching. It can be heard above the orchestra, yet it can be toned down to a low sweetness—lilting and sonorous in quality. Power, yes, and when you want it.

The very rare materials used in the construction are so disposed as to create a composite of lavish splendor. Exquisitely beautiful, harmonious in design and without equal for beauty of tone, power and elegance of ornamentation.

The neck of Tamatave ebony is hand carved and beautifully in-

# Recording
## Art Model

laid. Peg head and ebony fingerboard inlaid with pearl and hand engraved.

The resonator in black is inlaid with genuine wood inlays of matched color.

The heavily gold plated metal parts are hand burnished and hand engraved, presenting a dazzling and scintillating appearance that attracts and compels attention.

*The pegs (Hercules 3 to 1) are equipped with pearl buttons.*

The De Luxe "Epiphone" Recording Banjo — an instrument of unparalleled beauty, tone, and appearance and supreme over all.

De Luxe Model in either the Tenor or Plectrum complete in Keratol Plush Lined Case

**$375.00 Complete**

In full grain genuine cowhide Koverite feature case, solid brass nickeled fittings

**$415.00 Complete**

*(Melody banjo, mandolin banjo and five string banjo on order only).*

THE TENOR MODEL.
The De Luxe Art Model Banjo with the standard 23-inch scale, 19 frets. Ornamentation and proportions exactly as pictured here on this page.

THE PLECTRUM MODEL.
The De Luxe Art Model is also made in the 4-string Plectrum style with standard 27-inch scale, 22 frets. Similar to banjos as illustrated, except for scale length.

Rear View
Patented and other patents pending

Front View
Patented and other patents pending

The original four Epiphone Recording series banjos were introduced in 1924. By 1928 the line had doubled. The 1928 catalog included a list of Epiphone players and their home bases, ranging from Carl Kress, soon to become one of the first great jazz guitarists and playing at that time with the Victor staff orchestra in New York, to Miss Billie Farley with the Hollywood Redheads, whose current location was "enroute"—i.e., on the road.

The catalog pointed out that this was not the ordinary endorsement list. "You will note a total absence of the usual stilted testimonial letters and endorsements," the catalog said. "That these artists are using—*have paid for* [italics added]—Epiphone Recording Banjos, (a fact most carefully verified) is the most eloquent and convincing testimonial that could be offered."

All the banjos pictured, and the majority of Epi Recording banjos actually produced, were the tenor style—with four strings tuned in fifths, pitched a fifth below the mandolin—that has come to be associated with early jazz or "Dixieland" music. Epiphone also made some "plectrum" models—with four strings but with a longer scale (string length) than the tenors, essentially a five-string banjo but without the short fifth string. Five-string banjos, mandolin-banjos (eight strings strung in pairs and tuned like a mandolin), and guitar-banjos were offered by special order only.

The catalog emphasized the Epiphone neck construction, which consisted of several wood laminates and a reinforcing rod of "surgical steel." (The adjustable truss rod had been invented by this time, but Gibson held the patent, and no other companies could use it until the patent ran out in 1936.) The neck-body joint was adjustable by means of two metal coordinator rods.

The catalog also offered the usual accessories, including Epiphone-brand strings, geared tuning pegs, picks of genuine tortoiseshell or "finest" celluloid, prestretched heads, and even electric lights to keep the banjo head dry.

Recording models started at $150 with the Artist, an attractive creation with a walnut resonator and neck. In addition to "Epiphone" and "Recording" on the peghead, it had the letter "A."

The original 1924 Recording line had gone straight through the alphabet from A to D, but by 1928 some new models had been slipped in between the letters. A second letter-A model, the Alhambra, came next, above the Artist. It was an eye-catching study in Pyralin, a trade name for the simulated mother-of-pearl plastic commonly known as pearloid. The peghead, fingerboard, and resonator were all covered with Pyralin. The fingerboard was further ornamented by tinted figures. The back of the neck showed five multicolored wood laminates. The metal parts were plated with silver. It was a stunning piece, with a list price of $200, but it was only the sixth highest-ornamented in the Recording line. There was still a great deal of ornamentation to come.

The Bandmaster, the B model, boasted a tortoiseshell shade of Pyralin (rather than the more common mother-of-pearl imitation) covering the resonator and back of the peghead. The fingerboard and peghead front were adorned by engraved pearl inlays. Colored wood marquetry was inlaid at the edges. The neck was of rosewood, an unusual wood for a neck, but highly figurative. All the metal parts were gold-plated. List price: $250.

The Concert presented, according to the catalog, "a wealth of contrasting colors." The

## Epiphone

*At the top of the line rested the Emperor, another name that would eventually become famous on an Epiphone guitar.*

fingerboard and peghead face were covered with Pyralin, which was then engraved and tinted with multicolored floral images. The neck heel was ornately carved. The tortoiseshell Pyralin covering the resonator was inlaid with multicolored wood marquetry in three rings and two straight lines. The metal parts—gold-plated, of course—were engraved with the floral motif, and the tuner buttons were of real mother-of-pearl. List price: $300.

The Concert Special, "a symphony in white and gold," had a resonator and neck of "the most beautiful of woods—white holly—without a mark of grain or color." Otherwise it was similar to the Concert, and priced the same: $300.

In contrast to the Concert Special, the De Luxe had a rich dark look, with an ebony neck and fingerboard. (The De Luxe name would go on to become to Epiphone guitars what the L-5 was to Gibson: the model that represented the pinnacle of craftsmanship and design.) The back of the resonator was covered with a wide outer ring of black Pyralin. The center of the resonator and the fret markers on the fingerboard were of gleaming white Pyralin, extensively engraved and tinted in a floral pattern. Price: $350.

The Dansant brought the precious metal hues of silver and gold to the Pyralin. The outer ring of the resonator was gold-flecked Pyralin, the center silver-flecked. Both rings were elaborately engraved and tinted, with an Epiphone crest in the center of the resonator. The fingerboard alternated tortoiseshell Pyralin with white pearloid Pyralin. It should go without saying that the neck heel was carved and the metal parts engraved and gold-plated. "This model is for the fine orchestral banjo player and soloist," the catalog said. Indeed, a player would have to be a fine player to afford the Dansant at a price of $425.

At the top of the line rested the Emperor, another name that would eventually become famous on an Epiphone guitar. In 1928, though, it was "Truly the Emperor of the banjo world," according to the catalog. The neck was of ebony—not just the Gaboon ebony of some of the other models, but African Tamatave—"polished by hand until the luster of the wood is like a gleaming black diamond." The neck featured nine laminates of multicolored wood. The peghead was bordered with rhinestones. The blue-white Pyralin covering the resonator featured the Epiphone crest, which the catalog claimed was "the guild mark of the builders of the Epiphone—carvers, engravers and artists whose master work is here represented." (The guild reference was ironic in light of union problems that would later plague Epiphone.) The fingerboard was covered in alternating black and white Pyralin. The metal parts were engraved and gold-plated, but that just doesn't adequately describe them. "The gold work is exquisite beyond belief," the catalog exclaimed. With case, the Emperor listed for $500.

Epi also offered some entry-level banjos, below the Recording series. The Mayfair, Rialto, and Peerless were priced at $50, $75, and $100, respectively, all with case. The budget models were distinguished from the Recording line by, among other things, their short 21" scale; the Recording models had a 23" scale.

With a complete line of banjos, ranging from basic no-frills to ornate "beyond belief," with an established respected name in the banjo world, and with the Jazz Age in full swing, the Epiphone Banjo Company seemed set for a long and prosperous run. But just as Epi Stathopoulo had seen the coming of the tenor banjo as early as 1917, by 1928 he was seeing the end of the banjo boom, and he had already taken steps to move Epiphone on to the instrument that would replace the banjo.

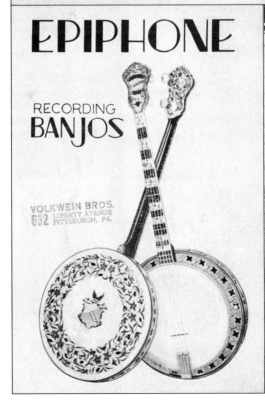

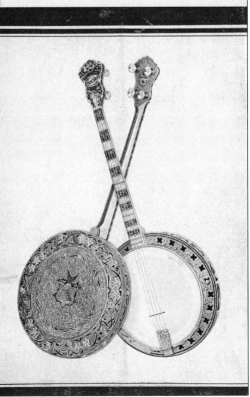

**Top:**
Epiphone Recording banjos were among the most respected in the industry, as illustrated on this page of the 1924 catalog.

**Bottom Left & Right:**
Front and back covers of the 1928 Epiphone Recording banjo catalog, featuring the new Emperor and Dansant.

# Recording Guitars

## THE NEW  GUITARS

*Recording*

REG. U.S. PAT OFF

---

**Special Features on ALL**

Back and sides of three-ply beautifully figured maple, cross grained for strength.

Top of close-grained, specially selected violin spruce, finished in natural color.

Violin blocking and lining.

Specially designed neck with three center strip veneers —dove-tailed into the body of the guitar.

**Epiphone Recording Guitars**

Standard professional 25-inch scale.

Extra wide frets of nickel silver.

Sunburst amber and red finish.

Banjo gear pegs.

Epiphone patented adjustable tension bridges.

Special Epiphone tailpieces.

### THE EPIPHONE MODEL E

*Recording*

### THE EPIPHONE MODEL C

*Recording*

Concert size $100
Auditorium $115

### THE EPIPHONE MODEL D

*Recording*

Concert size $125
Auditorium $140

Concert size $175      Auditorium $190

MODEL C is one that particularly appeals to the orchestra man. Top and back are carved and shaped. Fancy mother of pearl position marks decorate the genuine ebony fingerboard — slightly curved to make easier fingering. The neck is hand shaped — the edges of the fingerboard bound with white Pyralin. The well-shaped peg-head is engraved with a gold and black design. Patented Epiphone tension bridge and tailpiece—gear pegs. The tone is distinctive and has plenty of volume to meet any orchestral requirement.

THE hand-carved Stradivarius top—the exquisitely colored back and sides formed with violin artistry—the ebony fingerboard with inset position marks of pearl Pyralin, hand engraved and tinted—the exclusively designed finger rest of black Pyralin—the pearl Pyralin head plate upon which the variegated colors of the hand-engraved design sparkle—establish this model as unparalleled leader of modern master guitars.

Best quality gear pegs, gold plated and hand-engraved, equipped with gleaming genuine mother-of-pearl pegs; gold-plated Epiphone

A DE LUXE model Epiphone Recording Guitar. The top is deeply hand carved in a beautiful contour out of close-grained spruce. The back is beautifully shaped. The genuine ebony fingerboard is slightly rounded for easy playing and is bound on the edges with white Pyralin. Position marks of mother-of-pearl Pyralin, engraved in a pleasing design. Tone hole and edges are bound with Pyralin and bordered with an inlay of violin purfling. Special Epiphone finger rest. Finest gear pegs. Epiphone tailpiece and the new Epiphone self-adjusting tension bridge. The neck is beautifully shaped with large, engraved peg-head. This model is a revelation in guitar tone, and the appearance is strikingly beautiful.

*Epi's Recording guitars of 1928 were innovative, but not nearly as successful as the Masterbilt line that soon followed.*

The 1920s would go down in history as the Jazz Age, a decade of opulent good times. It was the era of speakeasies, flappers, and the Charleston, of red-hot bands playing the raucous new jazz music, of larger-than-life heroes like Babe Ruth, Jack Dempsey, and Charles Lindbergh. And banjos kept the beat of the times.

The minstrel banjo in the 1800s had had a run of popularity that lasted 50 years or more. The mandolin craze, which started in 1880, ran for 35 years before ending abruptly with World War I. The tenor banjo was such a vital part of the new music of the 1920s that tenor banjo makers might have reasonably expected 30 years or more of a booming market for banjos. The strong demand had spurred banjo makers into a flurry of innovations and ever-more-expensive ornamentation. But the stock market crash of 1929 put an end to all the excesses of the Jazz Age, including expensive tenor banjos.

The only banjo maker who had any vision of the future for stringed instruments was Epi Stathopoulo. Other East Coast companies, such as Bacon (whose B&D Silver Bells were Epi's main competition in the ultra-fancy arena), Paramount, and Vega had roots in the classic/minstrel banjo era and were run by longtime banjo people. Ludwig in Chicago was a drum company, owned by a drummer. Gibson in Kalamazoo, Michigan, was a mandolin and guitar company and had not even made its first banjo until 1918; in financial trouble in the early 1920s, Gibson elevated an accountant to general manager and then spent the rest of the decade frantically trying to catch up with other banjo makers. None of these companies paid more than passing attention to the public's changing musical tastes.

Epiphone was different. Epiphone was located in New York City, and its president was a musician and a gregarious socializer as well as an instrument maker. He was personally closer to what was happening in music than any of his major competitors. He had a crystal clear vision of the future. And the future was the guitar. Around 1928—at the height of the Jazz Age and the height of Epiphone's reputation as a banjo maker— Epi introduced an innovative line of five new guitars.

The Recording guitars were easily distinguished from those of any other maker by their odd body shape. They had a "cutaway" of sorts to allow easier access to the upper frets, but it was not the familiar scooped-out cutaway design that became popular in the second half of the twentieth century. Instead it was more like a bout-ectomy of the upper treble bout, looking like someone had simply lopped off that part of the guitar. Curiously, the Recording series flier did not tout this innovation. Instead, it extolled such virtues as a 25" "professional" scale length, an "adjustable tension" bridge (Gibson had patented a height-adjustable bridge), and three center veneers in the neck.

Like the banjos, the Recording guitars had alphabetical designations from A to E, but they had no full names like Dansant or Emperor. The lowest model, the A, had a flat top and back. The B had an arched back and flat top, and all the others had arched top

*Around 1928—at the height of the Jazz Age and the height of Epiphone's reputation as a banjo maker—Epi introduced an innovative line of five new guitars.*

and back. The tops were carved from solid spruce, in the style that Orville Gibson and the Gibson company had originated and popularized at the turn of the century.

The backs of the Recording guitars also had the violin-style curvature, as noted in the flier, but they were of three-ply laminated maple. The laminated construction gave the back added strength, and it allowed for more efficient use of highly figured maple. Years later, manufacturers would mention a laminated back in passing or in cryptic terms designed to disguise a cheaper manufacturing process, but Epiphone was proud of it. The three-ply back of highly figured maple was the very first feature listed in the flier.

All the Recording guitars featured a multicolored plastic-covered peghead with "Epiphone," "Recording," and the model letter engraved into the plastic. The upper models featured engraved and tinted Pyralin fingerboard ornamentation.

The guitar flier included another interesting innovation—the combination guitar and banjo case. This case held a banjo and a guitar—which fit into the lid—and it also had pockets for accessories and plenty of room for a stand. It was "not the least bit bulky or difficult to carry," according to the flier, but with the banjo about to go out and the Recording guitars not catching on, the all-encompassing case was doomed.

Although the idea behind the Epiphone Recording guitars—the belief that the guitar was the coming thing—was right on target, the execution and the timing were not right, and the Recording guitars went out with the Jazz Age. The next wave of Epiphone guitars, however, would rock the established guitar makers and lead a revolution in the fretted instrument industry. ◖

*Years later, manufacturers would mention a laminated back in passing or in cryptic terms, but Epiphone was proud of it.*

# THE EPI
# YEARS

The stock market crash of October 12, 1929, provides a convenient line of demarcation between the jazz banjo era and the guitar era, but the sounds of change—the sounds of the guitar—were already in the air by 1927. Jimmie Rodgers, who would become known as the Father of Country Music, made his recording debut with "The Soldier's Sweetheart" in 1927 and followed with "T for Texas" in 1928. The Carter Family, discovered at the same field recording session as Rodgers, debuted in 1928 with "Bury Me Under the Weeping Willow." Rodgers accompanied himself on guitar, filling in between vocal lines with single-note guitar runs; Maybelle Carter punctuated the Carter Family songs with a bass-string melody style that would set a new standard of guitar playing for generations to come.

In New York City, the dapper young president of the Epiphone Banjo Company might not have paid any attention to a couple of guitar-playing acts from this new genre of hillbilly music. But he could hardly have missed Nick Lucas on Broadway, singing the biggest song of 1929, "Tip Toe Through the Tulips." Lucas crooned his number onstage while he played a guitar, having long since abandoned the tenor banjo he had played in the early twenties. Another tenor banjo player by the name of Eddie Lang in Adrian Rollini's band had put down his banjo and begun making a name for himself as a guitarist. Fred Guy in Duke Ellington's band was holding forth on guitar in Harlem's famous Cotton Club. In 1928 Louis Armstrong's "Hotter Than That" featured not Johnny St. Cyr, his usual banjoist, but the great Lonnie Johnson on guitar.

The guitar was the coming thing, yes. Epi could see that. The catch was, Epiphone Recording guitars were *not* the coming thing.

None of these highly visible and influential players used an Epi. The reason should have been quickly obvious: Epi's guitars did not make enough noise. They were too small. With their curvy cutaway bout and intricate ornamentation they looked like delicate toys next to the big, workmanlike 16" Gibson L-4s that Lang and Guy wielded to cut through the blare of half a dozen brass instruments.

The guitar with the biggest punch (notwithstanding the super-loud sound of the National company's metalbody guitars, with their pie plate-like aluminum resonators) was Gibson's L-5, with a carved, arched top and violin-style *f*-holes. Gibson had brought the L-5 to market back in late 1922 as a member of a new line of mandolin-family instruments designed by the company's star engineer, Lloyd Loar. The Style 5 family was a commercial failure, contributing to Loar's resignation from the company in 1924. Gibson then focused its attention on banjos, seemingly unaware of what it had in the L-5. Even if someone at Gibson had been aware, the depression was so devastating to Gibson that the company probably wasn't in a financial position to capitalize on the L-5. In 1931 the L-5 was still Gibson's only *f*-hole archtop model.

Epi, as a major maker of fancy banjos, was certainly not immune to the tough economic times. After all, the depression had started in New York. But depression or no depression, if Epiphone were to survive, the company had to find a new identity as a guitar maker. With Gibson vulnerable, the time was right to strike, and Epi went for broke. (Sometime in the early thirties, according to Epi's sister Elly, and possibly at this point, Epi and Orphie strengthened their corporate power by asking Elly to sign her stock over to the company. She hesitated, but since the stock was not worth much at that time, she agreed.)

*Left:*
*The dapper Epi Stathopoulo was known to his friends as "The Duke."*
*(Courtesy Diane Cagianese)*

In June 1931 the Epiphone Banjo Company unveiled 12 new *f*-hole archtop guitars, a move designed to wrest the title of the world's leading archtop guitar maker away from Gibson. Epi even tried to usurp the name of Gibson's best models—the Master Model (Style 5) line of mandolins and guitars and the Mastertone banjos. Epi's models were called Masterbilt, and they said so right on the peghead. All had *f*-holes like Gibson's L-5, although Epi's *f*-holes were cut out in three segments rather than one continuous hole. The top Epi model, the De Luxe, was fancier and bigger (⅜" wider) than the Gibson. Where the L-5 had rectangular mother-of-pearl blocks on the fingerboard, the De Luxe had a more delicate, elegant pattern of hearts and diamonds. Where the L-5 had a small flowerpot as a peghead ornament, the De Luxe had two pearl banners engraved with "Epiphone" and "Masterbilt." Between the banners the model name was engraved. The peghead was topped off with a Gibson-type dip, but it was offset from the center, like a hat worn at a rakish angle.

The Epiphones even had classier names, like De Luxe, Broadway, Windsor, and Tudor, in contrast to Gibson's boring model nomenclature system: just the letter L followed by a number.

The introduction of the Masterbilts was intended to be a killing blow to a company that was already reeling from the depression. Gibson had practically shut down guitar production in 1931 and was staying alive by making wooden toys. But Gibson soon recovered enough to mount its own counterattack, and through the 1930s, these two heavyweights landed blow after blow on each other. But unlike boxers, they—and the guitar world along with them—rose to greater and greater heights as a result of the competition. ◖

*If Epiphone were to survive, the company had to find a new identity as a guitar maker.*

**Right:**
*Epi and his wife, Vickie, at the beach.*
*(Courtesy Diane Cagianese)*

# Masterbilt Guitars

*Just the word Masterbilt was its own piece of shrewd design.*

**Above:**
Lee Blair, with a left-handed Masterbilt De Luxe, during his stint with the Luis Russell Orchestra, 1934.
(Frank Driggs Collection)

**Opposite Page—
Top:**
Al Norris with the Jimmie Lunceford band in 1939, still playing his original Masterbilt De Luxe.
(Frank Driggs Collection)

**Center Left:**
Danny Barker accompanying Chippie Hill, circa 1946, still playing his 1934 De Luxe with "blossom" fingerboard inlay.
(Frank Driggs Collection)

**Center:**
Bobby McRae with a Masterbilt Broadway.
(Frank Driggs Collection)

**Bottom Left:**
Teddy Bunn leads the Spirits of Rhythm, circa 1934, with an original Masterbilt De Luxe.
(Frank Driggs Collection)

**Bottom Right:**
Bennie James, of the Blue Rhythm Band, poses in 1934 with his Masterbilt De Luxe.
(Frank Driggs Collection)

ust the word *Masterbilt* was its own piece of shrewd design. It sounded familiar yet it was new, and the unique spelling made it memorable. By using "Master," Epi capitalized on the familiarity and reputation of Gibson's Master Models and Mastertones. "Bilt" came from Epi's own marketing history. The first Epiphone banjo catalog, circa 1924, stated at the bottom of page 1: "Epiphone Recording Banjos are BUILT—not 'manufactured.'"

For the Masterbilt guitars, Epi departed from the ABCD nomenclature of the Recording series banjo and guitar lines. With the exception of the top model, the De Luxe, a new set of important-sounding names, though not necessarily all from the same context, graced the Masterbilt line. Some guitars carried a lofty British air with such names as Royal, Blackstone, Empire, and Bretton (notwithstanding that Bretons live in Brittany, in northwest France). The Olympic represented the pinnacle of the Stathopoulo family's Greek heritage. The Broadway represented the most famous and fantastic street of their new home town in America. And Zenith and Triumph simply meant "the tops."

Oddly, a guitar's name did not necessarily match its place in the line. The Zenith, for example, was closer to the bottom than the top. The Olympic was at the very bottom. Both the De Luxe and the Broadway triumphed over the Triumph. The tenor companion to the Broadway was the Bretton. But no matter. The point was that Gibson had only one guitar with ƒ-holes and an arched top. Counting tenor models (which had their own separate names), Epi could now boast nine.

The De Luxe was the original top-of-the-line Epiphone Recording Banjo, and it topped the Masterbilt guitar line, too. It was essentially a Gibson L-5—with a little

bit extra. It measured 16⅜" across the lower bout, which was just enough bigger than the Gibson to be noticeable. The back and sides were of maple and the top of spruce. The ƒ-hole shape was different—not continuous like the ƒ-hole on a violin or Gibson's L-5, but with scroll ends separated from the middle, dividing each ƒ into three segments or three actual holes. Rope-pattern purfling ran around the inner border of the top. Small heart and diamond shapes decorated the fingerboard, an elegant contrast to the huge rectangular pearl blocks on the L-5. The peghead was where the De Luxe strutted its best look. The front was overlaid with black plastic, with three inlaid mother-of-pearl banners, engraved (reading top to bottom) "Epiphone," "Deluxe," and "Masterbilt." Floral figures were inlaid between the banners. The appearance of binding was created by adding an underlayer of white plastic and then beveling the edges of the peghead so that the white layer was visible from the front of the guitar. The back of the neck had a shapely "volute," a violinlike feature, accentuated by binding. The top of the peghead had a most unusual dip, or notch, well to the right of center, that made the new Epiphone models instantly identifiable from a distance.

The Empire was essentially the same as the De Luxe except that it was a little smaller, 15½" wide, and was a tenor guitar—a four-stringed guitar tuned like a tenor banjo. Tenor guitars became popular in the late 1920s and early thirties as tenor banjo players looked for an easy way to switch to guitar. The Empire was the De Luxe's tenor companion, even though the names weren't related.

The Broadway was the same size as the De Luxe, but its back and sides were of walnut—an unusual choice of wood. Walnut had been Orville Gibson's choice of

# Epiphone

**Top:**
The Noble Sissle Orchestra, 1932, featuring Howard Hill on a new Epiphone Masterbilt De Luxe.
(Frank Driggs Collection)

**Center:**
Lee Blair, with Louis Armstrong's rhythm section (including Blair's former bandleader Luis Russell on piano), 1936, still playing his lefty Masterbilt De Luxe.
(Frank Driggs Collection)

**Bottom:**
Gene Brown's Epi Triumph leads the rhythm section of Floyd Ray's Harlem Dictators, circa 1935.
(Frank Driggs Collection)

**Opposite Page—**
**Top:**
Johnny Gomez, of the Emilio Caceres Swing Trio, 1937, with a De Luxe sporting what would become known as the "cloud" fingerboard inlay.
(Frank Driggs Collection)

**Bottom:**
1934 catalog.

wood when he made the first carved-top and carved-back mandolins and guitars, and the Gibson company's earliest offerings had been of walnut, but no high-quality guitars had been made of walnut in a quarter century. The Broadway had four-point stars for fingerboard inlay. It was not quite as deluxe as the De Luxe, but it still had the fancy Masterbilt peghead. The Bretton was the tenor companion to the Broadway, measuring ⅝" less across the body, but otherwise the same.

The Triumph, like the Broadway, had a walnut body. Small paired diamonds, like those of the old Recording C model, ornamented the fingerboard. Its tenor companion was the Hollywood.

The Royal was next, with a body width of 14¾" and back and sides of mahogany, which, like walnut, was not generally considered to be a suitable material for archtop guitars (except by Martin, which would make its archtop bodies just like its flat-tops, of mahogany and rosewood).

The Blackstone, also 14¾" wide, had back and sides of maple—curiously, the wood favored by Gibson for all archtop models and the wood used on Epi's top-of-the-line De Luxe. By this point in the lower part of the Masterbilt line, the fingerboard inlay was simple pearl dots.

The Zenith, even smaller than the Blackstone at 13⅝" wide, also had maple back and sides. The Melody, the Zenith's tenor companion, was not really the same guitar, having walnut back and sides.

The Olympic was the bottom of the new archtop line, 13" wide with mahogany back and sides. It did not have a Masterbilt peghead, or even a peghead logo.

It would be difficult to go below the Olympic, but the Beverly accomplished that feat with a flat top instead of a carved one. It still had *f*-holes. Like the Olympic, the Beverly was only 13" wide. It had no ornamentation whatsoever, not even body binding.

The 1931 Epiphone offering also included a pair of flat-top models and a family of mandolins, mandolas, and mandocellos. With the exception of the cheaper mandolins, Epiphone made very few flat-tops or instruments in the mandolin family in the 1930s.

Within three years, the line was changed and expanded. By 1934 the De Luxe sported the "vine" peghead inlay that would remain

**Top Left:**
*1936 catalog.*

**Top Right:**
*This four-in-one ad was the harbinger of a series of Epi ads featuring guitar stars of the late thirties and early forties.*

**Center Left & Right:**
*The Emperor's first catalog appearance, 1936.*

**Bottom Left:**
*Epiphone De Luxe from 1934 catalog, with "blossom" fingerboard inlay.*

**Bottom Right:**
*Carmen Mastren, later of the Tommy Dorsey band, plays a circa-1934 De Luxe with an early fan-shaped version of the "cloud" fingerboard inlay. (Frank Driggs Collection)*

**Opposite Page—**
**Top:**
*From the 1934 catalog.*

**Bottom:**
*Emperor and friend, on the back page of Down Beat magazine, September 1937.*

an Epi trademark through the rest of the century. The Tudor was added as a walnut guitar between the Broadway and Triumph. Then both the Tudor and Triumph switched from walnut to maple, the Royal from mahogany to walnut, the Blackstone from maple to mahogany (it also grew ¾" in width), and the Zenith from maple to walnut (it also grew, by 1⅛"). New additions were the Spartan, a maple guitar situated between the Royal and the Blackstone, and the Regent, a tenor version of the Royal.

Perhaps Epi had the foresight to know he'd need an ace in the hole in his battles of one-upmanship with Gibson. Despite the magnitude of the Masterbilt line, Epi still held something back. One had only to look at the old Recording series banjo line to see that the De Luxe was not the last word in Epi banjos. Nor would it the last word in Epi's archtop guitar line of the 1930s.

*One of the most memorable advertisements in the history of the guitar: Epi placed the guitar in the hands of a semi-nude woman.*

Gibson, on the road to recovery from the depression, shut down its toy-making operation in 1934 and launched a concerted counterattack on Epiphone by increasing the body width on all existing models and introducing a new super-sized 18"-wide archtop named the Super 400. Not to be outdone, Epi responded with an even larger model, 18⅜" wide. Where Gibson had again taken a rather simplistic approach to model nomenclature—naming the Super 400 after its relative size and its list price of $400 (a questionable ploy in hard times)—Epi went for a name that evoked a more opulent image than a pile of hard-earned cash. Epi had to look no

farther than the old Recording Banjo line to find a suitable name. He appropriated the name of his top banjo and christened his new guitar Emperor.

The Emperor debuted in 1935. To emphasize the Emperor's place in a class all its own, Epi came up with one of the most memorable advertisements in the history of the guitar. At the risk of diverting attention away from the product, Epi placed the guitar in the hands of a semi-nude woman. The photograph made such a strong impact on the industry that in 1937 *Down Beat*, the jazz magazine, ran it on the back cover—*not* as a paid ad, but as an item of interest to its readers. ◾

*I Cover the Water Front* . . . . . . .
Or Six G-Strings
Looking for "A Flat"

Latest fad for promoting interest in musical instruments is the hiring of first-class scenery for backgrounds. Biggest liability here is the background gets all the attention. Some piccolo or fife manufacturer ought to get hold of this idea.

ew York had been the home of many fretted instrument makers—C.F. Martin in the 1830s, a host of guitar makers in the parlor guitar era of the late 1800s, Dobson banjos in the classic banjo era—but the cities known as real centers in the various eras were places like Boston, Philadelphia, Kalamazoo, and Chicago. Finally, in the 1930s, the New York guitar community had its own shining star. He had a stylish waxed handlebar moustache and slicked-back hair parted in the middle. He went out on the town with his glamorous wife Vickie, a former "Ziegfeld girl," from the *Ziegfeld Follies* shows on Broadway. The guitars that bore his name were considered to be among the best in the world.

Despite Epi's personal presence in Manhattan, the company was still located in the borough of Queens, in the old Favoran factory in Long Island City. It wasn't very far from Manhattan—just a hop across the East River—but Epi's arch-rival Gibson had a strong presence in Manhattan in the form of its distributor, the New York Band Instrument Co., located in midtown Manhattan on 6th Avenue, around 46th and 47th Streets. Manhattan was Epi's home turf—he had been raised there, and the Epiphone brand had been born there. So in 1935, the same year the Emperor was introduced, he brought Epiphone back home, to 142 West 14th Street in downtown Manhattan. Also in 1935, Epi changed the official company name to reflect the changing times, from Epiphone Banjo Co. to simply Epiphone Inc.

Epi did more than just move the factory to Manhattan. He made his showroom a hangout for musicians. On Saturday afternoons in the late thirties, he and Orphie opened up the display cases and let players take their pick of instruments.

Epi's sister Elly had been married and uninvolved with the Epi company for over a decade, but she still stopped by the building on West 14th occasionally, and the experiences were memorable. "They used to come and play and people used to stand outside just to listen," she recalled.

*Epi made his showroom a hangout for musicians.*

"It was beautiful. They used to have Hawaiian people come in with the steel guitars. I have no thought of anything else but beautiful music, and I used to stay and listen to it."

Established players, like Harry Volpe, George Van Eps (with Ray Noble), Allen Hanlon (of the Red Norvo and Adrian Rollini bands), Frank Victor (also with Rollini), Zeb Julian (with Larry Clinton), and Teddy Bunn, would show up. New talents, like Tony Mottola and Al Caiola, were welcome, too. Occasionally someone would bring an upright bass or a wind instrument to join the jam.

Al Caiola would achieve fame as the staff guitarist for CBS and with hit singles in the 1960s of the themes from "Bonanza" and *The Magnificent Seven*. Tony Mottola would find fame with Frank Sinatra and a

40-year stint as NBC's staff guitarist. But in the 1930s they were just a couple of teenagers from Jersey. They had a band called the Blue Blazers, modeled after jazz guitar legend Django Reinhardt's band at the Hot Club in Paris, and they had their own show on WAAT in Jersey City. Both played Epiphones.

Caiola bought his first Epi in 1937. "I bought it right from the showroom," he recalled. "I picked it out. I tried it behind closed doors. They played a De Luxe, a couple of Broadways. I said, 'I'm gonna pick the third one.' I didn't know what I was looking at. I was just going by sound. That's the only way you're not influenced by what something looks like."

Surprisingly, the best-sounding guitar to Caiola's ear was not the De Luxe but one of the less-expensive Broadways. During his buying trip, he also learned of a regular Saturday afternoon jam session at the showroom. "A session would just start," he said, "just trying the guitars, just sitting around. I was a student. I would listen to Tony, and they all marveled at Tony's ability, and he was the young guy there among all the professionals already established. Tony hadn't joined CBS at that time."

The proprietors always seemed happy to have a showroom full of great musicians, Caiola recalled. "They were great people. I don't think they did any advertising. It was just a known place where the big boys would sit down behind a guitar.

"We at Epiphone were kind of partial and more or less felt that the Epiphone had a better orchestral sound, was a better cutting guitar. The Gibson was kind of a mellower-sounding guitar, a great accompanying guitar."

Mottola wasn't more than 15 years old—"just a kid on local radio," by his own description—when he started dropping by for Saturday jam sessions, but he was treated with as much respect as the star players. Epi put Mottola's photograph in the 1937 catalog over the caption "The Boy Wizard of Guitar."

"The thing I loved about the 14th Street factory," Mottola recalled, "you'd come into this place, the little showroom they had in the front. Epi and Orphie were great guys. We were young kids then. We hadn't made our mark yet. They were very nice to us. The thrill I got, we used to go into the showroom and there would be this galaxy of Broadway guitars and the De Luxe and later the Emperor."

Like his bandmate in the Blue Blazers, Mottola bought an Epiphone Broadway. He landed a job with George Hall's band. The Hall band had a small jazz group within the larger ensemble billed as Dolly Dawn (Hall's vocalist) and the Dawn Patrol, and it was with this group that Mottola played his first recorded solo—on his Epi Broadway—on a song called "Shine." He continued

playing the Broadway until 1938, when he joined forces with one of New York's best jazz players, Carl Kress (Mottola replaced Kress' former partner, Dick McDonough, who died in 1938). Kress was a Gibson man, and Mottola switched to a Gibson.

Another familiar face at the jams was that of Harry Volpe, a virtuoso who played everything from jazz to classical tunes. Fifteen years later Volpe would have his own Epiphone endorsement model. But in the thirties, Volpe said, "I didn't have an Epiphone then. I don't think I had any guitar. We played the guitars they had there."

Epi supplied the guitars. "We'd just go there to jam," Volpe said. "Epi used to do that for publicity. We'd all jam around there, all the great guitar players."

The only people who did not play, curiously, were Epi and Orphie. "I never saw a guitar in any one of their hands," Tony Mottola said. Nor did Harry Volpe: "I never heard him [Epi] play. He just was there. Had a nice moustache." 🎸

# Guitar Wars

Electric Musical Instruments

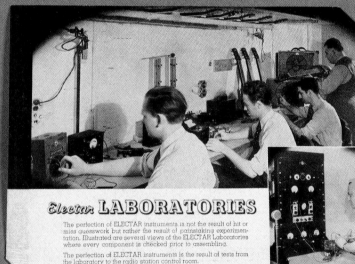

## Electar LABORATORIES

The perfection of ELECTAR instruments is not the result of hit or miss guesswork but rather the result of painstaking experimentation. Illustrated are several views of the ELECTAR Laboratories where every component is checked prior to assembling.

The perfection of ELECTAR instruments is the result of tests from the laboratory to the radio station control room.

TWO

espite the crushing depression that had ushered in the decade, the 1930s would be the most tumultuous, exciting, and innovative period in guitar development since the first six-string guitars emerged in Europe in the late 1700s. The guitar had become the most popular fretted instrument for the first time ever in America, and every guitar maker was fighting for a piece of this new territory, from the staid century-old Martin company in the East, with its new large-bodied acoustic flat-top guitars, to the brash upstart Rickenbacker company on the West Coast, with its revolutionary magnet-coil electric instruments. In the midst of these guitar wars of the thirties stood Epiphone and Gibson, each taking the other's best shot and coming back stronger.

Epi started the fight with the Masterbilts in 1931. Gibson countered with an expanded line, topped by the Super 400 and "advanced" body sizes, in 1934. Epi struck back in 1935 with the Emperor. And just for good measure, in July 1936 Epi one-upped Gibson's "advanced" models by increasing the size of the De Luxe, Broadway, and Triumph by a full inch so that once again they were ⅜" wider than the Gibsons.

In the meantime, the electric guitars that Rickenbacker had introduced in 1932 were beginning to find an audience, and Epi moved in mid-to-late 1935 to capture its share. As Epi had appropriated part of the Gibson Mastertone name to give the Masterbilt guitars an instantly familiar name, Epi played on a Rickenbacker name for his electric line. Rickenbackers had initially been marketed under the Electro brand; Epiphone's first electrics bore the brand name of Electraphone. Furthermore, Epi's pickups had the same horseshoe magnet shape as the Rickenbackers.

Whether the Electro String Instrument Co. (the official name of the company that made Rickenbackers) lodged a formal or even an informal complaint is unknown. Electro had already quit using "Electro" as a brand name; the peghead plates now said "Rickenbacher." (At the time the company used both this original spelling of the name, with the "h," and the anglicized version, with the "k.") In any case, Epi quickly discarded the Electraphone name but replaced it with one that was maybe even more ambiguous: Electar.

Electro/Rickenbacker may well have complained about Epiphone's similar-looking pickup—Epi was the only company that paid Rickenbacker a royalty on its pickup patent. (Electro had applied for a patent, but the approval process dragged on for so long that by the time the patent was granted the company felt it was useless to try to enforce it.) Epi changed its pickup style, but it may have been the result of innovation rather than infringement on a competitor's design.

Electro was a competitor, to be sure, but Epi's foremost competition would come from Gibson. The Electar line was announced in November 1935, just as Gibson was testing the waters with its first electric, a metalbody Hawaiian steel guitar. Although Rickenbacker's first offerings had been metal, metalbody guitars didn't fly under the Gibson banner, and Gibson replaced the model with a woodbody Hawaiian at the beginning of 1936. The Gibson pickup had a metal plate protruding from the coil upward toward the strings. The end of the plate was notched so that the three highest-pitched strings appeared to have individual polepieces. When Gibson put it on a standard guitar, there were initially no notches, but in later versions the area under the second string was

notched. Obviously the output was not always even across the entire pickup "bar" (to the player it looked like a bar rather than a plate).

Epiphone had a better idea. Epi salesman Herb Sunshine reasoned that if each string had its own adjustable pickup pole, then any problems resulting from uneven output could be solved by adjusting the polepieces up or down. The obvious choice for such a polepiece was a simple screw. So in 1937 Epi introduced a new, improved, and patent-applied-for "Master Pickup," easily identifiable by six large slot-head screws lined up under the strings. It was the first pickup with individually adjustable polepieces. It lacked the raw power of Rickenbacker's horseshoe or Gibson's bar, but power was not yet the primary issue in pickup construction. Proof of the correctness of this approach was not long in coming: Gibson ditched its bar pickup in 1939 for two new styles—both with screws for polepieces.

The first Epiphone Electar catalog, published in 1937, pictured an amplifier on the front cover and led off inside with an art deco Hawaiian guitar—a reflection of the style of music that first embraced the new electrics. Another Hawaiian lap steel and a doubleneck model endorsed by Tony Rocco of the Paul Whiteman Orchestra

preceded the single "Spanish neck," or standard electric model, in the catalog. An electric banjo, with a solid wood top, completed the Electar line.

Catalogs never showed it, but most of the Epi hollowbody electrics made prior to World War II had a large padded plate on the back that could be unscrewed and removed for easy access to the electronics. Although most musicians found it unnecessary to fiddle with the pickup and controls, it was that very feature that would bring an emerging guitar star named Les Paul into the Epi camp in the 1940s.

Epiphone electric guitars had another unusual feature: a metal plate noting that the instrument was made under license to Miessner Inventions, of Milburn, New Jersey. Miessner held several patents on electric keyboard instruments and claimed that all electric guitars utilized their patents. Epi complied with Miessner's licensing demands and listed 10 of Miessner's patent numbers on the metal plate attached to each instrument. Other makers fought Miessner, however, and Miessner's claims were eventually settled and dropped.

In a letter to dealers dated June 29, 1937, Epi reported that sales had doubled in the last year. The overall rise in popularity of the guitar undoubtedly contributed to the increase in sales. But part of Epi's success was based on its image as an innovative company, an image enhanced by the Master Pickup and a barrage of new features introduced in 1937, including the following:

- The Mastervoicer tone control, the catalog claimed, "enables the player to obtain a great variety of effects varying from a muted tone to that of the strident banjo with one turn of the knob." It was a basic tone

control system, for which Epiphone filed a patent application in 1937. Epi's efforts in this area led to the first "stacked" knob system, with tone and volume on a single shaft, officially introduced on the Zephyr De Luxe (an electrified De Luxe) on December 1, 1941.

- Epi's "thrust rod"—obviously a play on Gibson's truss rod—was, like Gibson's, an adjustable truss rod in the neck. But unlike Gibson's, which adjusted at the headstock end of the rod, Epi's adjustment was at the body end of the neck, and it did not require removal of a truss rod cover.

- The Frequensator tailpiece, one of the most identifiable pieces of Epiphone equipment, was essentially a two-piece version of the industry-standard "trapeze" tailpiece. The Frequensator gave the three bass strings a longer distance between bridge and string anchors than the three treble strings. The idea was to match the string lengths behind the bridge more closely to the string frequencies in order to enhance bass response from the bass strings and treble response from the treble strings. "Numerous tests were conducted with the oscillograph and at recording studios before this was perfected and adopted," the catalog said. The catalog also noted that the two "forks" of the trapeze were interchangeable, so that a player could reverse them to achieve more brilliant bass tone and deeper treble tone. The benefit was questionable, but the idea soon showed up in the "stairstep" tailpieces of Gretsch and D'Angelico and in the "harp" tailpieces of Guild.

The Rocco Tonexpressor may well have been the most advanced innovation of 1937. It was 30 years or more ahead of its time. Named after Anthony Rocco, a prominent Hawaiian guitarist whose Electar doubleneck model had just been introduced, the Tonexpressor was a variable pedal that controlled volume when pushed in the usual up-and-down motion. But it also rotated in a side-to-side motion to act as a tone control, making it a forerunner of the wah-wah pedals of the late sixties.

- The Resonoscope, another device that was years ahead of its time, was essentially an electronic tuner.

Gibson did not sit idly by during this period. L-5s and Super 400s started showing up with a gleaming natural finish.

Epi responded with natural-finish options on the Emperor and De Luxe in 1938. Two years later Epi devoted an entire catalog page "For Those Who Prefer Blondes." It featured three low-end acoustic archtops in natural finish. In addition, the top-of-the-line electric instruments—banjo and mandolin as well as guitars—were featured in blonde.

Gibson had, from its earliest years, helped promote publishers whose music was written for the type of instruments made by Gibson. In 1935, Gibson went a step farther and hired Julius Bellson, a musician from Minneapolis, to write instructional courses for the company to sell. Epiphone took the high road in its response to Gibson, offering guitar arrangements by George Van Eps, well-known guitarist with the Ray Noble band. The first three Van Eps pieces were "Squattin' at the Grotto," "Study in Eighths," and "Queerology."

*Opposite Page:*
*Freddie Green, of the Count Basie band, 1938, with an Emperor with separated V-block inlay. (Frank Driggs Collection)*

*Top Left:*
*Maurice and the Three Notes, with Maurice on a late-thirties De Luxe. (Frank Driggs Collection)*

*Top Right:*
*The Count Basie rhythm section, 1938, with Freddie Green, Jo Jones on drums, Walter Page on bass, and the Count on piano. (Frank Driggs Collection)*

*Bottom Left:*
*Lawrence Lucie on Epiphone Emperor, Billie Holiday on vocals for this Vocalian Records session, February 29, 1940. (Frank Driggs Collection)*

*Bottom Right:*
*Al Hendrickson plays an Emperor on this 1940 session with Artie Shaw's Gramercy Five. (Frank Driggs Collection)*

In 1939 Gibson introduced a major advance in Hawaiian guitar design: the Electraharp, with six pitch-changing pedals. Epi countered that same year with the Varichord, an electric Hawaiian with calibrated pitch-changing mechanisms mounted on the guitar itself, at the player's fingertips. The catalog called the Varichord "The Startling New Sensation." Chordal possibilities were virtually unlimited, the catalog said: "Just imagine an instrument of this type wherein the only chord not obtainable is 'The Lost Chord.'"

Also in 1939 Gibson introduced a family of violin instruments (the company had had violin connections as far back as the 1920s, when Gibson distributed violins made by the Virzi Brothers). Epi's father Anastasios had made violins, so Epi was not afraid of Gibson's challenge. He did, however, decide to let Gibson fight it out with established violin makers and to take on Gibson only in the upright bass arena. Epi introduced a line of basses in January 1941. Both companies' bass production would be curtailed by World War II, but Epiphone basses endured into the postwar period and would eventually be the attraction that prompted Gibson's parent company to buy Epiphone.

The one area where Epiphone made only a half-hearted attempt to compete was flat-top guitars. A full line of models was available, in Hawaiian as well as Spanish style, but in the glory years of the big band era, Epiphone focused on acoustic and electric archtops.

All the new models and accessories required a larger catalog, and in 1939 Epiphone put everything into an 8½"x11" format—larger than Epi's previous catalogs and, of course, larger than Gibson's. The 1941 version was 46 pages long and included nine acoustic archtops, four flat-

Ads from the Epi years. Bottom right:
Epi countered Gibson's natural finish with a new line of blondes.

tops, five mandolins (plus mandolas and mandocellos), five upright basses, eleven banjos (all of the models from the 1920s were still offered), four electric guitars, two electric banjos, two electric mandolins, six Hawaiian lap steels, three amplifiers, a microphone, stands, picks, steels, plus lots of prose about tunings, case construction, guitar construction, scale lengths, neck construction, the Frequensator tailpiece, electronics, etc.

The guitar wars pushed manufacturers to dizzying heights of innovation and expansion. The only force powerful enough to stop their progress was a real war. When the Japanese bombed Pearl Harbor on December 7, 1941, all of America—guitar makers included—dropped what they were doing and joined the war effort.

# FADING
# GLORY

*"Epiphone always made a good guitar."*—Les Paul

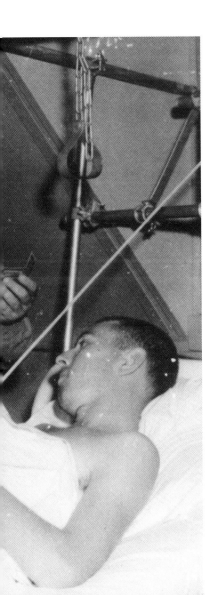

**Top Left:**
Al Casey plays an electrified De Luxe with the Bobby Hackett band at the Pied Piper club in New York, 1944. (Frank Driggs Collection)

**Bottom Left:**
Bill Flannigan, of Guy Lombardo's orchestra, with a blonde Emperor featuring the abalone and mother-of-pearl "wedge" inlay. (Frank Driggs Collection)

**Bottom Right:**
Al Caiola entertains soldiers with his Epi Triumph at a hospital in Espíritu Santo, in the New Hebrides, December 1944. (Courtesy Al Caiola)

**Top Right:**
Les Paul with his "Bread Wrapper" Epi, a Zephyr that he hot-rodded with his own electronics.

As World War II began, Epiphone had an impressive lineup of acoustic guitars, electric guitars, Hawaiian guitars, and upright basses. Even though the company curtailed guitar production to support the war effort, Epiphone guitars received coast-to-coast exposure, thanks to players like Al Caiola and Les Paul.

Caiola enlisted in the Marines in 1942 and took his Epi Broadway with him to Virginia and later to California. He sent the guitar back home when he went overseas, but even in the South Pacific he found an Epi to play. Back home after the war, he had John D'Angelico, the premier maker of archtop guitars, refinish the old Broadway. Then he sold it in 1946 and bought an Emperor.

That same year, Caiola landed a job as staff guitarist for the CBS network. Like many guitarists, he had already made the switch from acoustic to electric, adding a DeArmond pickup to his old acoustic Broadway and later to the Emperor. With the CBS job he became an official Epiphone amplifier endorser. The deal included a couple of free guitars and an amp.

Epiphone also enjoyed some free exposure from two of Les Paul's guitars, although a guitarist could not buy an Epi—or any other brand of guitar, for that matter—and get the same equipment Paul used. Paul typically built his own pickups and was constantly tinkering with the electronics in his guitars.

Les Paul was one of the earliest proponents of the solidbody electric guitar, and in 1941 he built one using a 4"x4" piece of pine. Epi let

# Epiphone

**Top:**
Nappy Lamare, of the Bob Crosby band,
appears to be beyond happy with his blonde
Emperor, 1943.
(Frank Driggs Collection)

**Center:**
Nappy Lamare's Emperor drives the rhythm
section behind Peggy Lee as she records
"Sugar" and "Ain't Goin' No Place" for
Capitol Records in Los Angeles,
January 7, 1944.
(Frank Driggs Collection)

**Bottom:**
Andy Nelson (right), future Epiphone sales
representative, with a Triumph.
(Courtesy Andy Nelson)

**Opposite Page:**
Jim Daddy Walker, an early influence on jazz
legend Charlie Christian, 1944, with a
Triumph fitted with a DeArmond pickup.
(Frank Driggs Collection)

him use the Epiphone factory as a workshop, and Paul fastened the body sides of an Epi archtop to his pine centerpiece. The neck was also a stock Epiphone neck, although Paul used a fingerboard made by the Chicago-based Larson Brothers. The Log, as the instrument was nicknamed, attracted a great deal of attention wherever Paul played it over the next 10 years, in New York, Chicago, and Los Angeles. (In the early fifties, when Paul signed an endorsement agreement with Gibson, Gibson put a new veneer with a Gibson logo on the headstock of The Log.)

*Epi let Les Paul use the Epiphone factory as a workshop to build the solidbody guitar nicknamed The Log.*

Paul's other working guitar during the 1940s was a 1941 Epiphone Zephyr, although he more often referred to it as "The Clunker" or "The Bread Wrapper Guitar." He tells the story of how he acquired it: "I had left Fred Waring in 1941 and I was on my way to go with Bing Crosby on the West Coast, and I stopped off in Chicago and was offered a very very fine job that slowed me down in my quest of going to the Coast. I took a job as musical director in Chicago and in doing that I got a phone call from a fellow that said to me, 'Les,' he says, 'I got my hand caught in a bread wrapping machine and it's all mangled up and I cannot play a guitar anymore and I had this guitar and I'd like to give it to you.' I said, 'Well, what is it?' He said, 'It's an Epiphone.' I said, 'As much as I appreciate your offer, I have a Gibson.'

He said, 'I'm gonna give it to you.' I said, 'What kind is it?' He told me which one it was. I said, 'I kind of like that guitar because it's got a big trap door in the back of it and you can get in and work on the electronics.'

"Epiphone always made a good guitar," Paul continues. "I remember giving him $125 or something, and I thought this would be a good one to saw up rather than sawing up my nice Gibson, and I could mutilate, do hysterectomies on this one. I did my experimenting on this one; I was

deep into Epi and I used their factory to make The Log. I was very well acquainted with what Epi was doing. When I got the Epiphone, what I finally got in my experimenting was an extension of The Log. It was to lighten up on The Log. I fooled around with it and finally I got a sound out of that guitar that was the sound I'd absolutely dreamt of." ⬦

# End of the Epi Era

For most companies, and most Americans for that matter, America's entry into World War II meant that everyday life would be suspended, and when the war ended everything would return to normal. For Epiphone nothing could have been farther from the truth.

Epiphone had suspended guitar production to make aileron parts for aircraft. But the company emerged from the war with a different face, literally, from its prewar persona. Epi—the man whose name was on every guitar the company made—had died during the war, on June 6, 1943, and his passing turned out to be the first death knell for the company. The cause of death was pernicious anemia, a condition better known today as leukemia.

Other family-owned companies—Martin and Gretsch in particular—had survived and thrived after the unexpected deaths of their leaders. Epiphone, even without Epi, would seem to have been in the capable hands of two brothers who had grown up in the business. Orphie Stathopoulo's specialty was the financial end, and younger brother Frixo had developed a capable engineering and mechanical aptitude. The brand name was well known and very highly respected. But, as Epi's sister Elly so succinctly summed it up, "Epi was the brains."

From the outside, it looked like everything was just fine at Epiphone. Orphie was now president, Frixo vice president and still treasurer. Guitarists continued to play Epiphone guitars, and when World War II ended in 1945, Epiphone renewed its battles with Gibson. One of Gibson's prewar moves had been to introduce "cutaway" bodies, scooping out the upper treble bout to give the player easier access to the higher frets. Epi caught up after the war, offering the Emperor and De Luxe in cutaway versions in 1948.

In the electric arena, Epi jumped a step ahead of Gibson in 1941 with an electric version of a high-end archtop, the Zephyr De Luxe. Shortly after the cutaway version of the De Luxe was introduced, it too was electrified (by 1949). Gibson had been improving the look and sound of its electric line, but it was 1949 before Gibson introduced an electric with the high-end trim of the L-5, called the ES-5 (ES for Electric Spanish), and 1951 before true electric versions of Gibson's L-5 cutaway and Super 400 cutaway appeared.

On the marketing side, Epi showed more imagination. The electric cutaway De Luxe had the grandiose name of Zephyr De Luxe Regent. Although the Zephyr had been a separate model, the company appropriated the term "Zephyr" to mean an electric model. "Regent" denoted a cutaway. Thus when an electric cutaway version of the Emperor appeared in 1952, it was dubbed the Zephyr Emperor Regent. The Gibson electric L-5 and Super 400, by comparison, had what sounded more like a model code than a real name: L-5CES and Super 400CES, respectively, with CES standing for Cutaway Electric Spanish.

Both companies had been busy refining pickups and electronic designs. Herb Sunshine's prewar pickups, with large screw poles extending out of an oval coil, had a decidedly homemade look—as if the maker had used whatever spare screws he might have found in his toolbox. Epi's postwar pickups had metal covers—gold-plated metal—and six small gold-plated screws. In response to Gibson's three-pickup ES-5, Epiphone put three pickups on the Emperor, and where the ES-5 had only three volume controls and one master tone control, the Zephyr Emperor Regent sported a tone control system operated by six push-buttons in addition to tone and volume knobs.

*Jimmy Vivino, guitarist with Conan O'Brien's house band on "Late Night," with his early-fifties Emperor. (Anthony Stroppa)*

With hot competition spurring one innovation after another, the postwar era was shaping up to be as exciting and successful as the years just before the war. But something was wrong. It may be reading too much into an insignificant change, but guitarists with an eye for quality could not have helped but notice something different about the Zephyr Deluxe Regent (and not just the change in the spelling of De Luxe). The model that had topped the original Masterbilt line in 1931, the showcase of Epi quality, the model that had gone toe-to-toe with Gibson's legendary L-5, was now a plywood guitar. The top still looked like a high-quality carved spruce top, but it was laminated. A laminated top certainly didn't affect the sound (the greater strength could actually improve the sound by lessening feedback), but when Gibson came out with the L-5CES, buyers got the whole L-5C, including the solid carved top. The Epiphone Zephyr Deluxe Regent, on the other hand, was a laminated pretender, not quite all that the acoustic Deluxe was.

While Epi continued on the course it had set in the prewar years, the guitar market changed courses. The postwar crowd did not pick back up on the Hawaiian guitar craze. Popular music was about to go through a revolution that would elevate the guitar higher than anyone had ever imagined, but *not* the kind of jazz guitar that Epiphone made. To make matters worse, the union was knocking at Epi's door, trying to organize the work force.

Epi's chief competitor, Gibson, was not immune to the forces that threatened Epiphone. Gibson had been unionized during the war and, top-heavy with managers, had been losing money ever since the war had ended. But the giant Chicago Musical Instrument Co. had bought Gibson in 1944, and CMI could absorb Gibson's losses until a new general manager could be brought in and the company turned around.

In the corporate boardroom at Epiphone, Orphie and Frixo were not getting along. Frixo held the title of vice president, but Orphie had taken away most of Frixo's power and given it to George Mann, the sales manager. In 1948 a frustrated Frixo resigned and sold his interest to Orphie. Orphie had to borrow the buyout money, possibly as much as $10,000, from his wife, the former Anna Rende, whose father was the publisher of *Il Progresso*, the prominent Italian-language newspaper. With Frixo's departure, Anna Rende Stathopoulo gained a vested interest in Epiphone, and George Mann was installed as vice president.

Frixo relocated to Gloucester, Ohio, where his wife's family lived, with the intention of manufacturing upright basses. He bought a house and set up a production area in a barn. He stayed in close touch with his niece Diane (daughter of his sister Elly) and her husband, Dom Cagianese, from whom he

soon had to borrow money. In a letter to Cagianese, Frixo pointed out an unexpected obstacle to his plans. "First of all I cannot produce any more string basses because the firm that specializes in the production of fine spruce veneer in large widths and lengths has repeatedly refused to sell me," Frixo wrote. "Their excuses have been that they are out of logs suitable for this purpose. I have tried other companies and the result is the same. As for the original company I have been contacting without success, has been shipping steadily to the same veneer to Epiphone, Kay Musical Inst., King Band Inst. etc. Readily you can understand, someone is making it tough for me."

Frixo had another idea—Frixotone ukuleles and guitars. Arthur Godfrey had become a TV star, and his baritone ukulele had revived interest in ukes. Frixo drew up plans for two ukuleles—one a traditional flat-top design and one an archtop that would be "the same as an expensive miniature guitar," he wrote. He had set up production equipment to build from 40 to 100 a day and hoped to grow into producing guitars at a retail price of $35–$45. "I would be able to manufacture them the same way as the Ukulele and make a damn good profit," he wrote. "The method of fabrication is such that I am sure the other companies would give their eye teeth to find out." Frixo sent a uke to Dom and Diane Cagianese, but their young son Robert, who would grow up to be a professional guitarist, accidentally broke the instrument beyond repair.

Stymied in Ohio, Frixo returned to New York in 1951 to a home in Astoria, in Queens, near Long Island City. According to an account written by Dom Cagianese, Frixo "started to mend his fences with Orphie. This mending process was a painful and long one that, although Frixo finally agreed with Orphie to restart the Epiphone Company in late 1956

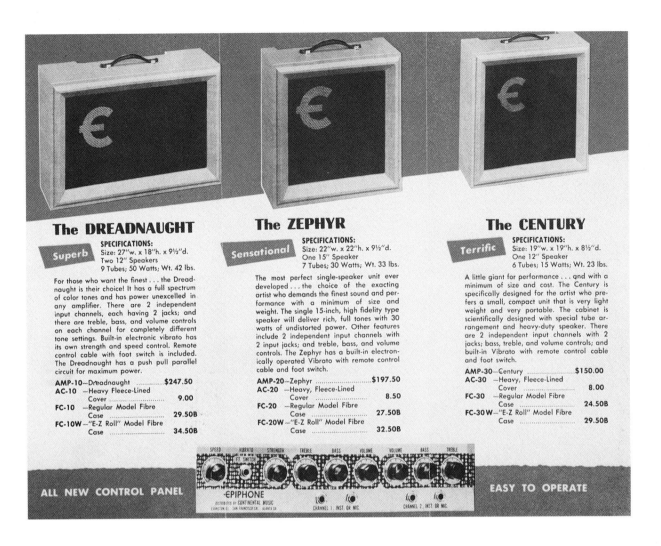

## The DREADNAUGHT

**Superb**

**SPECIFICATIONS:**
Size: 27"w. x 18"h. x 9½"d.
Two 12" Speakers
9 Tubes; 50 Watts; Wt. 42 lbs.

For those who want the finest . . . the Dreadnaught is their choice! It has a full spectrum of color tones and has power unexcelled in any amplifier. There are 2 independent input channels, each having 2 jacks; and there are treble, bass, and volume controls on each channel for completely different tone settings. Built-in electronic vibrato has its own strength and speed control. Remote control cable with foot switch is included. The Dreadnaught has a push pull parallel circuit for maximum power.

AMP-10—Dreadnaught ............$247.50
AC-10 —Heavy Fleece-Lined
    Cover ........................... 9.00
FC-10 —Regular Model Fibre
    Case ........................... 29.50B
FC-10W—"E-Z Roll" Model Fibre
    Case ........................... 34.50B

## The ZEPHYR

**Sensational**

**SPECIFICATIONS:**
Size: 22"w. x 22"h. x 9½"d.
One 15" Speaker
7 Tubes; 30 Watts; Wt. 33 lbs.

The most perfect single-speaker unit ever developed . . . the choice of the exacting artist who demands the finest sound and performance with a minimum of size and weight. The single 15-inch, high fidelity type speaker will deliver rich, full tones with 30 watts of undistorted power. Other features include 2 independent input channels with 2 input jacks; and treble, bass, and volume controls. The Zephyr has a built-in electronically operated Vibrato with remote control cable and foot switch.

AMP-20—Zephyr .....................$197.50
AC-20 —Heavy, Fleece-Lined
    Cover ........................... 8.50
FC-20 —Regular Model Fibre
    Case ........................... 27.50B
FC-20W—"E-Z Roll" Model Fibre
    Case ........................... 32.50B

## The CENTURY

**Terrific**

**SPECIFICATIONS:**
Size: 19"w. x 19"h. x 8½"d.
One 12" Speaker
6 Tubes; 15 Watts; Wt. 23 lbs.

A little giant for performance . . . and with a minimum of size and cost. The Century is specifically designed for the artist who prefers a small, compact unit that is very light weight and very portable. The cabinet is scientifically designed with special tube arrangement and heavy-duty speaker. There are 2 independent input channels with 2 jacks; bass, treble, and volume controls; and built-in Vibrato with remote control cable and foot switch.

AMP-30—Century .....................$150.00
AC-30 —Heavy, Fleece-Lined
    Cover ........................... 8.00
FC-30 —Regular Model Fibre
    Case ........................... 24.50B
FC-30W—"E-Z Roll" Model Fibre
    Case ........................... 29.50B

**ALL NEW CONTROL PANEL**　　　　**EASY TO OPERATE**

and early 1957, came too late." Frixo died in 1957 at the age of 52.

Back when Frixo left Epiphone, Orphie looked for help from the C.G. Conn company. Conn, based in Elkhart, Indiana, was a band instrument company, but its distribution arm, Continental, handled a full line of instruments. Conn's relationship with Epiphone went back to the 1920s, when Continental distributed Epiphone Recording banjos. Orphie granted distribution rights in some territories to Continental, and also some degree of control, although the exact financial arrangement is not known. Orphie did retain ownership of Epiphone.

The mounting pressure to unionize prompted Continental to move manufacturing from Manhattan to Philadelphia in 1953. Many of Epi's craftsmen refused to move, and they formed the backbone of the newly formed Guild company in New York. Conn was unable to help, according to John Stoltzfus, whose father managed the Philadelphia plant. "They were a brass manufacturer," Stoltzfus says. "They didn't know what to do with guitars, and as a result there were warehouses full of them. Guitars were coming out of cases with fuzz on them. They weren't moving it. They were storing the stuff in the wrong places. They were having a lot of trouble."

The few skilled craftsmen in the Philadelphia plant referred to the less-skilled workers as "butchers," Stoltzfus remembers, and to the guitars they made as "chair seats." Without its work force of skilled craftsmen, and without a dynamic personality in the leadership position, Epiphone was fast becoming a ghost of company. **€**

*Top:*
*Amplifiers in the Conn years, circa 1954.*

*Bottom:*
*C.G. Conn's Epiphone catalog, 1954.*

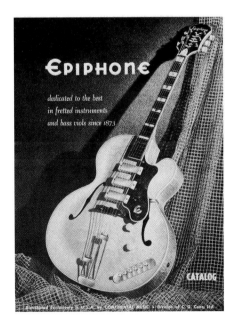

# The Harry Volpe Model

**Above:**
*Harry Volpe poses with the top model of the 1950s line, the Zephyr Emperor Regent.
(Courtesy Harry Volpe)*

**Below:**
*Harry Volpe (left), on a Zephyr Emperor Regent, swaps licks with Roy "Wizard of the Strings" Smeck at a 1954 convention.
(Courtesy Harry Volpe)*

**Opposite Page—
Top:**
*Harry Volpe leads his own trio with one of the rarest Epiphones of the early 1950s, a cutaway De Luxe flat-top.
(Courtesy Harry Volpe)*

**Bottom:**
*Harry Volpe, still playing the cutaway De Luxe flat-top with his trio of strolling musicians at Miami's Eden Roc hotel.
(Courtesy Harry Volpe)*

*E*piphone's last grasp at survival was the Harry Volpe model of 1955, a model that underscored Epiphone's need for quick sales.

In the 1990s, with the Epi name closely associated with such artists as Howard Roberts, Al Caiola, and Joe Pass, and the guitar industry permeated by such names as Les Paul, Chet Atkins, and B.B. King, an endorsement model seems like standard procedure, an obvious promotional move. But in 1954, it was a radical move. Epi had never had an artist's name on a standard guitar (the only endorsement model had been Tony Rocco's short-lived electric Hawaiian). But competition was heated enough in the early fifties to prompt Gibson to sign up Les Paul, Gibson's first endorser since Roy Smeck in the mid thirties, to make a big splash with a new model.

Epiphone's new endorser was a "New York plectrostylist," as a 1953 *New York Times* concert review once described him, a virtuoso guitarist whose repertoire ran from Rachmaninoff's "Prelude in C Minor" to pop and jazz tunes. Harry Volpe had been a star endorser for Gretsch, having scored a coup by putting a Gretsch guitar into the hands of French guitar legend Django Reinhardt. A photograph of the two musicians had been widely circulated in industry publications.

Ironically, it would seem, Epiphone's Harry Volpe model was not a virtuoso's guitar but a student model, an inexpensive beginner's guitar. It made good business sense, however. The lowest-priced models are often the biggest sellers, and Epi needed

*Harry Volpe, playing a cutaway Emperor, and singer Jimmy Durante. (Courtesy Harry Volpe)*

sales. Volpe could make as much or more off of the high-volume sales of a student guitar as he could off the occasional sale of a high-dollar model.

Volpe was born in 1904 in Sicily, the son of an accordion maker. His father made frequent trips to the United States, and the family followed him to America during World War I. By the time Volpe was 15 he was playing and teaching banjo. By the 1930s his prowess with classical pieces had gained him a great deal of notoriety, and Al Caiola was one of the up-and-coming players who engaged Volpe as a teacher in order to have access to Volpe's arrangements of classical music. Volpe often joined in the Epiphone jam sessions on West 14th, and he also hosted jams at his own guitar studio, the Volpe Guitar Center, on 48th Street.

Volpe doesn't remember if he even owned a guitar at the time he jammed at the Epiphone factory. He did play a Gibson L-5 with the NBC network orchestra in 1934, and Gibson gave him a new Super 400 in 1935 when he was on tour with the Vincent Lopez band. His first good guitar, he recalls, was a Gretsch that was given to him by the Brooklyn-based company after the American Guild of Banjoists, Guitarists and Mandolinists had voted him the most popular swing guitarist of 1939. "All of a sudden I went with Gretsch," he says. "I don't know how I ever got with them. They gave me a lot of publicity, gave me a lot of guitars."

As a player and teacher, Volpe was identified with Gretsch for 15 years. Except for a 1953 tryout of Mario Maccaferri's new all-celluloid guitars, Volpe seemed to have a lifelong home at Gretsch. In 1954, however, Gretsch lost Harry Volpe just as suddenly as it had gained him.

"I was playing a concert, I don't know where, in Minneapolis somewhere, for Gretsch," he recalls. "And Jimmy Webster was there demonstrating a guitar. [Webster was a noted musician, the developer of the fingerboard tapping system, and Gretsch's "idea man," who came up with the company's colorful guitars of the mid fifties.] My time was to go up there and demonstrate what I could do with my Gretsch guitar. Webster had his guitar tuned very high because he used to demonstrate the DeArmond thing, the touch system. [DeArmond made the pickups on Gretsch electrics.] I thought he was going to leave the guitar there, but he took his guitar."

Volpe was scheduled to play next, but he had no guitar. Fortunately, Roy Smeck, the former vaudeville star known as the Wizard of the Strings, was in the audience and he lent his guitar to Volpe. Also in the audience was a representative of Continental Music, which now distributed Epiphone in the Midwest. The sales rep, seeing Volpe's anger at Gretsch, asked him on the spot if he would like to endorse Epiphones. "I was mad anyway," Volpe recalls. "I said okay."

Volpe, who had relocated to Miami by this time, signed an exclusive agreement with Continental on November 30, 1954. In return for playing Epiphones, consulting on the design of his own models, and allowing his name to be used, he received four free guitars and a five percent royalty on the wholesale price of all Harry Volpe models.

The Harry Volpe model, introduced in March 1955, was available in sunburst or natural finish. The neck and string spacing were wider than standard, according to Volpe's specifications, so that players could easily play with a flatpick or a fingerpick. The single pickup had no individual polepieces and was cheaper than that on most Epi models. "Every month they used to give me a good royalty check from Continental," Volpe says. "They must have sold a lot."

Whatever boost the Volpe model might have given to Epiphone, it was too little, too late. The model did not survive, but Harry Volpe did have a legacy of sorts in the Epiphones of the sixties. One of only two Epi endorsement models of the sixties was named for his former student Al Caiola.

Although all of Volpe's personal Epiphone guitars have since been stolen, photographs show that his free guitars were not his namesakes, but Epi's top-of-the-line models. Even after Epi abandoned him as an official endorser, he continued to play Epiphones. He used an electric Emperor for a concert with the Philadelphia Symphony Orchestra. He played an acoustic Emperor at his regular gig at the Eden Roc hotel in Miami. "All the great artists would come there and I played for them," he says. "I used the Emperor, and it had a big tone, because I used to walk around." He also had a flat-top cutaway version of the Deluxe, one of the rarest of Epi models.

After the Eden Roc engagement Volpe found a permanent home for his music at the David Williams Hotel in Coral Gables. After 23 years at the David Williams, arthritis began to slow him down and he retired. He still lives in Miami. 🄴

*Even after Epi abandoned Harry Volpe as an official endorser, he continued to play Epiphones.*

# Gibson to the Rescue

**EPIPHONE ADS** (similar to the one above) are appearing regularly. They mean **MORE BUSINESS** for you. There's an *EPIPHONE BASS* for every popular price. *Send for folder.*

As Epi was fading in the early fifties, Gibson was regaining its old shine. Ted McCarty, an engineer by training and a 12-year veteran of the instrument business in various management positions, was installed as general manager of Gibson in 1948. He made Gibson profitable again within a few months and then pushed the company forward through the 1950s with such design innovations as a pickguard-mounted pickup that could easily convert an acoustic archtop to electric, the famous "Tune-O-Matic" bridge with individually adjustable saddles, and the semi-solidbody guitar.

*Epiphone bass brochure, early 1940s.*

By the mid fifties, McCarty's strongest competition was emerging from the West Coast, in the form of new solidbody electric guitars made by the Fender company. Epiphone guitars, McCarty recalls, no longer offered any competition to Gibson. "They were so poor you couldn't give them away," he says.

There was one area, however, in which Epi was still competitive and Gibson wasn't even in the race: upright basses. Although both companies had built basses before World War II, Gibson had not resumed production after the war. Epi had continued, and Epi basses were still among the most highly respected made by any American company.

McCarty recalls, "I was out in the state of Washington buying spruce. I got a phone call out there, and it was Orphie. He said, 'Ted, I've got to sell, I've got to get out. You once told me if I ever wanted to sell the bass business, you were interested.' I said, 'That's right.' And he said, 'Well, that's all I've got left is my bass viol business.' And he said, 'It's for sale.' I said, 'I'll have to get back to Kalamazoo and talk to Berlin, and I'll get back to you.' "

"Berlin" was M.H. Berlin, founder and president of Chicago Musical Instrument Co., Gibson's parent company. There was no other bass manufacturer in the CMI family, so he gave McCarty the okay to check out Orphie's bass operation. McCarty and his plant superintendent John Huis flew to New York, but discovered that the bass making equipment had been moved to the Conn facility in Philadelphia. So they went to Philadelphia, where they found not only the bass equipment and 17 finished basses, but also assorted guitar making equipment and some guitar parts, such as necks and pickups.

Telex communications of April 18, 1957, indicate that negotiations between McCarty and Orphie were secret. The Telex mentioned a possible legal entanglement regarding rights to the Epiphone name, although it didn't specify whether this involved Conn or Stathopoulo family members. It did say that the Conn people were desperately trying to find out who was making overtures to Orphie.

By the time of the McCarty-Orphie Telex, the deal was already done. Two days earlier, on April 16, Ward Arbanas, who would head up the Epi division for Gibson, was in New York packing up basses, and John Huis was in Philadelphia checking out the bass production molds. The deal was to include 35 basses, 17 of which were finished and already shipped to Kalamazoo. Huis had an additional 15 in New York, which he noted in a memo were mostly unfinished parts. The remaining three would have to be "recalled" from an Epiphone dealer in Denver.

Orphie wanted $20,000 for everything. He also requested that a portrait of his brother Epi be hung wherever Epiphone guitars were made. (The portrait ended up in the CMI offices in Lincolnwood, Illinois, hung next to a portrait of Orville Gibson. The two portraits moved to Nashville with Gibson headquarters in 1984, and they still hang side by side in the lobby of Gibson's corporate offices.)

McCarty paid Orphie the asking price and on May 10, 1957, announced the

After more than 80 years of making instruments, the Stathopoulo family was out of the instrument business.

acquisition with curious wording: "Epiphone, Inc. of Kalamazoo, Michigan, announces the acquisition of the business of Epiphone, Inc. of New York." Epiphone of Kalamazoo was, of course, a new corporation formed by CMI and made a division of Gibson.

After more than 80 years of making instruments, after more than 30 years as one of the premier names in the field, the Stathopoulo family was out of the instrument business. Frixo died that same year. Orphie retired, and preferred not to talk about Epiphone after that. His grandnephew Robert Cagianese (Elly's grandson) recalls as a teenager in the sixties taking his electric guitar over to uncle Orphie's. Orphie inspected the pickup but then ended any discussion of guitars before it had a chance to start. Cagianese recalls him saying, "No more, no more. We're out of the business. We're retired." Orphie died in 1973 at the age of 74. Orphie's grandnephew, under his professional name of Bob Cage, would eventually bring the Stathopoulo family back into the guitar world as a professional guitarist, recording a solo album, *Music from under a Tree*.

The loss of the family company saddened all the Stathopoulo family members, and apparently the feeling carried over to some employees. In March 1958 there was a belated funeral pyre of sorts at the Conn woodwind factory in New Berlin, New York, a small town a few hours northwest of New York City. Gibson representatives John Huis and Ward Arbanas were getting ready to leave Kalamazoo to take possession of the stock of Epi parts at New Berlin when they received a call from Continental president Paul Gazley. Gazley said a fire over the weekend had destroyed all the guitar parts, but he failed to mention the cause of the

fire. About a month later, a Gibson dealer in Oneonta (about 25 miles from New Berlin) let the truth slip out to his Gibson sales representative, Howard Kelley. On April 23, 1958, Kelley wrote a memo to the home office that began "Now I have heard everything." The story, as Kelley had heard it, was that Gazley gave employees any parts they wanted and then torched the rest in a bonfire behind the factory. €

CHICAGO MUSICAL INSTRUMENT CO.

**MEMORANDUM**

TED

RECEIVED

Date APR 23 1958

To Clarence Havenga
From H. Kelley
Subject Conn Wood-wind factory, New Berlin, N.Y.
Follow-up Date

Remarks:

Dear Clarence —

Now I have heard everything. My dealer in Oneonta told me this past week that there was a fire, but not the kind Mr. Gazley told you about.

It seems that Gazley gave many of the Epiphone parts to those employees who wanted them & then burned the remainder in a bon-fire out back of the factory. This is a fact, as my dealer's informant, who works at the Conn plant has some of the Epiphone parts in his possession.

Some cooperation, eh?

Howard

Epi employees "celebrated" the sale to Gibson with a bonfire of Epiphone guitar parts, according to this 1958 memo.

Epiphone

# EPIPHONES from KALAMAZOO

# From out of the Ashes

Upright basses—the reason Chicago Musical Instrument bought Epiphone—would turn out to be a disaster. But no matter. Before bass production ever got underway, Gibson president Ted McCarty had a better idea for Epiphone.

The unexpected stock of Epiphone necks and pickups inspired McCarty to revive Epiphone guitars and to make them exactly the same way Epi had in the company's golden years. Then an even better idea hit. A new, completely different Epiphone guitar line might be the solution to a growing problem concerning Gibson dealerships. Gibson's parent company, Chicago Musical Instrument, owned and distributed a variety of musical instruments, and after CMI's acquisition of Gibson in 1944, dealers began asking for the Gibson line. But Gibson had always protected its dealers' territories, so many of CMI's dealers were denied Gibson dealerships—unfairly, they felt. If Gibson had another brand to offer, then CMI dealers who couldn't get a Gibson could get the next best thing—a Gibson-made, Gibson-quality product, except that it would have another name on the peghead. A name like Epiphone. Gibson dealers would retain their territorial sovereignty, and all the other dealers could get a Gibson-made Epiphone.

This was in McCarty's mind by the time Gibson announced its acquisition of Epiphone on May 10, 1957. "It is planned that the famous line of Epiphone guitars, bass violins, and amplifiers will be continued by the corporation," the announcement said. "Bass violins will be available within the very near future and some models of the guitar line are expected to be ready this Fall. A complete list of models, including some new solidbody electric guitars and amplifiers, will be announced for shipment early in 1958."

McCarty's initial idea of reproducing Epiphones in the traditional Epi manner would have required reproducing Epi's production equipment, too. According to John Huis, McCarty's factory superintendent and the man who, with Ward Arbanas, delivered CMI's check for the purchase of Epiphone to Orphie, Epiphone no longer had any guitar production equipment. "The only thing I got out of Philadelphia was some forms," Huis says. In New York there wasn't much more. "He [Orphie] had a switch box there that had been newly installed and had a brand-new spray booth and then these basses. I'm trying to think of what equipment. He really didn't have much equipment, because he had it all done outside. All he had was a bunch of clamps to put the stuff together. They weren't making anything."

Epiphone had made a respectable mandolin prior to World War II, but there was only one complete mandolin and a few necks in

Dealers who couldn't get a Gibson could get the next best thing—a Gibson-made product with another name on the peghead. A name like Epiphone.

Orphie's inventory. "The only mandolin he had was stolen by some guy on a truck when they were loading up," Huis says. "When it got back to Kalamazoo we opened up the case and it was a block of wood in there."

Nevertheless, Huis says, "It was worth the money. What the hell, $20,000?"

There was no room for Epiphone at Gibson's famous plant at 225 Parsons Street in Kalamazoo, so Gibson rented a floor of the Grace Corset building at 224–242 Eleanor Street, less than a dozen blocks from Parsons Street. The different addresses helped to keep the Epi image separate from Gibson's. When the Parsons Street plant was expanded in 1960, Epi production was moved into the new space, but the image of two separate brands was maintained by making Epiphone's official address 210 Bush Street. The enlarged Gibson plant covered most of a city block, and Bush Street was the back boundary, so 210 Bush was literally the back door of the Gibson plant.

In retrospect, it was a symbolic move. With a few notable exceptions, Epiphone models would always be sort-of almost-Gibsons. Some small facet—the size of the humbucking pickups, the thickness of the solidbodies—would always keep Epiphone slightly in the shadow of Gibson. 🄴

*When the Parsons Street plant was expanded, Epi production was moved into the new space, but the image of two separate brands was maintained by making Epiphone's official address 210 Bush Street—literally the back door of the Gibson plant.*

# A New Line

**S**ome of Gibson's first Epiphones appeared to be nice re-creations of the Epis of old. Some were "almost-Gibsons"—slightly cheaper, slightly less than a similar model available under the Gibson brand. But the Gibson-made Epiphone line soon developed its own identity. Some models would pioneer areas unexplored by Gibson, such as a double-cutaway solidbody, a triple-pickup thinline, a "square-shouldered" Martin-style dreadnought flat-top, and an oval-hole archtop electric. Others, like the Professional electric or the Excellente acoustic, would be more innovative or imaginative than anything Gibson had to offer.

At first most of the Epi parts and bodies were built at the Gibson plant on Parsons Street and then sent over to the Grace building for assembly. Production did not proceed smoothly. Before any guitars appeared, Gibson had to spend almost $19,000—almost as much as Epiphone had cost—on repairing equipment, repairing the building, and other expenses.

The fall of 1957 came and went with no Epi guitars and no basses. Bass production was supposed to have been easy, with Epi's tooling intact and no new models to develop. But according to John Huis, "We built very few basses. We just weren't equipped for them. The Epi equipment, they didn't have anything in what you call real good equipment. I think they had gotten rid of it before we got hold of it."

Ward Arbanas was put in charge of the Epiphone division, and he was at first optimistic about bass production, suggesting in a memo to McCarty on

Gibson president Ted McCarty initialed this proposed Epiphone line in the upper right corner.

December 20, 1957, that a cello should be added to the line. (Gibson's own prewar cello forms were apparently still intact.) On February 13, 1958, however, Arbanas brought bad news from the bass production line. The Grace building was not climate-controlled, and abrupt changes in temperature and humidity had caused the finish on the Epi basses to "check," or crack. The real cause, according to John Huis: "We rented the space and then the guy turned off the heat over the weekend. We had to pay some extra rent to keep the heat on." Every single bass, even the ones that Gibson had bought in a finished state, had to be stripped and refinished. Furthermore, when the basses finally did hit the market they listed for 25 percent higher than comparable models offered by Kay—$345 for the Epi B-4, $275 for the Kay C-1. By 1961, with Epi guitar sales growing steadily, McCarty abandoned upright basses altogether.

News of the delays in bass production couldn't have been less welcome in Ted McCarty's office. Early in 1958, the projected date for an announcement of a full line of guitars, McCarty met with CMI head M.H. Berlin, CMI sales manager Clyde Rounds, and Gibson sales manager Clarence Havenga to decide just what that line would include. In their February 6 meeting, they did decide on the types of guitars, but several models still lacked names. The new Epiphone line would include some familiar names from Epi tradition, but most of the guitars would be different from anything that had ever appeared under the Epiphone brand name.

The first model on the list, the Century, was a case in point. The Century had been an inexpensive full-depth archtop electric in the Epi line of the early fifties. McCarty's description of the new Century: "Just like old Epiphone but thin rim." From the front the Century would look like the old Century, but from the side it was definitely a Gibson—Epiphone had never made a thinline guitar body. The Deluxe was continued as both an electric and an acoustic, but the electric version, like the Century, was something new and quite different: "...thin body, like Gibson ES-335." The ES-335 was McCarty's new creation: a semi-hollowbody guitar (an archtop electric, double-cutaway, with a solid block down the middle of the body). It was just in the process of being introduced as the Epiphone model-naming committee was meeting, but McCarty obviously had enough confidence in the idea—and high enough hopes for the Epiphone brand—to include a similar model in the Epi line. By June 30, 1958, when the final lineup was approved, the model name would be changed to Sheraton.

The solidbodies had an intriguing model name: Moderne Black. The Gibson Moderne, unveiled in 1958 with two other "Modernistic" models, the Explorer and the Flying V, would become the guitar equivalent of the lost city of Atlantis—no examples have ever been found. The Moderne, like its sister models, was made of "korina," or African limba wood, a light colored relative of mahogany, and given a natural finish. On the original artist's rendering of the Moderne, however, the finish was black.

*The new line would include some familiar names, but most of the guitars would be different from any previous Epiphone model.*

The Epiphone solidbody electric was a double-cutaway, a style unavailable under the Gibson brand until the Les Paul Junior debuted it in mid 1958. With the Epi double-cutaway, McCarty had something different in mind. The Epi body shape was based on a Fender Telecaster, the model that in its initial incarnation as the Broadcaster had opened up the market for solidbodies back in 1950. The Telecaster was a single-cutaway guitar, but the Epi model featured the same cutaway shape in a mirror image on the upper bass bout. It was essentially a double-cutaway Telecaster.

In the flat-top line, McCarty went after another competitor: C.F. Martin. Gibson's dreadnought-size flat-tops (16" wide) had always had a "round-shouldered," or "slope-shouldered," body shape—narrower across the upper bout than the Martins, whose wider look gave them a "square-shouldered" appearance. It seems like a minor difference, but Gibson had its body shape, Martin had a different one. Gibson was too proud to copy Martin—at least under the Gibson brand. The Epiphone brand was another story. McCarty's notes on the Flattop Jumbo, as it was initially called, left no doubt about his intent: "Copy Martin D'naught size." The Epi would be made of maple rather than the mahogany or rosewood of Martins, and it would be named the Frontier.

By May 29, the solidbody electrics still had asterisks beside them, with the note "Temporary description. These will be given names later." Finally on June 30 a revised price list came through with the new names.

A year had gone by since the acquisition of Epiphone, and there were still no Epiphones to show. On May 16, 1958, two months before the annual National Association of Music Merchants (NAMM) trade show, McCarty sent a memo to key Gibson and Epi personnel, among them John Huis, Ward Arbanas, personnel director Julius Bellson, and engineer Walt Fuller. McCarty demanded product: "It is absolutely imperative that everyone's cooperation be given to rushing the sample guitars and production guitars bearing the Epiphone name.... Anyone causing any delay of these instruments will be held personally responsible for the delay.... The success or failure of our operation of Epiphone depends upon your complete support and cooperation, which I know we shall receive."

# Finally, New Epis

The revived Epiphone line of 1958 used the familiar guitars of earlier years as a starting point. The Emperor, Deluxe, and Triumph all continued as acoustic archtops with cutaway bodies, and the Zenith returned in its non-cutaway version. However, the image of the old Epiphone company disappeared quickly when it came to the electric archtops.

All but one of the electric hollowbodies were thinline guitars, which Epiphone never made in New York. The Emperor still held its place at the top of the line. It retained the three pickups of the old

version and, oddly, the body width. At 18½" wide, it was a monstrous thinline, more than an inch wider than Gibson's widest, the 17" Byrdland.

The Sheraton had no history whatsoever as an Epiphone, except for its Epi neck and pickups. Otherwise it was constructed essentially the same as Gibson's ES-335. The Epi version outdid its Gibson counterpart in the area of ornamentation, however, with such features as Emperor-style V-block fingerboard inlays and vine inlay on the peghead.

*As Gibson was working on a new Epi line, the old models continued to show up in places like the house band for the 1958 March of Dimes Fashion Show, shown here serenading Dody Goodman, of Jack Paar's "Tonight" show.*
*(Frank Driggs Collection)*

# Epiphone

*Solidbodies had never borne the Epi brand before. Now there were two.*

The Broadway, which had never been available as an electric in the old Epi line, was now available *only* as an electric in the Gibson-made offering, and it was the only electric with a full-depth hollow body.

The double-pickup, single-cutaway Zephyr and single-pickup, noncutaway Century, both thinlines, completed the new Epiphone electric archtop line.

Many of the new Epis had old Epi necks, pickups, and tuners. The supply of necks and pickups lasted for several years, but the tuners were used up immediately. On September 26, 1958, Ward Arbanas sent a memo to McCarty regarding the need for new tuners. McCarty memoed back the same day, saying the Epiphone tuners were hereby discontinued. Epis would now be fitted with the same tuners as Gibsons: Grovers on the more expensive models and Kluson Deluxes on the less expensive.

The Epiphone flat-tops were all new. The Frontier was a square-shouldered, mahogany-body dreadnought. As Ted McCarty had noted back in February, this was the Martin-style guitar, but it was also important because there was no comparable model in the Gibson line. The Texan, a round-shouldered (traditional Gibson shape) dreadnought, complemented Gibson's J-45 and SJ. It was distinguished by large parallelogram fingerboard inlays; the Gibson SJ had double parallelograms. The Cortez and Caballero were small-bodied flat-tops (14¾" wide)—Epi versions of Gibson's successful LG-2 and LG-0 models.

Solidbodies had never borne the Epi brand before 1958. Now there were two. The Crestwood had gold-plated metal parts and a Tune-O-Matic bridge (with its individually adjustable string saddles), but, curiously, the dot fingerboard inlay of a low-end model. The Coronet had one pickup and the bridge/tailpiece that Ted McCarty had originally designed for the low-end Gibson solidbody, the Les Paul Junior.

The new Epi electrics needed amplifiers, of course, and Epi offered a new line of amps: the Devon, Century, Zephyr, and Emperor. The Devon name was an odd choice, since it had been an acoustic guitar in the old Epi line and was never produced as a guitar model at all by Gibson. Zephyr, even though it, too, was never produced as a guitar by Gibson, made more sense as an amp name, because "Zephyr" had been an Epi electric model and the term meant "electric" in the old Epi model nomenclature. Behind the new model names and cabinets, however, the new Epi amps were nothing new at all. The Devon, Century, Zephyr, and Emperor had the same circuitry, respectively, as Gibson's Gibsonette, GA-20T, GA-40, and GA-77.

The splash created by the new Epi guitars seemed to obscure Epi's reason for being—the upright basses. The new line included three of them: the B-5 Artist, B-4 Professional, and BV Studio. ◧

# The Unveiling

The first Gibson-made Epiphone, an Emperor, on display at the July 1958 NAMM show at the Palmer House in Chicago. Proud "fathers" of the new Epi are (from left) Clyde Rounds, Ted McCarty, and Ward Arbanas.

The NAMM show of July 1958, held at the Palmer House hotel in Chicago, would *not* be remembered among aficionados of guitar history primarily for being the site of the resurrection of the Epiphone brand. McCarty had more than Epi to sell. He had his newly introduced double-cutaway thinline semi-solidbody ES-335. And he debuted his radical new Gibson models—the Flying V, Explorer, and never-to-be-seen-again Moderne. They all became legends—the "Modernistics" because they were so odd that no one wanted them and the ES-335 because it would be as widely accepted as the Modernistics were shunned.

The Epiphone room at the Palmer House did attract a crowd wishing to see the new models. A report from Epi division manager Ward Arbanas to Ted McCarty noted that among the visitors was former Epiphone vice president George Mann, "straining at the bit to see the new Epiphone line from the doorway, but not coming inside." The centerpiece of the display was an Emperor electric, which was designated as the first of the new Epis. The show generated modest orders: 226 guitars and 63 amplifiers.

Gibson had built prototypes to show, but may not have been ready to put the guitars into production. John Huis recalls: "There was a little delay there. We made some samples and took them to the show, then started production." If any were shipped in 1958, they weren't entered into Gibson shipping records that year.

Epi sales picked up in 1959, when Gibson shipped a total of 1,458 Epiphone guitars. After a small increase in 1960 to 1,750 units, Epiphones began to catch on. A total of 3,798 were shipped in 1961, accounting for about 10 percent of total units shipped out of Kalamazoo. By 1965, Epiphone's share of the total had risen to almost 20 percent. ◧

*Top Left:*
In July 1959 Gibson sent the best of its new Epiphones to a show in Moscow sponsored by the U.S. Information Agency.

*Top Right:*
Carl Perkins livens up the Johnny Cash and June Carter show with his electric Emperor at the Newport Folk Festival in July 1969. (Fred Ramley Jr., Frank Driggs Collection)

*Right:*
Gibson's first Epiphone bass flier, 1958.

# EPIPHONE
## BASS VIOLS

*world's most honored name in basses*

### model B5
*. . . the Artist*

A superb instrument for the exacting artist who requires the very finest. Of the most choice woods . . . straight-grained spruce arched top, select curly maple full arched back and sides, finest maple neck, natural Brazilian rosewood fingerboard and rock maple tailpiece. Hand polishing brings out the beautiful flame of the wood. Exquisite hand inlaid triple purfling ornaments top and back. Gold plated, full plate engraved machine heads. Adjustable end pin. Famous George Van Eps adjustable bridge, sloping shoulders, narrow fingerboard. In shaded (rich Cremona brown) or natural finish. Three-quarter size only.

B5 NATURAL $475.00

B5 SHADED $400.00

# Surpassing Gibson

Epiphone in the sixties is usually regarded as an almost-Gibson line—primarily because Epi pickups were a bit smaller and Epi solidbodies were a bit thinner than those of their Gibson cousins—but the Epi line of the early sixties included some models that rivaled or even surpassed anything in the Gibson line, in price as well as in appeal. According to Ted McCarty, Les Propp deserves credit for keeping the Epis up with the Gibsons. Propp moved from a job in the CMI offices to become Epi sales manager. "All Les was interested in was that his guitars were just as good and fancy as Gibson," McCarty says. "We'd come up with a new Gibson and he wanted something similar."

In the early sixties, the Epiphone Emperor electric with natural finish listed for $850—$250 more than the top Gibson thinline, the Byrdland, and about $40 more than even Gibson's highest-priced model, the Johnny Smith (which was a full-depth archtop). The Sheraton, at $580, was about $20 less than the most expensive Gibson semi-hollowbody, the ES-355. Nothing in the Gibson line matched the electronic innovations of the Professional, which had a set of amplifier controls mounted on the guitar.

In 1963, a deluxe flat-top model joined the Epiphone line and brought with it a something-more-than-a-Gibson look. At $535, the Excellente was $100 more than Gibson's venerable "King of the Flat Tops,"

*Above:*
*Andy Nelson demonstrates the new Professional of 1962, the only Epi (or Gibson) model with amplifier controls mounted on the guitar. (Courtesy Andy Nelson)*

*Right:*
*A drawing of what became the Excellente, from Andy Nelson's design sketchbook, 1962.*

the J-200. The Excellente also challenged the J-200 aesthetically, with a huge piece of pearl in the peghead, Deluxe-style "cloud" fingerboard inlays, and rosewood back and sides (rosewood was unavailable in a Gibson guitar at the time).

The idea for the Excellente came from Andy Nelson. Nelson had been a staff guitarist on Chicago's WGN radio and, since 1957, a clinician for CMI. He was technically a salesman, but he demonstrated Gibson products at music store clinics and trade shows. His repertoire of "commercial jazz" included such diverse tunes as "Steel Guitar Rag," "Star Dust," "Flight of the Bumblebee," and "Night Train." Nelson was full of opinions and ideas for guitars, and his relationship with CMI was unsteady. On the road, he constantly offered artists custom features on guitars, which created extra work back at the factory. At one point he was fired for showing low sales in a slow territory in Chicago, then rehired with a raise.

Gibson sales manager Clarence Havenga was "my star," Nelson says. "When he died it was a different thing for me. For one thing I am fairly vocal—was at that time. He saved me from a real chewing or whatever." Upon Havenga's death in 1962, Nelson moved from Gibson sales to Epiphone. He takes credit for several changes in the line, including:

• Designing the Excellente.

• Bringing jazz star Howard Roberts into the Epiphone camp.

• Redesigning the solidbody line, streamlining the bodies and giving them a new headstock with a six-on-a-side tuner configuration. The headstock shape is known among collectors as "bat-wing," but the treble-side edge actually forms a letter *E*.

• Bringing reverb to amplifiers. "I got that from a dealer out in the south end of Chicago—Aurora," he says. "He was a Hammond [organ] dealer and he put it together and showed me, and I brought it to Clarence and Mr. Berlin. About a year or something later it came out and our business went up 100 percent for that one thing alone." (Amplifier sales by units actually decreased from 1961 to 1962, the first years of reverb-equipped models, but reverb-equipped amps did account for about a third of sales. The biggest-selling Gibson or Epi amp in 1962 and 1963 was the reverb-tremolo model GA-19RVT; the Epiphone EA-28RVT accounted for almost 25 percent of Epi amp sales in 1962 and 1963. Epiphone amp sales did grow by more than 100 percent from 1963 to 1964.)

Nelson left Gibson in 1965 to work for Fender. Now living in Florida, he has weathered a series of health problems, but is still playing and is working on his own book. And he is still working on new designs for Epiphone guitars. ■

The Epiphone Excellente was the fanciest flat-top made in Kalamazoo in the 1960s. (Guitar courtesy Nick Skopelitis, photo © 1995 Anthony Stroppa)

*Andy Nelson's relationship with CMI was unsteady. At one point he was fired for showing low sales, then rehired with a raise.*

The Gibson-Epi line couldn't have debuted at a better time. By the end of the fifties, rock 'n' roll had brought the electric guitar into the mainstream of popular music. And by the early sixties, the rising folk music scene did the same for the acoustic guitar. The music was mostly of the three-chord variety, easy to play, and the guitar quickly became the instrument of the people. Everybody played guitar, and Gibson met the growing demand with an explosion of new models in both the Epi and Gibson lines.

The folk movement brought a new interest in classical guitars and eventually a hybrid "folk" guitar, which was essentially a classic guitar body, with 12-fret neck and wide fingerboard, but with steel strings. Epi revived an old name from a prewar classical guitar, the Seville, and introduced two versions, one with a ceramic-magnet pickup in the bridge and one fully acoustic, in 1961. A year later, the mahogany-body Madrid joined the Epi classical line. It was followed in 1963 by a fancier maple model, the Espana, and a 3/4-size classical, the Entrada.

An indisputable sign of the folk influence appeared in the Epi line in 1962 in the form of a 12-string guitar, a type of guitar that had almost become extinct until folk musicians revived the music of Leadbelly

*Al Caiola poses with his own Epi Caiola model, 1963.*
*(Popsie Randolph, Frank Driggs Collection)*

**Top Left:**
Al Caiola's 1963 Casino, with single-coil P-90 pickups, offered a change in sound from the mini-humbucking pickups of his Epi endorsement model. (Popsie Randolph, Frank Driggs Collection)

**Top Right:**
Robbie Robertson, of The Band, 1969, in the house that became known as Big Pink, playing an Epiphone Howard Roberts. (© David Gahr)

**Right Center:**
Louisiana slide guitarist Sonny Landreth (right) got his start on a mid-sixties Epiphone Olympic Double. His drummer, Tommy Alesi, would later join Beausoleil. (Courtesy Sonny Landreth)

**Bottom Right:**
Pop star-to-be Michael Bolton lays down a vocal track with the help of a Casino. (Frank Driggs Collection)

**Opposite Page—**
**Top:**
Howard Roberts plays a Howard Roberts Custom, the deluxe version of his Epiphone endorsement model. After Epi production moved overseas, the model was reintroduced under the Gibson brand. (Courtesy Guitar Player)

**Bottom:**
Paul Revere and the Raiders rocked in the sixties with a Sheraton guitar and a Newport bass. (Frank Driggs Collection)

plating of the Gibson. A smaller folk guitar, the Folkster, was introduced in 1966.

Acoustic archtop guitars were on the way out, as shown by the lack of new models in the Epi line. Electrics were another matter, however. In 1962 Epi introduced a sort of stepsister to the Sheraton, called the Casino. The Casino looked somewhat like the Sheraton, with a double-cutaway thinline body, but it had single-coil Gibson P-90 pickups and a fully hollow body, making it a companion to the Gibson ES-330. Also that year, the Granada appeared, offering Epi customers a budget-priced electric hollowbody—if they could live with the non-cutaway shape, the small single-coil pickup (the same as those on Gibson's budget-priced Melody Makers), and the controls built into a molded pickguard. At the other end of the line, the Professional introduced the innovative idea of putting amplifier controls where the guitarist can get to them—right on the guitar itself. The problem was that the companion amp would work only with the Professional guitar, since it had no controls of its own.

Epi also landed some big-name jazz players to compete with such Gibson endorsers as Johnny Smith, Barney Kessel, and Tal Farlow.

Al Caiola joined the Epi flock in 1963. "Les Propp had contacted me when they moved to Kalamazoo," Caiola says. "They said, 'Come out and try the instrument.' That was a model that they already had but they decided to put my name on it because I liked it. I was rewarded monetarily for all the units sold, but I didn't design all that." The Caiola had a bank of slide switches for tone adjustments. A cheaper version appeared in 1966 as the Caiola Standard, at which time the original was named Caiola Custom.

(writer of the Weavers' huge 1950 hit "Goodnight Irene"). Epi named its 12-string the Bard and followed with a smaller version, the Serenader, in 1963.

Also in 1963, the fancy Excellente led a trio of new steel-string flat-tops that included the mahogany El Dorado and maple

Troubadour, all with a square-shouldered body shape. The Troubadour was one of the new 12-fret, wide-fingerboard "folk guitars," and it was easily distinguishable by its double white pickguards. It was a clone of the Gibson FJN (Folksinger Jumbo, Natural), but the Epi version had gold-plated metal parts rather than the nickel

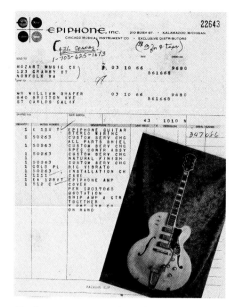

*The Emperor was not catalogued with stereo electronics, but anything was possible by special order.*
*(Courtesy Bradley Bolton)*

In 1964 Howard Roberts joined Epi with a unique, oval-hole archtop electric with a floating, Johnny Smith-style pickup. The oval hole was Roberts' idea. He liked to hear his guitar acoustically, even though he was playing it amplified, but on a conventional *f*-hole archtop, the pickguard covered up one soundhole and the player's arm covered the other. The oval hole solved his problem. A fancier, gold-plated version was added in 1965 and christened the Howard Roberts Custom.

The solidbody line got a complete overhaul that gave the models as much first-impression power as the new sharp-pointed, double-cutaway Gibson SG models. The Epis had been slimmed down almost immediately after their introduction to a body depth of only 1⅜", with rounded body edges. As soon as all of the old Epi pickups were used up, a new mini-humbucker was phased in. In 1963 the cutaway horns became slightly asymmetrical, and the higher models gained a "bat-wing" headstock, which also formed the outline of a script letter *E*, with all six tuners on one side. The six-on-a-side tuners represented another direct assault on a competitor, in this case Fender.

A fancy new solidbody, the Crestwood Deluxe, sported the new features in 1963. In later years, Gibson would use "Deluxe" in an ironic manner, usually on a lower-level model, but the Crestwood Deluxe was as advertised: more deluxe than the Crestwood, with three pickups and gold-plated metal parts.

The Wilshire, added to the solidbody line in 1959, had two white "soapbar" pickups, no doubt left over from the Gibson Les Paul's conversion from soapbars to metal-covered humbucking pickups. The white soapbars were replaced by black soapbars (which were still in use on some Gibsons) in 1961. A 12-string version was available from 1966 to '68.

On the low end, the Olympics (single pickup, double pickup, and ¾-size) appeared in 1960 as a mirror image of the Gibson Melody Makers. Like the Gibsons, they started as single-cutaways, then went to a double-cutaway shape in 1963. Even lower was the Olympic Special of 1962, which had a sort of semi-sharp cutaway.

Epi's first electric bass, the Rivoli, debuted in 1959, and it was the equivalent of Gibson's EB-2, a semi-hollowbody archtop modeled after the Gibson ES-335 and Epi Sheraton. Solidbody basses soon followed: the Newport in 1961 and the Embassy Deluxe in 1963. The Newport had a single pickup. When guitars went to the six-on-a-side, bat-wing headstock in 1963, the Newport followed, with all four tuners moving to one side. It was also available with fuzztone and in a six-string version beginning in 1962. The Embassy Deluxe had two pickups.

By 1965 Epiphone had a substantial line, with something to offer musicians in any style of music, at any budget level. Electric guitarists could choose from 14 archtops, six solidbodies, and three basses. They could play an Epi electric through any of 12 Epi amplifiers. For the folk and bluegrass crowd, Epi offered seven steel-string flat-top guitars, six classicals, three banjos, and a mandolin. Although upright basses were gone, the Epiphone tradition was still represented by four acoustic archtop guitars.

# Enter the Beatles

*The Beatles, featuring George Harrison and his Epiphone Casino, taping "Hello, Goodbye," from* Magical Mystery Tour.
*(© Hulton/Apple Corps)*

**N**ear the end of 1964, Epi scored an unexpected artist relations coup when the Beatles bought three Casinos—one each for George Harrison, John Lennon, and Paul McCartney.

McCartney recalled the circumstances for *Guitar Player* magazine in an interview in 1990: "My first Epiphone was one of them where I just went down to a guitar shop after having heard B.B. King, Eric Clapton and Jimi Hendrix. [McCartney may have been remembering a different guitar, because Hendrix was playing with the Isley Brothers in 1964 and didn't arrive in England until 1966] And I wanted something that fed back. He [the salesman] said, this Epiphone will do it because it was semi-acoustic, and he was right. The only reason I don't use it on stage is because it's a little too hot. It's great in the studio."

All three Casinos were sunburst, and George's had a Bigsby vibrola tailpiece.

McCartney put his on record almost immediately, playing the guitar fills on the group's 1965 hit "Ticket to Ride" on his Casino. At about the same time, McCartney acquired an Epiphone Texan flat-top, and he played that guitar, backed by a string quartet, in 1965 on what would become the most-recorded song ever written: "Yesterday."

Fans around the world saw the Casinos on the Beatles' world tour of 1966. The group used them on various recordings and promotional films, but their influence was not as profound as the Epiphone people might have hoped. By this time, the Beatles were using several different guitars, and no single model was closely identified with them (not in the way Harrison's Gretsch Country Gentleman or Lennon's Rickenbacker 325 had been in earlier years). On their TV broadcast "All You Need Is Love" in 1967 they played colorful custom-finished guitars—George had a Strat, Paul a Rickenbacker bass, and John

his Casino, the back of which he had painted white—but on the actual recording sessions for the songs, all three played Casinos. For Epiphone, that represented a huge lost opportunity, although it's unlikely anyone in Kalamazoo was aware of it.

The Casinos kept showing up with the Beatles. By the time the band appeared on the British TV show "Tops of the Pops" on September 19, 1968, Lennon's sunburst Casino had been transformed into a blonde. Harrison's, too, had acquired a natural finish. Actually the guitars had no finish at all, as Harrison explained to writer Dan Forte in the November 1987 *Guitar Player*: "John and I scraped the varnish off our Epiphone Casinos, and they became much better guitars. I think that works on a lot of guitars: If you take the paint and varnish off, and get the bare wood, it seems to sort of breathe." ◖

# Beyond the Boom

The guitar boom of the early to mid sixties was a dream come true for Gibson and other guitar makers. From 1961 to 1965, combined production of Gibson and Epi guitars almost tripled, from 35,000 to 102,000. Epi unit sales increased more than fivefold during that time, from 3,789 to 19,223. By the end of the decade, however, the dream would turn into a nightmare. The creatures of this nightmare did not look scary. They were inexpensive foreign-made guitars, and they looked good. Too good, actually. Too much like American guitars. And they devoured huge chunks of the American guitar market.

By 1969 total Gibson and Epi production had fallen to less than 60 percent of what it had been in 1965. Other companies were hit even harder. Kay and Harmony, the two most prominent American makers of budget-priced guitars, folded. Had Epiphone been a free-standing company, it too would have folded. In 1969 Gibson shipped out a mere 2,526 Epiphone guitars—an 86 percent drop from 1965. An Epi cost almost as much as a Gibson to manufacture, and consequently Epiphone was competing with Gibson more than with the imports.

Stan Rendell, president of Gibson from 1968 to 1976, sums up the problem: "Basically, Epiphone was always sold second to Gibson. In other words, if you were a music dealer in a given area and you wanted a guitar franchise, you were given Epi; then if you did a good job for a couple of years, you could move up to a Gibson. It just didn't work out. Even though they were both made in the same factory, Epi was always sold second to Gibson."

Bruce Bolen, who joined Gibson in the sixties as a guitar clinician, is even more succinct in his explanation of the relationship between Gibson and Epiphone: "Epi was a stepchild."

Gibson had other problems, too. Ted McCarty, the man who had guided the company out of hard times in the late forties to its most prosperous period ever, resigned in 1966. In an effort to meet the increase in demand for guitars, Gibson had let the quality of its product slip. Union problems didn't help the situation. In addition, CMI, the parent company, had built a new plant for its Lowrey Organ division, and it bled money from day one. By the time CMI closed the Lowrey plant, CMI's stock price was depressed. Watchful eyes on Wall Street saw a bargain, and in December 1969 the ECL corporation, an Ecuadorian company whose major product was beer, took over CMI. With top-level management populated by strangers to the musical instrument business—people who might be unappreciative, or at least unaware, of the traditional values of the Epiphone name—Epiphone was caught in a no-man's-land: not as good as Gibson, but too expensive to compete with budget-priced imports. The very survival of Epiphone guitars was once again threatened.

By the end of the decade, the dream would turn into a nightmare.

## Chapter 5

EPIPHONE

OVERSEAS

*Pick Epiphone*

Fighting Imports with Imports

Scrolls, Novas, and the First PRs

On to Korea

# *Fighting Imports with Imports*

**6730**

A traditional jumbo size and shape guita[r] the 6730 is a favorite among Country-Western and Blue Grass artists. Feature[s] slim, fast, low-action neck and quality spruce top.

**FEATURES:**

Selected natural spruce top with attracti[ve] fingerrest. Mahogany rims and back, multiple body binding and purfling. Slim fast, low-action three piece adjustable n[eck] with pearl dot inlays. Rosewood fingerbo[ard] and adjustable bridge. Chrome plated machine heads and parts. 16" wide, 19¾[" ] long, 4¾" deep; 25½" scale, 20 frets.

#810 Durabilt Case

**5102T**
This thin double-cutaway model with twin pickups produces clear, distinctive tones. The slim, fast, low-action neck allows easy access to upper register.

**FEATURES:**
Double-cutaway thin body with multiple binding, twin pickups with adjustable polepieces, slim, fast, low-action adjustable neck, high gloss cherry red finish, select hardwood top, rims and back. Adjustable precision bridge, rosewood fingerboard with block inlays, vibrola tailpiece, deluxe machine heads, chrome plated parts. 15¾" wide, 18¾" long, 1⅞" thin; 25½" scale, 22 frets.

**#805 Durabilt Case**

**1502T**
Modern deep cutaway design provides easy action and access to all frets. Response is from deep, rumbling bass sounds to treble biting tones.

**FEATURES:**
Thin modern cutaway design, high gloss cherry red finish. Slim, fast, low-action three piece adjustable neck, two powerful pickups with adjustable polepieces, pickup selector switch, rosewood fingerboard with pearl dot inlays, hand vibrola, chrome plated parts. 13¼" wide, 17¼" long, 1⅜" thin; 24¾" scale, 21 frets.

**#809 Durabilt Case**

---

here's a new line of import guitars available and just a few thousand sample deliveries have convinced us and all of the dealers that have received them that these are the finest import guitars ever offered in America."

That introduction was sent to dealers in a letter from CMI vice president Marc Carlucci, along with a price list dated October 10, 1970. The letter went on to point out that "Japan's finest guitar factory in close co-operation with our Kalamazoo experts have developed guitars that virtually sell themselves.

These were the new Epiphones. Bruce Bolen, an accomplished guitarist who at the time was working as both a clinician and a field sales manager, recalls what happened to the last of the old Epis. "I had the distinct pleasure of closing out the

American-made Epiphones," he says. "That was a blowout—substantial discounts, substantial inventory."

"In 1969, Marc Carlucci and I flew out to L.D. Heater [in Seattle], which at that point was our distributor for Gibson on the other side of the Rockies—'Zone 2.' They had been importing for years and years Japanese guitars bearing the name Lyle. My reason for going out there was to choose a selection of guitars that would become the new Epiphone line. We had some samples sent in, and they were in my office when M.H. Berlin came by, and he says, 'Young man, what are these?' I said, 'These are some samples. We're looking at some samples for the Epiphone line.' In no uncertain terms he said to me, 'As long as I am here we will not import this kind of product.' "

**Top Left:**
*The sole Epiphone hollowbody electric of 1971 had little in common with its American-made forerunners.*

**Top Right:**
*Epiphone's only solidbody electric in 1971 looked more like the guitars from Epi's competitors than a traditional Epiphone.*

**Opposite Page:**
*A flat-top from the first catalog of Japanese-made Epis, with an Epiphone peghead, but with body, pickguard, and bridge shape suggestive of a popular model from a competitor's line.*

The late Norton Stevens, who was the head of ECL and then of Norlin (the Norlin name was derived by pushing together *Nor*ton and Ber*lin*) confirmed that the decision to take Epiphone overseas was CMI's. "It was a big issue when we came on board," Stevens said. "I remember spending a lot of time when we first got involved up in the Kalamazoo plant, which was packed to the gunwales with inventory. So the imports were really impacting."

Despite M.H. Berlin's statement, CMI did put Japanese-made Epiphones in motion prior to the takeover by ECL in December 1969. Bolen chose 11 acoustic models from the existing Lyle line, which was made by the Matsumoku company. Located in the town of Matsumoto, in central Japan, west of Tokyo, Matsumoku was owned by the Singer sewing machine company. At the time it was known as the "other" factory in Japan, after Ibanez.

By the time of Carlucci's announcement, the Epiphone line included 13 models—an abrupt reduction from almost 50 models the year before. "We don't offer a lot of models," Carlucci's letter explained, "but we cover every sales opportunity."

The first catalog for the imported Epiphones, titled "Pick Epiphone," summed up the new Epi line: "Light price, heavy

sound, high quality. It's all together in this exciting new line of master crafted guitars and basses." The copy writers exercised their creative best in summing up the line: "Growling, acid rock. Gentle, breezy folk. And breathless, stirring classics."

These Epis had been made in Japan so that CMI could compete with Japanese guitars, and they gave up their own identity as Epiphones in the process. In principle that was nothing new. Back in 1958 Ted McCarty's first Gibson-made Epi line included a Martin-style dreadnought and a Fender-inspired solidbody. But this new bunch of Epis seemed to take it too far. Indeed, for the next 10 years the look of the Epiphone line would be inspired more by convenience—by what the Japanese contractors were already building—than by Epiphone tradition. Gibson was a production division and not directly responsible for sales and promotion of the guitars made in Kalamazoo. Since Gibson no longer produced Epiphones, there would be less and less direct involvement from Kalamazoo, as responsibility for design and production of Epiphones moved to the Norlin offices in Lincolnwood (a suburb of Chicago).

The first Japanese-made flat-tops looked pretty much like the most successful Japanese copies of the period, which is to say they looked like Martins. Body shape, pickguard shape, and bridge shape were Martin. Only at the fancier end of the line, where the models were decked out with large block inlays and wide rosette decals (soundhole ring ornamentation), did they look decidedly un-Martin. The bridges had a height-adjustable saddle with larger, more obtrusive screw-heads than the Gibson-made models of the sixties. And the pegheads lost the flared shape that distinguished Epis from Gibsons; now they just looked like Gibsons but with the Epiphone brand.

The solidbody guitar and bass had a body and pickguard modeled roughly on a Fender Stratocaster and Precision Bass, respectively. The guitar pickups, however, had a cheap, klunky look compared to the old Gibson-made metal-covered mini-humbuckers, and the vibrato tailpiece was a huge square device with a metal cover through which the arm protruded.

There was one thinline double-cutaway, a sort of poor man's Sheraton, and a companion bass, a poor man's Rivoli. Three classical guitars rounded out the line.

A blue rectangular label gave the impression that Epiphones were still made in Kalamazoo. It actually didn't say "Made

in…" anywhere. It just said "Epiphone, Inc. Kalamazoo, Michigan." But nowhere on the guitars was there a "Made in Japan" notice. The instruments bore a seven-digit serial number, the likes of which never appeared on a Gibson-made instrument.

The quickest and cheapest way to get a product line going was not to have the Japanese builders copy Epiphones, but to use what was already available. Tim Shaw, a longtime Gibson employee who would later be involved in the Epiphone line, has seen a number of these early guitars through his work as a repairman. "As far as I can see," he says, "there was no conscious effort in the early stuff to do anything more than just buy something plausible that they were pretty much already making. It was like, use parts and tooling you've already got and make me something that sort of looks like this old catalog.

"Some of those things I still see around," Shaw adds. "I had one of those Epiphone J-200s, those big blond suckers, in the shop, and they've held up remarkably well. These are 20-, 25-year-old Japanese guitars."

The line was unimpressive in every aspect except for price. The *highest*-priced model, a cedar-topped classical, listed for only $159.50. The lowest model, a mahogany-

*The quickest and cheapest way to get a product line going was not to have the Japanese builders copy Epiphones.*

body flat-top, could be had for a list of only $79.50—quite a contrast to Epi's last U.S.-made line, which ranged from the Caballero flat-top at $149.50 to the Emperor electric at $1,125.

While the cheap price may have attracted some buyers, the Epiphone name was of little value on guitars that had nothing in common with traditional Epis. Consequently, Gibson and CMI soon started bringing back some recognizable Epi features.

The guitars in the 1971 catalog had four-digit model numbers and no model names. The old Gibson-made Epis, in addition to their familiar model names, had a model number consisting of a letter prefix—EA for electric archtop, FT for flat-top—followed by two or three digits. In 1972, a system similar to the old one was instituted on the imports. Also revived was a familiar Epi body style, the slightly asymmetrical double-cutaway solidbody from the mid sixties. The new model was called the ET-278.

The response to the new Epis was strong enough to prompt an expansion of the line. By 1973 there were 10 steel-string flat-tops (including two 12-strings), with none listing over $200, plus five classicals. Three solidbodies, one semi-hollowbody, two basses, and a banjo completed the line.

By the early part of 1976 Gibson and CMI had further expanded the Epi line and given it some new flair. The Monticello, taking inspiration from the U.S. bicentennial, became the first of the new Epis to have a real model name. It sported an eagle carved into the headstock face and small stars for fingerboard inlays. All this for only $199.50. The *pièce de résistance*, however, was the FT-550, a dreadnought flat-top (also available as a 12-string) with a flashy three-piece back made of two pieces of jacaranda wood (a nicely figured South American wood) and a contrasting center piece of curly maple. List price: $299.50.

On the electric side, the double-cutaway thinline was upgraded considerably, with an attractive walnut body, a Frequensator tailpiece, Gibson-style humbucking pickups, and gold-plated metal parts. The solidbody line now featured a gleaming natural-finish maple model, the T290N, with humbuckers, maple fingerboard, and gold-plated parts. **ε**

*Gibson and CMI soon started bringing back some recognizable Epi features.*

# Scrolls, Novas, and the First PRs

## Scroll Series

**Scroll 550N**—Epiphone has brought back a symbol of tradition, quality and utmost craftsmanship...to stand as the hallmark of a new series of superior guitars—the scroll.

The Scroll 550N has the versatile electronics you need with today's versatile music. For high energy rock, the two gold plated, fully adjustable humbucking pickups give you all the power you need. For more subtle situations, flip the coil tap switch to get a more fundamental, funky, non-humbucking sound. The solid maple body helps deliver a solid sound with "cutting power." And the maple neck is extra rigid, with the wood grains of the three pieces running in opposite directions.

The Scroll 550N is one beautiful guitar, and there's a lot more than meets the eye. So experience it for yourself soon.

Two gold plated, fully adjustable, humbucking pickups. Three-position pickup selector switch. Two-position coil tap switch for non-humbucking tonalities. Master volume and tonal controls with linear potentiometers. Solid maple body full balanced for comfort. Bridge adjustable for height and intonation. Three-piece maple neck. Adjustable truss rod. Ebony fingerboard. Block inlays. 24 frets. Gold plated hardware. Natural finish.

**SC550B—(Not Shown)** Same features as SC550N except in ebony finish.

Cases for the above models—
**D-90**—Deluxe Plush Durabilt Case
**830**—Durabilt Case

©1977

2

**Scroll 350**—The scroll motif is a symbol of superior craftsmanship, and Epiphone's Scroll 350 guitar is a fine example of that craftsmanship—and musical engineering. The balanced styling is balanced in weight, so the Scroll 350 is a comfort to play while you move around the stage. The scroll and cutaway also leave plenty of room to roam around the 24th fret.

The hot humbucking pickups are fully adjustable for your kind of balance and sensitivity. And you can count on plenty of years of good times with the Scroll 350. The three-piece bolt-on neck, with grains running opposite directions, and the adjustable truss rod assure you of the touch, intonation and versatility you've grown so familiar with. And the sound of those superb electronics will always be outstanding. But then, this whole instrument is outstanding—the Epiphone Scroll 350.

Two chrome plated, fully adjustable humbucking pickups. Three-position pickup selector switch. Master volume and tone controls with linear potentiometers. Solid mahogany body fully balanced for comfort. Bridge adjustable for height and intonation. Three-piece bolt-on mahogany neck. Adjustable truss rod. "Ebonized" maple fingerboard. 24 frets. Chrome plated hardware. Lustrous mahogany finish.

Case for the above model—
**D-90**—Deluxe Plush Durabilt Case
**830**—Durabilt Case

**Scroll 450N**—Same as Scroll 450 (shown elsewhere) except in natural finish.

3

---

*The Scroll guitars, from the 1976 catalog, were among the most memorable Epiphones of the seventies.*

In 1976 the Epi line took a radical step forward, but also reached back for some familiar features from Epi tradition. On the radical edge were the new scroll-body electrics. The catalog copy, ironically, was formal and stuffy, stating: "The scroll motif is a symbol of superior craftsmanship." These were weird, cool-looking guitars, with the upper bass bout carved into a scroll. Old-time craftsmanship was hardly the selling point, and after an initial splash, the sales of the scrolls subsided. Bruce Bolen recalls: "Everybody was under the opinion that we needed a facelift with Epiphone, a new look. Like anything new back in those days that wasn't traditional, it died."

The scroll-body guitars were available in three versions with mahogany or natural maple finish. The upper two models had coil-tap capability (using only one coil of a double-coil pickup). More important to Epi tradition, the scrolls marked the return of the flared peghead style, which hadn't been seen on an Epi since the sixties. A double-scroll bass also joined the line.

The flat-top line was topped by a new Presentation series, which marked the beginning of the PR model designation. The first of these was the Presentation 765, a rosewood dreadnought featuring the traditional Epi "vine of life" peghead inlay, revived from the old Deluxe and Emperor.

## Nova Series

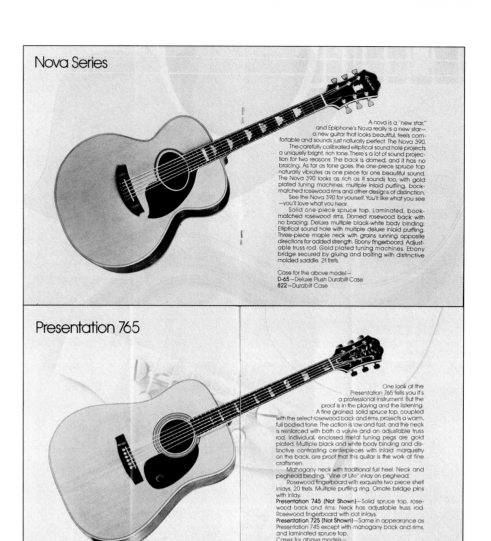

A nova is a "new star," and Epiphone's Nova really is a new star—a new guitar that looks beautiful, feels comfortable and sounds just naturally perfect. The Nova 390.

The carefully calibrated elliptical sound hole projects a uniquely bright, rich tone. There's a lot of sound projection for two reasons: The back is domed, and it has no bracing. As far as tone goes, the one-piece spruce top naturally vibrates as one piece for one beautiful sound. The Nova 390 looks as rich as it sounds too, with gold plated tuning machines, multiple inlaid purfling, bookmatched rosewood rims and other designs of distinction.

See the Nova 390 for yourself. You'll like what you see —you'll love what you hear.

Solid one-piece spruce top. Laminated, bookmatched rosewood rims. Domed rosewood back with no bracing. Deluxe multiple black-white body binding. Elliptical sound hole with multiple deluxe inlaid purfling. Three-piece maple neck with grains running opposite directions for added strength. Ebony fingerboard. Adjustable truss rod. Gold plated tuning machines. Ebony bridge secured by gluing and bolting with distinctive molded saddle. 21 frets.

Case for the above model—
D-65—Deluxe Plush Durabilt Case
822—Durabilt Case

## Presentation 765

One look at the Presentation 765 tells you it's a professional instrument. But the proof is in the playing and the listening. A fine grained, solid spruce top, coupled with the select rosewood back and rims, projects a warm, full bodied tone. The action is low and fast, and the neck is reinforced with both a volute and an adjustable truss rod. Individual, enclosed, metal tuning pegs are gold plated. Multiple black and white body binding and distinctive contrasting centerpieces with inlaid marquetry on the back, are proof that this guitar is the work of fine craftsmen.

Mahogany neck with traditional full heel. Neck and peghead binding. "Vine of Life" inlay on peghead.

Rosewood fingerboard with exquisite two piece shell inlays, 20 frets. Multiple purfling ring. Ornate bridge pins with inlay.

**Presentation 745 (Not Shown)**—Solid spruce top, rosewood back and rims. Neck has adjustable truss rod. Rosewood fingerboard with dot inlays.

**Presentation 725 (Not Shown)**—Same in appearance as Presentation 745 except with mahogany back and rims, and laminated spruce top.

Cases for above models—
D-25—Deluxe Plush Durabilt Case.
814—Durabilt Case.

## Electric

**ET-290N**—The moderately priced ET-290N isn't a moderate performer. It's one of the best electric guitars you can get. The two gold plated Humbucking pickups are hot and sensitive so you can turn on some real hard rock. Your leads will pierce right through the loudest rhythm section. It's all under the control of two sensitive tone controls, two volume controls and a three position pickup selector switch. Highly polished, select maple body. Gold plated bridge, hardware. You know it's the best just looking at it. A beautiful instrument—a beautiful sound.

Deluxe professional highly polished natural Maple solid body. Two gold plated Humbucking pickups. Two volume and tone controls. Three position toggle switch.

**ET-290**—Same as above, but with cherry sunburst finish and rosewood fingerboard with block position markers.

**ET-276 (Not Shown)**—Original Epiphone body design. Mahogany finish. Hardwood adjustable neck. Rosewood fingerboard with dot inlays. Two pickups. Volume and tone controls. Pickup selector switch. Chrome plated hardware.

Cases for above models—
D-43—Deluxe Plush Durabilt Case.
811—Durabilt Case.

**EA-255 Electric-Acoustic (Not Shown)**—Deluxe professional thin electric with two Humbucking pickups. Frequensator tailpiece. Naturally finished select walnut top, rims and back. Three piece slim adjustable neck with block inlay, rosewood fingerboard. Multiple body bindings. Adjustable bridge. Two volume and two tone controls. Gold plated hardware.
D-30—Deluxe Plush Durabilt Case

**ET-285-Bass**—Other basses in this price range give you a "muddy" sound without much "definition." But the ET-285 has a rich, clean, distinctive sound that studio engineers love to work with. The powerful bass pickups and hard, solid body design give it that sound. The action is effortless and the intonation is flawless. The double cutaway makes it easy to get at the high notes for playing the funkiest rhythms. And the sunburst finish really sparkles.

Original Epiphone solid body, electric bass design. Sunburst finish. Double cutaway. Adjustable hardwood neck. Rosewood fingerboard with dot inlays. Two powerful pickups. Toggle switch. Adjustable bridge. Foam rubber mute. Volume and tone controls. Chrome plated hardware.

Cases for above model—
D-47—Deluxe Plush Durabilt Case.
821—Durabilt Case.

In addition, a completely new flat-top line debuted in 1976, called the Nova series. These had a body shape similar to that of the Gibson J-185, with a circular lower bout, but from there they were off on their own. The bridge shape curved into a wide smile. The pickguard looked something like the sail of a sailboat. And the soundhole was elliptical. The top model, the Nova 390, sported the cloud fingerboard inlay shape from the old Epi Deluxe and the fat, squat, columnlike peghead inlay found on the old Triumph acoustic and Broadway electric.

By 1979 the Epi line seemed healthy, with over 20 steel-string flat-top models, four classicals, a pair each of banjos and mandolins, the Scrolls, and a new solidbody series, the Genesis. The three Genesis models were made in Taiwan and sported a new double-cutaway shape similar to the old Olympic Special, but with nubbier horns. The Sheraton-like T290N

# EPIPHONE GENESIS CUSTOM

**BODY SPECIFICATIONS**
- Solid, double cutaway mahogany body for total access to all 22 frets.
- Carved top.
- Gold plated parts.
- Fully adjustable tune-o-matic bridge.
- Top and back bound with deluxe black/white laminate binding.

**NECK SPECIFICATIONS**
- One-piece mahogany.
- Rosewood fingerboard bound with deluxe laminate binding.
- Headpiece bound with deluxe laminate binding.
- Simulated abalone Epiphone insignia inlaid on headpiece.
- Revealed edge truss rod cover.
- Individual, gold plated deluxe tuning machines.
- Fully adjustable truss rod.
- 24¾" scale.

**ELECTRONICS SPECIFICATIONS**
- 2 powerful, gold plated humbucking pickups.
- 3-position toggle switch.
- Coil-tap switch for humbucking/non-humbucking tonalities.
- 2 volume and one master tone controls.

**AVAILABLE FINISHES**
- Ebony, Dark Sunburst.

**Epiphone**
Another Quality Product from Norlin
7373 No. Cicero Avenue, Lincolnwood, IL 60646
In Canada: 51 Nantucket Blvd., Scarborough, Ontario

*Epiphone*

The constant changes in the line reflected the efforts of Norlin's sales and marketing people to find a way to compete with the imports.

---

*Above:*
*The Genesis line of 1979 borrowed its body shape from Gibson's double-cutaway Les Paul Junior and Les Paul Special.*

*Opposite Page—*
*Top:*
*This Nova, from 1976, combined traditional Epi inlay patterns with new bridge and pickguard shapes.*

*Center:*
*The Presentation model debuted in 1976, and the PR designation still lives in the Epi line of today.*

*Bottom:*
*Solidbody electrics of 1976 returned to a body shape based on the Epi solidbodies of the sixties.*

had been dropped from the line, as had the basses and assorted solidbodies.

The constant changes in the Epi line reflected the efforts of Norlin's sales and marketing people to find a way to compete with the influx of imports. "What was really occurring," says Bill Nothdorft, Epi marketing director in the early eighties, "is that the model changes were a by-product of committee, and we were changing presidents about every 18 months, and everybody had an idea about which way it should go. And of course Epiphone was a stepchild. Oftentimes it was the whim of whoever." Although Epiphone had been divorced from Gibson for a decade, Gibson

people were still called on for help. According to Nothdorft, Gibson plant manager Jim Deurloo had some influence on the Epi line, and Nothdorft eventually sent Gibson technicians to the overseas plants to help with production problems.

Norlin CEO Norton Stevens recalled, "Everybody was doing it on a price basis, and everybody was just figuring out how to deal with that new world. We felt we were taking the high road, maintaining or improving the quality. I always feel we did the best we could in the things we thought were important: maintain quality, improve it, be good to the clients, and also try to make a little money for the shareholders."

## Epiphone

The shrinking of the guitar industry was illustrated in the Epi line. By the beginning of 1980, the Scroll series was gone, the Novas were gone, the classicals were gone, and the eight student-model flat-tops were gone.

Stevens went the extra mile to learn the secrets of his competitors. "I used to go over to Japan a lot," he said. "I lived there for three years and spoke the language a little bit. I nosed around and tried to find their secret. With the Yamaha people, single-minded dedication was an important part of their stuff. They were able to do things others couldn't because they made all their money locally and they could dump overseas. That was very clever. In a way some people claimed it was unfair. I never could take that line. You had to be able to figure out how to compete with them on quality, availability, and service."

By the end of the 1970s the musical instrument market had begun to turn away from the guitar—American-made as well as imported—in favor of new, innovative keyboard instruments. The shrinking of the guitar industry was illustrated in the Epi line. By the beginning of 1980, the Scroll series was gone, the Novas were gone, the classicals were gone, and the eight student-model flat-tops were gone. The 36-model line of 1979 was slashed to 20. In mid year, however, the line was expanded a bit, with a Genesis bass, another mandolin, and four new Presentation series flat-tops. By this time, Epiphones were coming from several sources, including Aria, Matsumoku, Iida, and Terada.

Also in or around 1980, a new sub-budget line of acoustic flat-tops appeared briefly. Bearing the "Epi" brand (not Epiphone, just Epi), these were made by the Marina company in Taiwan, in the city of Chuanyin, just outside of Taoyuan. Tim Shaw recalls, "The quality was so bad nobody was willing to put *Epiphone* on it. It was just *Epi.* Silkscreened on. They were real pigs. The factory is outside on a mountain in Taipei. We could talk about good climates in which to build guitars. That would not be my first choice."

These guitars were so bad that CMI had to send Bill Nothdorft to Seattle to set up a final assembly facility. "They came in needing final adjustment anywhere from straightening reverse bows in the neck to whatever happens to an electric and acoustic guitar," Nothdorft says.

The Genesis series was scrapped in 1981, leaving the Epiphone line totally acoustic and entirely built by the Aria company. But not for long. In 1982, at a time when Gibson had discovered great market interest in reissues of fifties Les Pauls, four names from the old Gibson-Epi days were revived in the Epiphone line. Bill Nothdorft recalls these, like all the more expensive Epis, as being made by the Terada company. At the top of the line once again was the Emperor, available in a full-depth or a thinbody version—both 17" wide, rather than the 18" of the original. Below it were the Sheraton, Riviera, and Casino. At prices ranging from $595.95 for the Casino to $989.95 for the Emperor, these guitars were reasonably priced, but certainly not aimed at the buyer on a budget. €

# On to Korea

Times were bad for guitar makers in the early 1980s, thanks to a surge of innovation in electronic keyboards. Times were even worse for Norlin. Norlin had mismanaged all of the divisions of the old CMI empire into a shambles, and Gibson was about to go on the auction block. The Epi line seemed to have found a solid identity in 1982, but it was too late, as the cost of Japanese guitars was increasing. Japanese makers had begun moving their production to Korea as far back as the early seventies, when American makers had first started looking to Japan. Now the Japanese-made Epiphones were too expensive to compete with imports from Korea.

Norlin decided to send Epi production to Korea around 1983. Tim Shaw recalls that the move mirrored the earlier move to Japan in terms of model lines. Samick was chosen as a manufacturer. "They basically just got the Samick catalog, '83 or '84. This is Samick, which was at the time building the fantastically successful Hondo line. It was a matter of talking directly to Samick and saying, 'Do you want to build Epiphones?' and they said, 'Sure.'"

*The Emperor, available with the full-depth body (F) or thin (T), represented the upscale turn taken by the Epi line in 1982, just before production was moved to Korea.*

The only Epiphones made in the United States in the seventies and eighties, these map-shaped guitars of 1983 were designed for a Gibson promotion, but some were made for Epi dealers, too.

In the early 1980s it's likely that few people in the Norlin corporate offices cared who was making Epiphones. The company was struggling, selling off its music divisions and even its Ecuadorian beer industry holdings in an effort to survive. In August 1984 Rooney Pace, a New York brokerage house, took over Norlin, but Rooney Pace was anything but a savior for Gibson and Epiphone, the last of Norlin's music divisions. In an official corporate statement, the head of the corporation rejoiced when Gibson (and Epiphone along with it) was finally unloaded in January 1986.

The new owners—Henry Juszkiewicz, David Berryman, and Gary Zebrowski— were Harvard MBAs who had turned around a failing Oklahoma company that made tape decks for computers. They hoped to bring back Gibson to its former position of respect and prosperity. Epiphone was a different matter.

"The state of Epi at the end of 1985 was pretty dismal," Berryman says. "No one spent any time on it. It was thrown in with the Gibson company." He sums it up this way: "No one was Epiphone."

Right:

*A* pair of Recording
Bandmaster models from the
late 1920s, with tenor neck
and the longer plectrum neck.
(Banjos courtesy Gruhn
Guitars)

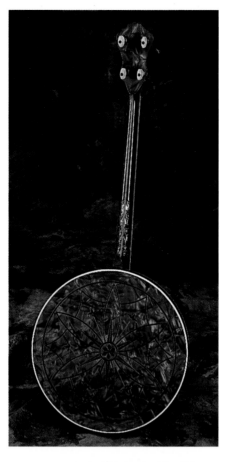

Above:

*The highly ornamented Recording Concert banjo was Epiphone's mid-line model of the 1920s.*

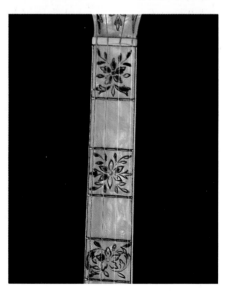

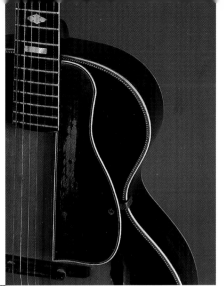

Right:

*D*e Luxe, 1932, the top model of the original Epiphone Masterbilt line of 1931.

*(Guitar courtesy Gruhn Guitars)*

Left:

*Model M lap steel and amp, circa 1939—two models from the original Electar catalog of 1937.*

Right:

*Epiphone's answer to the pedal steel: the Varichord, with pitch changing mechanisms mounted on the body of the guitar itself, providing "every chord but 'The Lost Chord,' " according to Epi literature.*

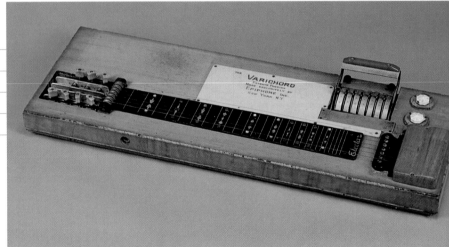

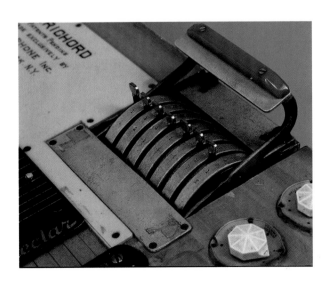

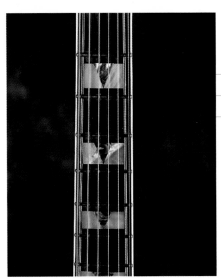

Left:

*A*n Emperor in natural from the early fifties. (Guitar courtesy Gruhn Guitars)

Right:

*B*londes in the garden: a '59 Sheraton (with "New York" knobs and pickups), an acoustic Emperor from the forties, and a '58 Emperor. (Instruments and photo courtesy Lark St. Music)

**Right:**

*Jim Vivino, guitarist on Conan O'Brien's "Late Night" TV show, plays a cherry Riviera from the late sixties. An early-fifties Zephyr Emperor Regent waits in the background. (© 1995 Anthony Stroppa)*

**Below:**

*Collector Steve Johnson with a 1957 Coronet, the model originally named the Moderne. (© 1995 Anthony Stroppa)*

**Bottom Left:**

*Musician and collector Nick Skopelitis with a 1965 Texan.*

*(© 1995 Anthony Stroppa)*

**Bottom Right:**

*Kevin Kuhn, guitarist for the Broadway production of* Tommy, *with an Emperor.*

*(© 1995 Anthony Stroppa)*

Top Left:

Collector Frank Daley with a late-sixties Casino.

(Guitar courtesy Rudy's Music Stop, photo © 1995 Anthony Stroppa)

Top Right:

Session guitarist Eddie Martinez with a Dwight—a Coronet made for a dealer brand.

(© 1995 Anthony Stroppa)

Left:

A late-sixties Riviera in metallic burgundy.

(Guitar courtesy Chelsea Second Hand Guitars, photo © 1995 Anthony Stroppa)

Right:

Blues great Stevie Ray Vaughan playing a Riviera.

Above:

*The Beatles perform on the BBC in 1966, with George Harrison and John Lennon playing Epi Casinos. (© Hulton/Apple Corps)*

Bottom Left:

*John Lennon and his Casino, 1966, during the Beatles' Abbey Road studio sessions for "Paperback Writer" and "Rain." (© Hulton/Apple Corps)*

Bottom Right:

*George Harrison and his Casino take center stage for the Beatles' taping of "Hello, Goodbye," 1967. (© Hulton/Apple Corps)*

Above:

*A*llen Woody, bass player with the Allman Brothers Band, holds a rare sunset

yellow Newport bass.

*R*ivoli hollowbody bass, 1960s vintage, from

the collection of Allen Woody.

Bottom Right:

A sampling of electrics from Epiphone's

1965 catalog.

Bottom Left:

A pair of Epiphone Cortez models, owned by Allen

Woody, of the Allman Brothers Band. Only the all

mahogany Caballero outsold the Cortez in the

Kalamazoo-made Epi flat-top line.

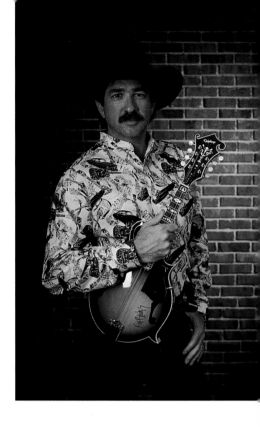

Top Left:

*G*lenn Maxey, of Brother Cane, with the El Capitan electric/acoustic bass.

Top Right:

*Country star Kix Brooks (of Brooks & Dunn) created his own signature model by signing an Epiphone MM-50 mandolin.*

Bottom Center:

*J*ohn Ricco, of Warrior Soul, with a U.S.-made Coronet. (© 1991 Anthony Stroppa)

Bottom Right:

*Joe Taylor, of the Lita Ford Band, with an EM-1 Rebel Standard. (© 1991 Anthony Stroppa)*

*Emperor reissue.*

Right:

*Hot rocker Lenny Kravitz modeling the latest*

*fashion, an Epi Riviera.*

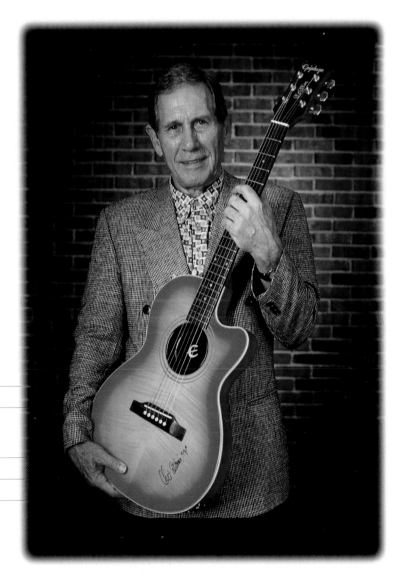

Left:

*Blues great John Lee Hooker in 1994 with a new Sheraton.*

*(© 1995 Al Pereira)*

Above:

*Jeff "Skunk" Baxter and his signature Epi model.*

Right:

*Guitar legend Chet Atkins with an Epi version of his solidbody*

*acoustic guitar.*

Above:

*Robert Cagianese with his grandmother, Elly Stathopoulo Retsas, the last surviving child of Anastasios and Marianthe Stathopoulo.*

Right:

*The Stathopoulo family plot in Astoria, New York.*

# EPIPHONE
## TODAY

# From Dozens to Thousands

Epiphone

David Berryman (left) and Henry Juszkiewicz revived Epiphone along with Gibson after acquiring the company in 1986.

The sale of Gibson and Epiphone in January 1986 to Henry Juszkiewicz, David Berryman, and Gary Zebrowski was hardly the rescue operation for Epiphone that Gibson's acquisition of Epi had been 29 years earlier. The task of reviving Gibson required an enormous amount of attention, and Epiphone had fallen so low—under $1 million in revenues for 1985, according to the sketchy sales figures provided by Norlin—that the new owners had no grand plans for Epiphone. In fact, they didn't even have any small plans for the "stepchild" company.

"When we first bought the company Epiphone sales were so small that frankly it wasn't really anything that we even thought about," says Juszkiewicz,

chairman and CEO of Gibson Guitar Corp. "I'm not even sure that the little that we did sell was profitable. There was also a significant perception that Epiphone was really bad product, so in the beginning, we really didn't think there was much potential in it."

"We didn't really see a future for Epiphone," concurs David Berryman, president of the new ownership group. "We talked about it, and obviously no time was being spent on it, but the problems at Gibson were so serious that it really didn't command a lot of time or attention, unfortunately. We didn't have the people to put on it, nor did we have the management time to really spend and focus on Epiphone."

The new owners had no background in the guitar market, but they needed only a quick look to find a place for Epiphone. "Very early into the situation, I had a chance to take a look at the product and understand a little bit more about the Epiphone history and see what was happening in the guitar business," Juszkiewicz says. "Basically all the most popular instruments in 1986 were sourced in the Far East. Charvel was making big gains. Kramer was basically a Korean product. Just about all the big names were basically Asian at that point in time. So I said, hey, we have a product made in the Far East, they have a product made in the Far East. They're selling thousands, we're selling dozens. Maybe this is something we should look at. So I looked at it and decided that if Kramer can do it, we can do it. But it's certainly going to be a long-term program."

Berryman was tied up managing the Gibson plant in Nashville, where Gibson had moved its headquarters in 1984. Juszkiewicz tried to get Epiphone rolling again, making a trip to Korea in 1986 to visit Samick, the primary Epiphone supplier. "We were a puny little customer, but they knew Gibson," he says. "I remember sitting with the owner of the factory. He said 'What do you think you're going to do in the future?' And I told him, and he just about fell out of his chair. He said, 'That's a pretty big increase.' I said, 'Yep.' Koreans are pretty aggressive businessmen and they kind of liked that, but in the first year or so I'm pretty sure they didn't believe we were going to revive this brand name. It certainly was a long shot." Juszkiewicz also added the Cort and Peerless companies to the list of Epiphone's Korean suppliers.

Juszkiewicz's perspective on Epiphone in the late eighties differs from Berryman's. "I'm not so sure that Epiphone got less management attention and focus as that there wasn't that much to do, and the [Gibson] factory was a lot more challenging than ordering models," Juszkiewicz says. "I think that we went about as fast as our resources allowed at the point. I was on top of it. There's only just so much you can do with an import line. Once you choose the product and you order it, then you've got to sell it. The fact is, we were experiencing 100, 200 percent growth every year. You can't do much better than that. It was our highest-growth line right from the get-go."

Juszkiewicz emphasizes that Epiphone did command a great deal of his attention. "I actually put the full-court press on it," he says. "It was difficult. The first thing I had to do was convince our sales force that the product was good, and it was a major component of our effort from 1986 on. There was just a lot of work to be done in terms of ensuring the quality of the product. The biggest problems in the first few years were supply problems, because of production delays at the Korean factories. They had labor riots, they had a flood, the factory burned down. So besides the normal customary way of doing business, they had supply disruptions. It was very difficult maintaining a consistent flow of product, but it was a growth line pretty much from the outset.

"I had a fairly good feel for what the market wanted, but a lot of it was based on

"Just about all the big names were basically Asian at that point in time. So I said, hey, we have a product made in the Far East, they have a product made in the Far East. They're selling thousands, we're selling dozens."

# Epiphone

*The rising Japanese yen made it impossible to meet the target price point, and the Nouveaus were dropped after 1989.*

some instinct and also looking at historical results. I placed fairly conservative orders, and basically I was pretty confident I could sell anything I ordered. Fortunately, that was true. I never really had a problem moving any product. I was pretty accurate in ordering. It took me a couple of years to establish a good feeling for market acceptance of various models, and that was made very difficult because supply would come and go. It was real hard to figure out what the market really wanted when product didn't show up, then it showed up three container loads at a time. So it took me a couple of years to figure out with those elements what the product demand really was. The strategy for Epiphone got refined progressively as we got more experience and became a bigger factor in the market."

Juszkiewicz also explored the possibility of renewing Japanese production. Even traditional, conservative American companies like Martin were taking advantage of import opportunities with Japanese-made guitars and Japanese-made "kits"—unfinished necks and bodies that were assembled and finished in the United States, thus avoiding a "Made in Japan" tag. Juszkiewicz ordered some kit guitars from Japan and outfitted them with inlay patterns from what he calls "the scrap-heap archives—random thoughts by old-time Gibson designers." These models were introduced in 1987 under the "Nouveau by Gibson" banner. The next year they were moved to the Epiphone line. The rising

Japanese yen made it impossible to meet the target price point, and the Nouveaus were dropped after 1989. The only subsequent Japanese production came at about the same time, with limited production of carved-top instruments. The Casino, Riviera, and Sheraton were manufactured in Japan, for the Japanese market only, by Aria under a licensing agreement.

Juszkiewicz considered other supply sources for Epiphone besides Korea and Japan. "We tested other suppliers," he says. "We had a supplier in Taiwan, which was pretty interesting because it was a new factory, but it had too much moisture in the product. The product looked pretty good but it would explode in the stores. Not one of our most successful. We tested other factories continuously. We looked at Eastern Bloc, East Germany, but never were able to find anybody who had the same level of quality versus pricing [as Korean sources]. Within three years we became a major customer at Samick, so we had a lot of clout."

Tim Shaw, who would move from Gibson's engineering department to help with Epiphone, saw a profound difference in the way Epiphone was run after the arrival of Juszkiewicz and Berryman. Before, he says, the sales department was somewhat in control, "ordering based on gut instinct and the phases of the moon. How many of these did we sell this last month? Electric guitars for Norlin were bumped into product line 40 at the time. Hell, we just bought 'em. Bought 'em and shipped 'em. Henry and Dave were the first people to quantify an ordering model, which is a spreadsheet the size of a table that actually tracks historical sales data."

By 1988 the Epiphone line had begun to look better. The acoustic offering featured a revamped PR series of square-shouldered dreadnoughts that, with belly bridges and tortoiseshell teardrop-shaped pickguards, looked a lot like Martins. In the sixties tradition of Gibson-styled guitars, the line also included a version of the Gibson J-180, which was a revival of the sixties Everly Brothers model (but without the Everlys' endorsement). Three classical guitars, a banjo, and a mandolin rounded out the line.

The Epi electric catalog of 1989 illustrated several of the directions the Epi line would follow in the nineties. The featured solidbody models followed the lead of the acoustic line, drawing on designs of the most popular models of the day, regardless of whether they were associated with the Gibson/Epi tradition.

By this time, Juszkiewicz was well aware of, and catering to, a market that was different from the average buyer of a Gibson. "We were selling generally to first-time users," he explains. "That's very fashion-oriented. Most of the fashion was in colors. Back in the late eighties they had the zebra stripe, the camouflage, the hideous yellow. They were real big on

provocative colors, then the market swung to real conservative within about three months, so you had to be really on top of what was happening. But at the same time we took a really conservative look at it, unlike some other companies that had the 'flavor of the month.' Our S-310 [one of the "copy" models] today is pretty much the same guitar it was back then—much better made, and we've refined a lot of stuff, put our own pickup designs in, but effectively it's still a fairly conservative, three-single-coil guitar."

Significantly, the 1988 line also included some new Epi versions of famous Gibson models: the Flying V, SG, even a Les Paul Standard and Les Paul Custom. More recent Gibson models, such as the Chet Atkins Country Gentleman and the Howard Roberts Fusion (both $f$-hole archtops), were now available in the Epi line. And finally, a new Sheraton, called the Sheraton II, represented the Epiphone line of 25 years earlier. €

*The featured solidbody models followed the lead of the acoustic line, drawing on designs of the most popular models of the day.*

# Turning up the Gas

## Epiphone

By 1992 Epiphone sales had grown from less than $1 million to $10 million. A thousand percent growth in just five years.

In 1991 the Epiphone line boasted 43 models, including all types of electric and acoustic guitars, electric basses, and a mandolin and banjo. In addition, the new Epiphone Orville series brought back memories of an older Epiphone company that often beat Gibson to the punch with Gibson's own ideas. In this case, Epiphone appropriated the name of Gibson's founder, Orville Gibson, and several of his well-known design elements: the star-and-crescent inlay on a "paddle" peghead and an ornate butterfly inlay between the bridge and soundhole. In the meantime the Coronet solidbody was revived—but with the addition of active electronics—in a limited run built in the United States. These two moves helped reestablish Epiphone as a company with a freer, more adventuresome spirit than its parent, Gibson.

"Still," Berryman says, "Epiphone was sold alongside Gibson, and everything was shared. The marketing was shared, the sales management and sales support was shared, the people in the distribution center were working on both Gibson and Epiphone, and we just didn't get the benefit of having a dedicated focus and dedicated work force until late 1993, and when we did that, it really catapulted us to a new level.

By 1992 Epiphone sales had grown from less than $1 million to $10 million. A thousand percent growth in just five years—still without a dedicated staff—screamed out for attention, and David Berryman took over the Epi line. He found that Epiphone's problems were more deeply rooted than just a lack of someone's undivided attention. "It goes back to the

*Above:*
*The Epiphone version of one of the most famous models of all time, the Gibson Les Paul Standard goldtop.*

*Opposite Page:*
*Jim "Epi" Rosenberg arrived in 1992 to help bring autonomy to the Epiphone line.*

The first step in "turning up the gas" was to open an office in Seoul. As a result, Berryman was more easily able to expand the supply base to include more manufacturers and also to keep better control over design, as well as the quality of the product.

"It was only in 1992, when we began to staff it separately, with Jim Rosenberg in a product management role, totally focused on the product, and had separate distribution center employees and separate quality control people, again only focused on Epiphone, did we really start to reap the benefits," Berryman says. "We really took off, because we were concentrating on the product and marketing of the product, product design, product specifications. So now it's in a whole different light. Epiphone is its own company, truly."

Jim Rosenberg arrived in April 1992 from E-mu Systems (the synthesizer company), where he had been director of product marketing. "I think when I started, the Epi line was at a respectable point," he says. "People had done a lot of work to get it where it was. But it was really, 'Let's just come out with some models that are like other people's.' We did have the Les Paul, similar to Gibson's. We did have the Emperor and the Sheraton. But there wasn't a lot of attention being paid to, 'Let's do something unique to Epiphone, new or historical.' "

Rosenberg also recognized and ran up against the same problem that had held Epiphone back since the late fifties. And he uses the same term to describe Epiphone that had been used for 30 years. "One of the big problems that existed when I got here, in a sense of not being able to take Epiphone to its fullest potential, was that most people looked at Epiphone as

fact that Epiphone really didn't benefit by Gibson buying it and incorporating it, even up in Kalamazoo," Berryman says. "It's the age-old problem that when you incorporate something like that into the organization, it's non-Gibson, so it doesn't belong. So if you don't have dedicated people—where

all they do is Epiphone—it dies, because people think they're Gibsons.

"Epiphone was the red-headed stepchild, all the way through, until we separated it out and really turned up the gas."

secondary to Gibson—the red-headed stepchild," he says. "I think it goes back historically. I talked to Andy Nelson [an Epi rep from the sixties; see Chapter 4], and we had long conversations about the Epiphone line. He kept saying, 'I know what you're up against. Those bastards at Gibson, they're always putting you down. You can do something better.'"

Rosenberg fought that problem with the one thing Epiphone had been lacking for a quarter century: complete dedication. "I think what I brought to the Epiphone line was the idea that Epiphone is as important as Gibson in my mind—well, even more so." To illustrate his dedication, Rosenberg

began signing his name, which appears on the Epiphone guarantee, "Jim Epi Rosenberg."

At the time Rosenberg arrived, reissues of the Emperor, Howard Roberts, and Zephyr were about to begin production in Japan. These were made by Fujigen, probably the most modern, most automated guitar factory in the world. At one time they were the leading manufacturer in Japan. "These were limited editions—limited to the price of the yen," Rosenberg recalls. "They became impractical to produce because of the change in the yen." Also, the Emperor's 18½" body caused problems, particularly in natural finish, because of the unavailability of suitable wood for the large solid-wood tops. The first shipment of Emperors arrived around the end of 1992 and was only about 36 guitars, followed by another seven or eight. The multi-ply binding of the Howard Roberts caused production problems, and the first shipment consisted of 42 guitars, followed by another five. Only about 13 Zephyrs were made. Their pickups were Japanese-made in the old New York style, which required tooling for the pickup rings and the octagonal control knobs.

Despite the limited production and high costs, the endeavor was a success. "We still have people asking for them," Rosenberg says. "I think it brought a lot more awareness to the name and also put some attention on our heritage as being a great name in archtops."

Epiphone had also just introduced the Epiphonic V, a preamp with five-band parametric equalization. Designed by Gibson's Oberheim keyboard division, the Epiphonic V showed a new, innovative side of Epiphone. By the time of the NAMM show in January 1993, Rosenberg had expanded the acoustic-electric line with some thinbodied models and put electronics into almost all the Epiphone flat-tops. It served notice to the industry that Epiphone was intent on being a leader in product development and could respond to new market demands. "Those thinbodied acoustic-electric guitars were what people were looking for," Rosenberg says. "There weren't many who had electronics. We were not the first, but we were among the first to recognize the need. The PR-6Es had beautiful flame maple tops and great colors. The PR-7 had a bird's-eye top and a wide selection of translucent colors."

Also at NAMM 1993, Rosenberg unveiled the LP-100, an entry-level guitar with the shape of Gibson's classic Les Paul model. "That's when people really started looking at Epi and saying, 'There's a lot in the line here and it's a real good value,' " according to Rosenberg.

The NAMM show established Epiphone as a force in the market for innovative new guitar styles. Later in 1993, Epiphone recognized its own rich tradition. At Henry Juszkiewicz's suggestion, the Riviera and Sheraton were reissued in a limited run of 250 made in Gibson's Nashville plant. "They sold out immediately," Rosenberg says. "There was a lot of demand for us to build more, but the fact is it wasn't practical to build them in the Nashville plant because the Gibson Nashville plant had their hands full building their own ES models [Electric Spanish, Gibson's terminology for hollow and semi-hollow electrics], and actually the equivalent model in the Gibson line, like the ES-335, was easier to produce and less costly to produce than the Sheraton model."

Gibson's Montana division, which makes all Gibson flat-tops, jumped on the U.S.-made Epi bandwagon with limited editions of the Excellente, Frontier, and Texan. Each sold out its run of 250 instruments.

Although the U.S.-made models were special events, they had an immediate positive effect on the Epiphone line. "After seeing the response, the success of the archtops out of Nashville, that inspired us to bring out all the archtops that we have now in the line produced in Korea—the Casino, Riviera, Sorrento, Emperor Regent, and Rivoli bass," Rosenberg says. "Except for the Emperor Regent, which is a Gibson L-5 type guitar with a floating pickup, those models

*The first step in "turning up the gas" was to open an office in Seoul. As a result, Berryman was more easily able to expand the supply base to include more manufacturers and also to keep better control over design, as well as the quality of the product.*

are very authentic replications of the originals. It took significant development time to have those produced at that price point. We had to tool a lot of the components, like the Frequensator tailpiece, the pickguards, the metalplate *E* on the pickguard, the dog-eared pickup covers, etc. We started in early '93 and weren't able to introduce them until NAMM 1994."

The historic value of the Epiphone name also affected the new Epiphone amplifier line. Epiphone amps were revived in 1993 with black vinyl coverings. In 1994 the covering was changed to a textured vinyl with a vintage tweed look (although it was the look of a competitor's vintage amps). In 1995 the demand for vintage Epi guitars prompted Rosenberg to look to vintage Epiphone amplifiers for future models.

In the meantime, Rosenberg and Berryman were working behind the scenes to change the perception of Epiphones among distributors and dealers. "We were working with our dealers and positioning Epiphone differently versus Gibson," Berryman says. "People were thinking of Epiphone just as a cheap Gibson, and that's not the case. And now people are realizing that. Also our international distributors I don't think took the line seriously back in the late eighties. Now our domestic dealers and our international distributors and their dealers see Epiphone as one of the highest profit potentials of any guitar line that they can

handle. We have the broadest offering of product of any of our competitors, and at all price points. And our key—the premise that we've been going on for many, many years, and people are starting to take notice of—is value. Value is the combination of quality and price. And at the retail price of our instruments, we feel we offer the best quality that's available in the marketplace, period."

Rosenberg explains one of the reasons behind Epiphone's success and reputation among imported brands: "Epiphone is different from other brands that have guitars produced offshore. We're very much involved in the manufacturing of the instruments, and we determine the product specification of each one of the instruments. We also specify where it is produced. We have an office full-time in Seoul, Korea, to help manage that process, so I think of those factories as extensions of us here in Nashville."

# The Epi Bandwagon

Epiphone salesman Joe Terhesh posed for the official "Mark of a Great Guitarist" photo.

The new, improved Epiphone guitars caught the ears of a group of players who hadn't paid any attention to Epiphones for 30 years—professional musicians. "After we started the U.S.-made models and the reproductions of the original models, people started looking at the quality and looking at the value," Rosenberg says. "I was approached by a number of artists after they had played them, and they were excited about putting their name on a guitar that had great quality, sounded good, was easy to play, and yet didn't cost an arm and a leg."

Jazz great Joe Pass adopted the Epiphone Emperor II, a classic jazz guitar shape with rounded cutaway, as his own signature model. Then Chet Atkins, who already had a successful line of solidbody acoustics under the Gibson brand, was approached by Rosenberg.

"Chet Atkins wanted to have a model with his name on it that would be much more affordable and accessible for the masses," Rosenberg says. "So we built a prototype of the SST and took it to him. I remember being in his office. He said, 'Let me try this thing out.' He went out on this back porch

area where he has his amp. He checked out the intonation, the output of each string, checked it over, and said, 'Boy, this is a pretty good guitar. I think I like it.'"

An all-new Epiphone endorsement model, the first since the 1960s, came from Jeff "Skunk" Baxter, former member of the Doobie Brothers. "He had said he visited Gibson several years before and was looking for a guitar and tried a number of acoustic guitars and didn't find one he liked," Rosenberg says. "They were all good guitars; they just didn't have one that appealed to him, sound characteristic-wise.

**Top Left:**
Epiphone "tattooed" thousands with "The Mark of a Great Guitarist" at the 1993 NAMM show in Nashville.

**Top Right:**
For the EO-2, Epiphone appropriated the butterfly and the star-and-crescent inlay from a guitar made by Orville Gibson circa 1900.

**Center Left:**
Chet Atkins with his hands full of Epi models.

**Center Right:**
Jazz great Joe Pass was the first to endorse a 1990s Epiphone.

**Bottom Left:**
The Epiphonic V on-board electronics system.

**Opposite Page—**

**Top Left:**
The Jeff "Skunk" Baxter signature model.

**Top Right:**
The "solid" body of Epi's Chet Atkins is heavily routed to provide tone cavities.

**Bottom Right:**
Country star Kix Brooks signs a mandolin for Jim "Epi" Rosenberg.

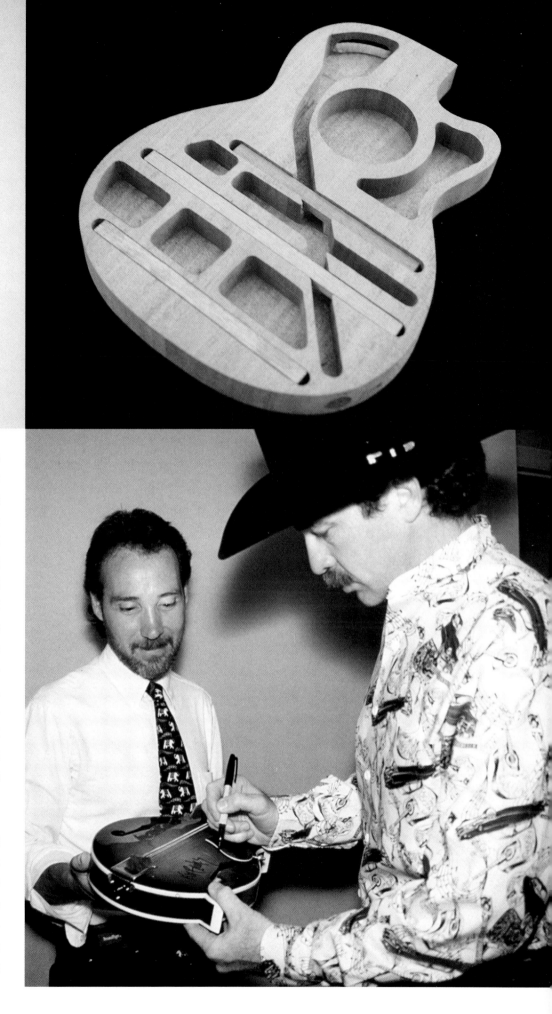

He looked over in the corner. There was a dusty guitar in the corner. He said, 'What about that guitar?' The people in the factory said, 'You don't want to look at that one; it's an Epi.' He blew off the dust, tried playing a few notes, and said, 'Wow, can I have this guitar?' He took it home, did some work on it, polished up the frets, and he has been playing it for about two years in the studio. His friends had been commenting on it, saying, 'That's a great-sounding guitar. What is it?' He had to say, 'Prototype, not available.' He had so many people asking about it he called me up and said, 'I think you can really sell this if you came out with it. The soundhole says its an EA-75.'

"We don't have an EA-75," Rosenberg continues. "It was similar to a PR-5, except the depth was more like a dreadnought. So I started working on doing one exactly like his. He added a few touches cosmetically—gold hardware, 'Skunk' inlay on the twelfth fret. He chose the colors. That's the Skunk Baxter signature model." ◪

# The Future of Epiphone

In less than 10 years Epiphone has grown from a minor import line to become one of the most important guitar brands in the world—and, arguably, the most popular. In 1994, international sales of Epiphones exceeded U.S. sales for the first time in Epi history.

On November 1, 1995, Epiphone moved into its own manufacturing facility at 645 Massman Drive in Nashville, next to Gibson's electric guitar factory. With the move, Epiphone came full circle, bringing production of some models (beginning with the Casino) back to the U.S.

Epiphone has grown from a stepchild brand name with no future to its own corporate division (as of 1994)—one with a broad but clear future, as detailed by Dave Berryman:

- "First of all, there is the Epiphone historic product—which is of course the Sheraton, Emperor, Casino, Riviera, Rivoli bass, Excellente—that whole area of rich heritage that Epiphone has, being known for making great instruments. We're bringing those back.

- "At the same time, we're the makers of Gibson-authorized replica product, such as the Les Paul, the SG, the J-200.

- "Then we have the 'commodity' styles. What I mean by that is basic shapes at basic price points, like basic dreadnought guitars, an entry-level guitar, a mid-level guitar, a little higher-level guitar with more features and benefits to it, but just general shapes.

• "And finally we have the fun product, innovative product—new shapes, new electronics, new things. That's one area where we will especially concentrate, because Gibson is a very traditional company, that's where it has its roots, and people expect certain things of a Gibson. Epiphone is different.

"Epiphone, I think, is more of a renegade. It marches to the beat of a different drum. Always has. When you look at the people who played Epiphone, when you look at the kind of product that was designed, it's different. We want to maintain and enhance that image. That's what we're about and that's what we're going for.

"That's the future of Epiphone." 🄴

*Top:*
*Epi president David Berryman shows his Epi tattoo.*

*Bottom:*
*Ribbon cutting at the new Epiphone headquarters, October 31, 1995. From left are Jim Rosenberg, Dave Berryman, and Henry Juszkiewicz.*

**EPIPHONE**

dedicated to the best
in fretted instruments
and bass viols since 1873

**APPENDICES**

Distributed Exclusively in U.S.A. by CONTINENTAL MUSIC

# Catalog History

## Recording Banjo Catalog, circa 1924

| | |
|---|---|
| De Luxe Art | .$375 |
| Concert | .$300 |
| Bandmaster | .$225 |
| Artist | .$150 |

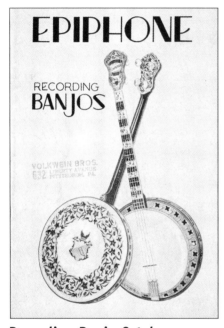

## Recording Banjo Catalog, circa 1928

| | |
|---|---|
| Emperor | .$500 |
| Dansant | .$425 |
| De Luxe | .$250 |
| Concert Special | .$300 |
| Concert | .$300 |
| Bandmaster | .$250 |
| Alhambra | .$200 |
| Artist | .$150 |

*Non-Recording models*

| | |
|---|---|
| Peerless | .$100 |
| Rialto | .$75 |
| Mayfair | .$50 |

## Recording Guitar Flier, circa 1928

| | |
|---|---|
| Recording E | .$175/$190 |
| (concert size/auditorium size) | |
| Recording D | .$125/$140 |
| Recording C | .$100/$115 |
| Recording B | .$75/$85 |
| Recording A | .$50/$60 |

## Masterbilt Guitar Catalog, 1931

*All have 3-segment f-holes, asymmetrical Masterbilt peghead...*

De Luxe: 16³/₈" wide, maple back and sides
Tudor: 16³/₈" wide, maple back and sides
Broadway: 16³/₈" wide, walnut back and sides
Triumph: 16³/₈" wide, walnut back and sides
Royal: 14³/₄" wide, mahogany back and sides
Blackstone: 14³/₄" wide, maple back and sides
Zenith: 13⁵/₈" wide, maple back and sides
Olympic: 13" wide, mahogany back and sides
Beverly: 13" wide, flat top, mahogany back and sides

*Tenors (related six-string model)*

Empire (De Luxe): 15¹/₂" wide
Bretton (Broadway): 15¹/₂" wide
Melody (Zenith): 13¹/₄" wide, walnut back and sides

## 1934 Catalog

*Top models no longer have triple-banner peghead ornamentation but have asymmetrical peghead with notch to right of center. The Triumph and lower models have a simple rounded-peak peghead.*

De Luxe: maple back and sides, $275
Tudor: maple back and sides, $225
Broadway: maple back and sides, $175
Triumph: maple back and sides, $125
Spartan: round hole, maple back and sides, $100
Royal: 14³/₄" wide, mahogany back and sides
Blackstone: 15¹/₂" wide, mahogany back and sides, $75
Zenith: 14³/₄" wide, walnut back and sides, $50
Olympic: 13⁵/₈" wide, mahogany back and sides
Beverly: $35

*Tenors (related six-string model)*

Empire (De Luxe): $250
Bretton (Broadway): walnut back and sides, $175
Hollywood (Triumph): $125
Regent (Spartan): $95
Melody (Zenith): $50

*Mandolins*

Windsor Special: scroll body, f-holes, maple back and sides, $200
Windsor: $150
Strand: Florentine body with two upper body points, f-holes, walnut back and sides, $75
Rivoli: A-style (pear-shaped), f-holes, walnut back and sides, $50
Adelphi: A-style (pear-shaped), f-holes, maple back and sides, $35

*Mandolas*

Strand: $110
Rivoli: $75
Adelphi: $50

*Mandocellos (guitar bodies)*

No. 1 (Blackstone): $95
No. 2 (Triumph): $150
No. 3 (De Luxe): $275

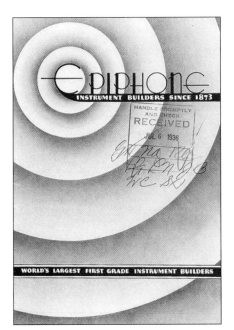

## 1936 and 1937 Catalogs

*Except for the substitution of several pictures of artists, the listings in these catalogs are identical. The 1936 edition has an orange cover and lettering; the 1937 is blue. All models now have conventional f-holes (rather than 3-segment style).*

Emperor: 18½" wide, $400
De Luxe: 17⅜" wide, $275
Broadway: 17⅜" wide, $175
Triumph: 17⅜" wide, $125
Spartan: 16⅜" wide, f-holes, $100
Blackstone: 16⅜" wide, maple back
  and sides, $75
Zenith: 16⅜" wide, walnut back
  and sides, $50
Olympic: 15¼" wide, mahogany back
  and sides, $35

*Tenors*

Broadway: $175
Triumph: $125
Spartan: $100
Blackstone: $50
Zenith: $50
Olympic: $35

*Flat-tops*

F.T. 75: 16½" wide, $75
F.T. 37: 15½" wide, $37.50
F.T. 27: 14½" wide, $27.50
Madrid: 16½" wide, Hawaiian, maple back
  and sides, $90
Navarre: 16½" wide, Hawaiian, mahogny
  back and sides, $50

---

*Mandolin family, same as 1934 except:*

Windsor Special changed to Windsor
Windsor changed to Artist
Windsor mandola added: $200
Artist mandola added: $150

## Electar Catalog, 1937

Model M lap steel and amp: black-on-black
  art deco pattern, angular body shape,
  horseshoe pickup; tweed-covered amp 12"
  speaker, stylized E on grille cloth, flip
  down panel to protect grille
Model C lap steel and amp: guitar shaped,
  maple top with sunburst finish, bar
  pickup; tweed amp with 10" speaker
Rocco double neck Hawaiian: horseshoe
  pickups, "Rocco Model" between necks
Super Amp: grained plastic covering
Spanish Guitar: horseshoe pickup
Tenor Guitar: four-string, horseshoe pickup
Banjo: tenor neck, plectrum available
  by special order, maple top,
  horseshoe pickup

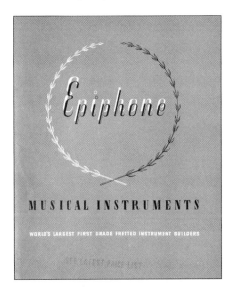

## 1939 Catalog

*All acoustics are unchanged from 1936–37, except for the addition of truss rod and Frequensator tailpiece. Natural finish is offered on the Emperor and De Luxe at no extra charge.*

---

*Additions*

F.T. De Luxe: flat top, maple back and sides,
  cloud inlay, $200
Concert: classical, 16½" wide, $225
Alhambra: classical, 14⅜" wide, maple
  back and sides, $105
Seville: classical, 14⅜" wide, mahogany
  back and sides, $65

*Electrics*

Zephyr Hawaiian, 6-/7-/8-string
  . . . . . . . . . . . . . . . .$90/$100/$110
Zephyr Spanish . . . . . . . . . . . . . . .$100
Zephyr Banjo . . . . . . . . . . . . . . . .$100
Zephyr Mandolin . . . . . . . . . . . . . .$100
Zephyr Amp, AC/DC . . . . . .$134.50/$149.50
Century Hawaiian, 6-/7-/8-string
  . . . . . . . . . . .$62.25/$72.25/$82.25
Century Spanish . . . . . . . . . . . . .$72.25
Century Banjo . . . . . . . . . . . . . . .$72.25
Century Mandolin . . . . . . . . . . . .$72.25
Century amp, AC/DC . . . . . . .$62.25/$72.25
Coronet Hawaiian . . . . . . . . . . . . .$35
Coronet Spanish . . . . . . . . . . . . . .$40
Coronet amp . . . . . . . . . . . . . . . . .$40
Solo Console, 6-/7-/8-string
  . . . . . . . . . . . . . .$120/$130/$140
Duo Console . . . . . . . . . . . . . . . .$185

## 1941 Catalog

*This catalog is similar to 1939. A separate price list notes up-charges of from $10 to $25 for natural finish (except on the Emperor). Most prices are still the same as 1936.*

*Changes and additions:*

Blackstone . . . . . . . . . . . . . . . .$79.50
Zenith . . . . . . . . . . . . . . . . . . . .$59.50
Ritz . . . . . . . . . . . . . . . . . . . . .$47.50
Olympic . . . . . . . . . . . . . . . . . .$39.50
F.T. 75 . . . . . . . . . . . . . . . . . . .$79.50
F.T. 37 . . . . . . . . . . . . . . . . . . .$42.50
F.T. 50 . . . . . . . . . . . . . . . . . . .$57.50
B-5 bass . . . . . . . . . . . . . . . . . .$250
B-4 bass . . . . . . . . . . . . . . . . . .$175
B-3 bass . . . . . . . . . . . . . . . . . .$150
B-2 bass . . . . . . . . . . . . . . . . . .$125
B-1 bass . . . . . . . . . . . . . . . . . .$105
Varichord . . . . . . . . . . . . . . . . . .$295
Zephyr Hawaiian, 6-/7-/8-string
  . . . . . . . . . . . . . . . .$96/$106/$116
Zephyr Spanish, Banjo, Mandolin . . . . .$106
Zephyr Amp, AC/DC . . . . . . . . . .$100/$115
Dreadnought Amp, AC/DC . . . . . .$140/$155
Century Hawaiian, 6-/7-/8-string
  . . . . . . . . . . . . . . . .$66/$76/$86
Century Spanish, Banjo, Mandolin . . . . .$76
Century amp, AC/DC . . . . . . . . . . .$66/$76
Coronet Hawaiian . . . . . . . . . . . .$37.25
Coronet Spanish . . . . . . . . . . . . .$47.25
Coronet amp . . . . . . . . . . . . . . .$42.25

## 1946 Price List

*Revised prices for catalog V (1941).*

*Many items were not yet back in production after World War II. These were noted by asterisks, with the explanation: "prices to be furnished when production is resumed."*

| | |
|---|---|
| Emperor, natural/sunburst | .....$410/$400 |
| De Luxe, natural/sunburst | .....$360/$350 |
| Broadway, natural/sunburst | ...$225/$250 |
| Triumph, natural/sunburst | ....$170/$160 |
| Spartan, natural/sunburst | .....$135/$125 |
| Blackstone, natural/sunburst | ....$110/$100 |
| Zenith regular | .................$75 |
| Olympic | .....................*** |
| Ritz blonde | ...................*** |

*Tenor versions of Olympic through De Luxe at same price as regular guitars.*

| | |
|---|---|
| FT 79 | ......................*** |
| FT 110 | .....................*** |
| FT 50 | ......................*** |
| FT 45 | ......................*** |
| FT 30 | ......................*** |

*Mandolins and mandolas*

| | |
|---|---|
| Windsor | ....................*** |
| Artist | ......................*** |
| Strand | .....................*** |
| Rivoli | ......................*** |
| Adelphi | ....................*** |

*Mandocellos*

| | |
|---|---|
| Blackstone | ..................*** |
| Triumph | ....................*** |
| Deluxe | .....................*** |

*Bass Viols*

| | |
|---|---|
| B-1 | .........................*** |
| B-2 | .........................*** |
| B-3 | .......................$190 |
| west of Rockies | ...............$199 |
| B-4 blonde or colored | ...........$235 |
| west of Rockies | ...............$243 |
| B-5 blonde or regular | ...........$325 |
| west of Rockies | ...............$333 |

*Banjos*

*Same offering as 1928, not in production.*

*Electrics*

| | |
|---|---|
| Zephyr De Luxe | ..............$225 |
| Zephyr Spanish | .............$125 |
| Century Spanish | .............$90 |
| Coronet Spanish outfit | ...........*** |
| Zephyr Hawaiian 6-/7-/8-string | |
| | ...........$112.50/$125/$137.50 |
| Century Hawian 6-/7-/8-string | |
| | ...............$75/$85/100 |
| Coronet outfit | ................*** |
| Varichord | ...................*** |
| Electar Grand | ................*** |
| Zephyr mandolin | ..............*** |
| Century mandolin | .............*** |
| Zephyr amp, AC/AC-DC | .......$132/$152 |
| Dreadnought amp, AC/AC-DC | ....$180/$210 |
| Century, AC/AC-DC | ..........$90/$100 |

## 1951 Electar Catalog

*Three different pickup styles debut in this catalog, including large rectangular metal covers on the Zephyr De Luxe, but not what will eventually be known as "New York" style.*

| | |
|---|---|
| Zephyr De Luxe Regent | ........$325/310 |
| (natural/sunburst) | |
| Zephyr De Luxe 2 pickups | .....$265/$250 |
| Zephyr De Luxe 1 pickup | .....$240/$225 |
| Zephyr | ..............$162.50/$150 |
| Century | ....................$110 |
| Kent | ......................$51 |
| Zephyr, 6-/7-/8-string | |
| | ............$112.5/$125/$137.50 |
| Century, 6-/7-/8-string | .....$75/$85/$95 |
| Kent steel | ...................$50 |
| Duo Console | .................$215 |
| Solo Console, 6-/7-/8-string | |
| | ...............$150/$160/$170 |
| Dreadnought amp, non-vib/vib | |
| | ...............$192.50/$202.50 |
| Zephyr amp, non-vib/vib | ......$154/$165 |
| Century amp, non-vib/vib | ......$110/$125 |
| Kent amp | ....................$54 |

## 1954 Catalog

| | |
|---|---|
| Emperor cutaway | ..........$565/$540 |
| (natural/sunburst) | |
| Emperor non-cutaway | .......$515/$490 |
| Deluxe cutaway | ...........$505/$485 |
| Deluxe non-cutaway | ........$450/$430 |
| Broadway cutaway | .........$355/$335 |
| Broadway non-cutaway | ......$315/$290 |
| Triumph cutaway | ..........$260/$240 |
| Triumph non-cutaway | .......$230/$210 |
| Triumph tenor | ............$230/$210 |
| Devon | .................$185/$179 |
| Zenith | .................$140/$125 |
| Zenith tenor | ............$140/$125 |
| Flat Top 110 | ............$180/$165 |
| Flat Top 79, sunburst | .............$125 |
| Emperor electric | ..........$535/$510 |
| Deluxe electric | ...........$425/$400 |
| Zephyr cutaway | ...........$245/$225 |
| Zephyr non-cutaway | ........$205/$285 |
| Zephyr tenor | ............$205/$185 |
| Century | ................$145/$130 |
| Triple-neck console | .........$365/$350 |
| Double console | ...........$305/$290 |
| Zephyr Hawaiian, 6-/7-/8-string | |
| | ...............$150/$160/$175 |
| Century Hawaiian, 6-/7-/8-string | |
| | ...............$100/$110/$120 |
| Zephyr mandolin | ..........$185/$170 |
| Strand mandolin | ...............$140 |
| Rivoli mandolin | .................$95 |
| B-4 bass | ...............$340/$310 |
| B-5 bass | ...............$395/$375 |
| Dreadnaught amp | ............$247.50 |
| Zephyr amp | ................$197.50 |
| Century amp | .................$150 |

**1955**

*The Harry Volpe model appeared only in advertisements.*

## 1961 Catalog

| | |
|---|---|
| Emperor electric | $775/$750 |
| (natural/shaded) | |
| Sheraton | $475/460 |
| Broadway | $350/335 |
| Zephyr | $280/265 |
| Windsor, 2 pickups | $300/285 |
| Windsor, 1 pickup | $240/225 |
| Sorrento, 2 pickups | $270/255 |
| Sorrento, 1 pickups | $210/195 |
| Century | $159.50 |
| Crestwood Cust | $265 |
| Wilshire | $195 |
| Coronet | $132 |
| Olympic | $99.50 |
| Olympic 3/4 | $99.50 |
| Frontier | $225/$210 |
| Texan | $145 |
| Cortez | $105 |
| Caballero | $75 |
| Emperor acoustic | $675/$650 |
| Deluxe | $565/$555 |
| Triumph | $295/$285 |
| Zenith | $157.50 |
| Rivoli electric bass | $300/$285 |
| B5N bass | $495/$425 |
| B4B bass | $375/$345 |
| BV bass | $299.50 |

*Amps*

Emperor EA5: 1-15", 6 tubes, $295
Deluxe EA10: 1-15", 6 tubes, $260
Zephyr EA15T: 1-12", 7 tubes, $215.
Century EA25T: 1-12", 7 tubes, $189.50
Triumph EA30: 1-12", 5 tubes, $137.50
Devon EA35: 1-10", $87.50
Pacemaker EA50: 1-8", $64.50

## electric spanish guitars

| | | |
|---|---|---|
| EA 8P | PROFESSIONAL OUTFIT guitar/amplifier combination with all controls in the guitar —35-watt amplifier | $595.00 |
| EA 7P | PROFESSIONAL OUTFIT guitar/amplifier combination with all controls in the guitar —15-watt amplifier | 495.00 |
| 1519 | Case, hard shell, plush-lined | 50.00 |
| 1304 | Case, Archcraft | 26.00 |
| 1104 | Case, chipboard | 15.00 |
| E 112T | *EMPEROR, thin body cutaway, shaded finish, 3 pickups | $825.00 |
| 1111 | Case, hard plush-lined | 60.00 |
| E 212TNV | SHERATON, thin body double cutaway, natural finish, 2 pickups and Tremotone vibrato | 580.00 |
| E 212TN | SHERATON, thin body double cutaway, natural finish, 2 pickups | 525.00 |
| E 212TV | SHERATON, thin body double cutaway, shaded or cherry finish, 2 pickups and Tremotone vibrato | 565.00 |
| E 212T | SHERATON, thin body double cutaway, shaded or cherry finish, 2 pickups | 515.00 |
| 1519 | Case, hard shell, plush-lined | 50.00 |
| CAIOLA | Al Caiola Model, thin body double pickup, Tonexpressor, Royal Tan | 495.00 |
| 1519 | Case, hard shell, plush-lined | 50.00 |
| E 252N | BROADWAY, full body natural finish, 2 pickups | 380.00 |
| E 252 | BROADWAY, full body cutaway, shaded finish, 2 pickups | 365.00 |
| 1105 | Case, hard shell, plush-lined | 56.00 |
| E 360TD | RIVIERA, thin body double cutaway, Royal Tan finish | 325.00 |
| 1519 | Case, hard shell, plush-lined | 50.00 |
| 1104 | Case, chipboard | 15.00 |

*Special order—120-day delivery

## electric spanish guitars (cont.)

| | | |
|---|---|---|
| E 452TDN | SORRENTO, thin body cutaway, natural finish, 2 pickups | $295.00 |
| E 452TD | SORRENTO, thin body cutaway, Royal Olive or shaded finish, 2 pickups, nickel plated parts | 280.00 |
| E 452TN | SORRENTO, thin body cutaway, natural finish, single pickup | 230.00 |
| E 452T | SORRENTO, thin body cutaway, Royal Olive or shaded finish, single pickup, nickel plated parts | 215.00 |
| 1519 | Case, hard shell, plush-lined | 50.00 |
| 1304 | Case, Archcraft | 26.00 |
| 1104 | Case, chipboard | 15.00 |
| E 230TDV | CASINO, thin body double cutaway, Royal Tan or shaded finish, 2 pickups, nickel plated parts, Tremotone vibrato | 314.50 |
| E 230TD | CASINO, thin body double cutaway, Royal Tan or shaded finish, 2 pickups, nickel plated parts | 275.00 |
| E 230TV | CASINO, thin body double cutaway, Royal Tan or shaded finish, single pickup, nickel plated parts, Tremotone vibrato | 269.50 |
| E 230T | CASINO, thin body double cutaway, Royal Tan or shaded finish, single pickup, nickel plated parts | 230.00 |
| 1519 | Case, hard shell, plush-lined | 50.00 |
| 1304 | Case, Archcraft | 26.00 |
| 1104 | Case, chipboard | 15.00 |
| E 422T | CENTURY, thin body non-cutaway, Royal Burgundy, or shaded single pickup, nickel plated parts | 172.50 |
| 1519 | Case, hard shell, plush-lined | 50.00 |
| 1304 | Case, Archcraft | 26.00 |
| 1104 | Case, chipboard | 15.00 |
| E 444T | GRANADA, thin body built-in pickup, shaded finish | 149.50 |
| 1519 | Case, hard shell, plush-lined | 50.00 |
| 1304 | Case, Archcraft | 26.00 |
| 1104 | Case, chipboard | 15.00 |

## electric spanish guitars, solid body

| | | |
|---|---|---|
| SB 232 | CRESTWOOD DELUXE, solid body double cutaway, cherry red or white finish, three pickups, Tremotone vibrato | $425.00 |
| 1635 | Case, hard shell, plush-lined | 55.00 |
| SB 332 | CRESTWOOD CUSTOM, solid body double cutaway, cherry red or white finish, two pickups, Tremotone vibrato | 325.00 |
| 1535 | Case, hard shell, plush-lined | 50.00 |
| 1115 | Case, chipboard | 16.00 |
| SB 432MV | WILSHIRE, solid body double cutaway, Red Fox or Cherry finish, 2 pickups, Maestro Vibrola | 262.50 |
| SB 432 | WILSHIRE, solid body double cutaway, Red Fox or Cherry finish, 2 pickups | 235.00 |
| 1535 | Case, hard shell, plush-lined | 50.00 |
| 1115 | Case, chipboard | 16.00 |
| SB 533MV | CORONET, solid body double cutaway, Silver Fox or Cherry finish, single pickup, Maestro Vibrola | 181.00 |
| SB 533 | CORONET, solid body double cutaway, Silver Fox or Cherry finish, single pickup | 154.00 |
| 1535 | Case, hard shell, plush-lined | 50.00 |
| 1115 | Case, chipboard | 16.00 |
| SB 722D | OLYMPIC, solid body cutaway, Sunburst finish, two pickups | 160.00 |
| SB 722 | OLYMPIC, full size solid body cutaway, Sunburst finish, single pickup | 129.50 |
| 1115 | Case, chipboard | 16.00 |
| SB 721 | OLYMPIC JR., full size solid body Sunburst finish | 109.50 |
| 1115 | Case, chipboard | 16.00 |

### electric bass

| | | |
|---|---|---|
| EB-DL | EMBASSY DELUXE, solid body electric bass, cherry red, double pickup | $299.50 |
| 1727 | Case, hard shell, plush-lined | 65.00 |
| EB-S | NEWPORT, solid body electric bass, Red Fox finish, or Cherry nickel plated parts | 235.00 |
| 1627 | Case, hard shell, plush-lined | 60.00 |
| 1330 | Case, Archcraft | 26.50 |

## classic guitars—nylon strings

| | | |
|---|---|---|
| EC 300 | BARCELONE, natural top, maple back and rim, authentic mosaic inlay sound hole, fan bracing, French heel | $325.00 |
| EC 200 | ESPANA, natural top, maple back and rim, authentic mosaic inlay sound hole, fan bracing, French heel | 215.00 |
| EC 150 | CLASSIC, natural top, mahogany back and sides, authentic mosaic inlay sound hole, fan bracing, French heel | 169.50 |
| EC 100 | SEVILLE, natural top, mahogany finish | 119.50 |
| EC 90 | ENTRADA, natural top, mahogany finish | 119.50 |
| 1137 | Case, Archcraft | 13.50 |
| EC 30 | MADRID, classic guitar high gloss finish, natural top | 109.50 |
| 1415 | Case, hard shell, plush-lined | 44.50 |
| 1317 | Case, Archcraft | 24.00 |
| 1117 | Case, chipboard | 14.00 |

### amplifiers

| | | |
|---|---|---|
| EA 500T | PANORAMA, one 15" and two 10" speakers with Tremolo | $575.00 |
| 610-C | Cover | |
| EA 4TL | EMPEROR, Jim Lansing 15" and 10" Speaker with Tremolo | 575.00 |
| EA 4T | EMPEROR, 15" and 10" speakers with Tremolo | 460.00 |
| EA 6T | EMPEROR, two 12" speakers | 410.00 |
| 600-C | Cover | |
| EA 72 | CONSTELLATION, bass amp, 12" speaker | 369.50 |
| 610-C | Cover | |
| EA12RVT | FUTURA, Four 8" speakers w/Tremolo and Reverberation | 299.50 |
| 510-C | Cover | 15.50 |
| EA15RVT | ZEPHYR, 15" speaker w/Tremolo and Reverberation | 249.50 |
| 510-C | Cover | 13.50 |
| EA28RVT | PATHFINDER, 12" speaker w/Tremolo and Reverberation | 189.50 |
| 195-C | Cover | 9.75 |

## amplifiers (cont.)

| | | |
|---|---|---|
| EA33RVT | GALAXIE, 10" speaker w/Tremolo and Reverberation | $149.50 |
| 195-C | Cover | 9.75 |
| EA 35T | DEVON, 12" speaker w/Tremolo | 129.50 |
| 195-C | Cover | 9.75 |
| EA 50T | PACEMAKER, 10" Speaker w/Tremolo | 87.50 |
| EA 50 | PACEMAKER, 10" Speaker | 69.50 |
| 195-C | Cover | 4.50 |

### Epiphone Tremotone/Maestro Vibrola

EPIPHONE TREMOTONE vibrato available for conventional type and solid body guitars.
Nickel Plating  $39.50
Gold Plating  35.00

MAESTRO VIBROLA available for solid body guitars.
Nickel Plating  $27.50

## flat top guitars

| | | |
|---|---|---|
| FT 120 | EXCELLENTE, deluxe, flat top | $535.00 |
| 1515 | Case, hard shell, plush-lined | 50.00 |
| FT 98 | TROUBADOUR, flat top with classic neck, Frontier body natural top | 265.00 |
| 1515 | Case, hard shell, plush-lined | 50.00 |
| 1115 | Case, chipboard | 14.50 |
| FT 112 | BARD, twelve strings natural top, adj. bridge | 254.50 |
| 1545 | Case, hard shell, plush-lined | 57.50 |
| 1345 | Case, Archcraft | 26.50 |
| FT 110N | FRONTIER, jumbo, natural finish, adj. bridge | 265.00 |
| FT 110 | FRONTIER, jumbo, shaded finish, adj. bridge | 250.00 |
| 1515 | Case, hard shell, plush-lined | 50.00 |
| 1115 | Case, chipboard | 14.50 |
| FT 90 | ELDORADO, jumbo, natural top, adj. bridge | 195.00 |
| 1515 | Case, hard shell, plush-lined | 50.00 |
| 1115 | Case, chipboard | 14.50 |

## flat top guitars (cont.)

| | | |
|---|---|---|
| FT 85 | SERENADER, 12-string, flat top | $179.50 |
| 1147 | Case, chipboard | 16.00 |
| FT 79N | TEXAN, jumbo, natural finish, adj. bridge | 159.50 |
| FT 79 | TEXAN, jumbo, shaded finish, adj. bridge | 159.50 |
| 1515 | Case, hard shell, plush-lined | 50.00 |
| 1115 | Case, chipboard | 14.50 |
| FT 45N | CORTEZ, natural top | 127.50 |
| FT 45 | CORTEZ, shaded finish, adj. bridge | 115.00 |
| 1415 | Case, hard shell, plush-lined | 44.50 |
| 1117 | Case, chipboard | 14.00 |
| FT 30 | CABALLERO, light mahogany high-gloss finish | 95.00 |
| 1317 | Case, Archcraft | 24.00 |
| 1117 | Case, chipboard | 14.00 |

## acoustic spanish guitars

| | | |
|---|---|---|
| A 112N | *EMPEROR, full body cutaway, natural finish | $740.00 |
| A 112 | *EMPEROR, full body cutaway, shaded finish | 715.00 |
| 1110 | Case, hard shell, plush-lined | 60.00 |
| A 212N | *DELUXE, full body cutaway, natural finish | 620.00 |
| A 212 | *DELUXE, full body cutaway, shaded finish | 610.00 |
| 1105 | Case, hard shell, plush-lined | 56.00 |
| A 412N | *TRIUMPH, full body cutaway, natural finish | 315.00 |
| A 412 | *TRIUMPH, full body cutaway, shaded finish | 305.00 |
| 1105 | Case, hard shell, plush-lined | 56.00 |
| A 622 | *ZENITH, full body non-cutaway, shaded finish | 172.50 |
| 1515 | Case, hard shell, plush-lined | 50.00 |
| 1103 | Case, chipboard | 15.00 |

*Special order—120-day delivery

## mandolin

| | | |
|---|---|---|
| EM 66 | VENETIAN MANDOLIN carved spruce top, F-holes, nickel plated parts | $159.50 |
| 1365 | Case, hard shell plush-lined | 40.00 |
| 1101 | Case, chipboard | 16.00 |

## banjo

| | | |
|---|---|---|
| EB 188 | PLANTATION, long neck 5-string banjo | $295.00 |
| 1520 | Case, hard shell plush-lined | 57.50 |
| EB 88 | MINSTREL, flat head, mahogany back, 5-string banjo | 265.00 |
| 1523 | Case, hard shell plush-lined | 42.00 |
| 1121 | Case | 15.00 |
| EB 44 | CAMPUS, long neck 5-string, open back | 179.50 |
| 1123 | Case, Archcraft | 16.00 |

## bass viols

| | | |
|---|---|---|
| B 5N | THE ARTIST, natural finish | $525.00 |
| B 5S | THE ARTIST, shaded finish | 450.00 |
| B 4B | THE PROFESSIONAL, blonde finish | 395.00 |
| B 4S | THE PROFESSIONAL, shaded finish | 375.00 |
| B V | THE STUDIO, shaded finish | 325.00 |
| 2404Z | Bass bag, zipper fastener, side opening, canvas, dark brown, ¾ size (Standard) only | 31.50 |

Effective July 1, 1963. All prices subject to change without notice. To improve the design, quality, and performance of our units and to make use of the best available materials at all times, we reserve the right to change specifications without notice.

PRINTED IN U.S.A.

ЄPIPHONE

# guitars
# amplifiers
# basses

EPIPHONE, INC., KALAMAZOO, MICHIGAN

July 1, 1963
Price List

ADD # 55 °° FOR YEAR 68

## electric spanish guitars

| | | |
|---|---|---|
| EA 8P | PROFESSIONAL OUTFIT guitar/amplifier combination with all controls in the guitar —35-watt amplifier | $670.00 |
| EA 7P | PROFESSIONAL OUTFIT guitar/amplifier combination with all controls in the guitar —15-watt amplifier | 560.00 |
| 1519-L | Case, hard shell, plush-lined | 60.00 |
| 1304-L | Case, Archcraft | 26.00 |
| 1104-L | Case, chipboard | 15.00 |
| 510-C | Amp cover for EA-8P | 15.50 |
| 195-C | Amp cover for EA-7P | 9.75 |

| | | |
|---|---|---|
| E 112T | *EMPEROR, thin body cutaway, shaded finish, 3 pickups | $935.00 |
| 1111 | Case, hard shell, plush-lined | 72.00 |
| E 212TNV | SHERATON, thin body double cutaway, natural finish, 2 pickups and Tremotone vibrato | 645.00 |
| E 212TN | SHERATON, thin body double cutaway, natural finish, 2 pickups | 595.00 |
| E 212TV | SHERATON, thin body double cutaway, shaded or Cherry finish, 2 pickups and Tremotone vibrato | 635.00 690.00 |
| E 212T | SHERATON, thin body double cutaway, shaded or Cherry finish, 2 pickups | 580.00 625.00 |
| 1519-L | Case, hard shell, plush-lined | 60.00 |
| CAIOLA | AL CAIOLA Model, thin body double cutaway, double pickup, Tonexpressor, Royal Tan or shaded | 550.00 |
| 1519-L | Case, hard shell, plush-lined | 60.00 |
| E 252N | BROADWAY, full body cutaway, natural finish, 2 pickups | 435.00 |
| E 252 | BROADWAY, full body cutaway, shaded or Cherry finish, 2 pickups | 415.00 |
| 1105 | Case, hard shell, plush-lined | 67.50 |
| E 360TD | RIVIERA, thin body double cutaway, Royal Tan or shaded finish, 2 pickups | 369.50 |
| 1519-L | Case, hard shell, plush-lined | 60.00 |
| 1304-L | Case, Archcraft | 26.00 |
| 1104-L | Case, chipboard | 15.00 |

*Special order—120-day delivery

## electric spanish guitars (cont.)

| | | |
|---|---|---|
| HR CUSTOM-E | HOWARD ROBERTS Model Walnut Finish with jazz pickup installed | $610.00 |
| HR-NE | HOWARD ROBERTS Model Natural top, walnut rims, back and neck with jazz pickup installed | 375.00 |
| HR-SE | HOWARD ROBERTS Model Sunburst top, walnut rims, back and neck with jazz pickup installed | 355.00 |
| 1515-L | Case, hard shell, plush lined | 60.00 |
| 1303-L | Case, Archcraft | 26.00 |
| 1103-L | Case, chipboard | 14.50 |
| E 452TDN | SORRENTO, thin body cutaway, natural finish, 2 pickups | 337.50 |
| E 452TD | SORRENTO, thin body cutaway, Royal Olive or shaded finish, 2 pickups, nickel plated parts | 315.00 |
| E 452TN | SORRENTO, thin body cutaway, natural finish, single pickup | 262.50 |
| E 452T | SORRENTO, thin body cutaway, Royal Olive or shaded finish, single pickup, nickel plated parts | 245.00 |
| 1519-L | Case, hard shell, plush-lined | 60.00 |
| 1304-L | Case, Archcraft | 26.00 |
| 1104-L | Case, chipboard | 15.00 |
| E 230TDV | CASINO, thin body double cutaway, Royal Tan or shaded finish, 2 pickups, nickel plated parts, Tremotone vibrato | 349.50 |
| E 230TD | CASINO, thin body double cutaway, Royal Tan or shaded finish, 2 pickups, nickel plated parts | 310.00 |
| E 230TV | CASINO, thin body double cutaway, Royal Tan or shaded finish, single pickup, nickel plated parts, Tremotone vibrato | 299.50 |
| E 230T | CASINO, thin body double cutaway, Royal Tan or shaded finish, single pickup, nickel plated parts | 260.00 |
| 1519-L | Case, hard shell, plush-lined | 60.00 |
| 1304-L | Case, Archcraft | 26.00 |
| 1104-L | Case, chipboard | 15.00 |
| E 422T | CENTURY, thin body non-cutaway, Royal Burgundy or shaded, single pickup, nickel plated parts | 195.00 |
| 1519-L | Case, hard shell, plush-lined | 60.00 |
| 1304-L | Case, Archcraft | 26.00 |
| 1104-L | Case, chipboard | 15.00 |
| E-444TC | GRANADA, thin body cutaway, built-in pickup, shaded finish | 215.00 |
| E 444T | GRANADA, thin body non-cutaway, built-in pickup, shaded finish | 170.00 |
| 1519-L | Case, hard shell, plush-lined | 60.00 |
| 1304-L | Case, Archcraft | 26.00 |
| 1104-L | Case, chipboard | 15.00 |

ADD # 55 °° FOR YEAR 68

## electric spanish guitars, solid body

| | | |
|---|---|---|
| SB 232 | CRESTWOOD DELUXE, solid body double cutaway, cherry red or white finish, three pickups, Tremotone vibrato | $455.00 |
| 1710 | Case, hard shell, plush-lned | 49.50 |
| SB 332 | CRESTWOOD CUSTOM, solid body double cutaway, Cherry red or white finish, two pickups, Tremotone vibrato | 340.00 |
| 1710 | Case, hard shell, plush-lined | 49.50 |
| 1115 | Case, chipboard | 16.00 |
| SB 432 | WILSHIRE, solid body double cutaway, Red Fox or Cherry finish, 2 pickups, Vibrola | 265.00 |
| 1710 | Case, hard shell, plush-lined | 49.50 |
| 1115 | Case, chipboard | 16.00 |
| SB 533 | CORONET, solid body double cutaway, Silver Fox or Cherry finish, single pickup, Vibrola | 175.00 |
| 1710 | Case, hard shell, plush-lined | 49.50 |
| 1115 | Case, chipboard | 16.00 |
| SB 722D | OLYMPIC, solid body double cutaway, Sunburst or Cherry finish, two pickups, Vibrola | 189.50 |
| SB 722 | OLYMPIC, solid body double cutaway, Sunburst or Cherry finish, single pickup, Vibrola | 149.50 |
| 1115 | Case, chipboard | 16.00 |
| SB 721 | OLYMPIC SPECIAL, solid body double cutaway, Sunburst finish, 1 pickup, Vibrola | 136.50 |
| 1154 | Case, chipboard | 12.00 |

## electric bass

| | | |
|---|---|---|
| EB-DL | EMBASSY DELUXE, solid body electric bass, Cherry red, double pickup w/mute | $289.50 |
| 1727 | Case, hard shell, plush-lined | 65.00 |
| EB-S | NEWPORT, solid body electric bass, Red Fox or Cherry finish, nickel plated parts, single pickup w/mute | 240.00 |
| 1720 | Case, hard shell, plush-lined | 60.00 |
| 1330 | Case, Archcraft | 26.50 |
| EB-232N | RIVOLI, thin body double cutaway, natural finish | 325.00 |
| EB-232 | RIVOLI, thin body double cutaway, shaded finish | 310.00 |
| 1539 | Case, hard shell, plush lined | 77.50 |
| 1339 | Case, Archcraft | 27.00 |
| 1139 | Case, chipboard | 16.50 |
| | FUZZTONE provides new bass sound—new guitar sound—including batteries | 39.95 |

*Custom colors for solid body and bass guitars—$15.00 additional*

## amplifiers

| | | |
|---|---|---|
| EA-500T | PANORAMA one 15" and two 10" speakers, with Tremolo | $650.00 |
| 610-CA | Cover, amp | 6.00 |
| 610-CC | Cover, cabinet | 18.00 |
| EA-400T | PANORAMA V one 15" and one 10" speaker, with Tremolo | 600.00 |
| 710-C | Cover | 16.50 |
| EA-4TL | *EMPEROR one 15" Jim Lansing and one 10" speaker, with Tremolo | 650.00 |
| EA-4T | EMPEROR one 15" and one 10" speaker, with Tremolo | 525.00 |
| 600-CA | Cover, amp | 6.00 |
| 600-CC | Cover, cabinet | 18.00 |
| EA-300RVT | EMBASSY two 12" speakers, with Tremolo and Reverberation | 469.50 |
| 510-C | Cover | 15.50 |
| EA-72 | CONSTELLATION bass amplifier with one 15" speaker | 415.00 |
| 610-CA | Cover, amp | 6.00 |
| 610-CC | Cover, cabinet | 18.00 |
| EA-71 | CONSTELLATION V bass amplifier with one 15" speaker | 379.00 |
| 710-C | Cover | 16.50 |
| EA-12RVT | FUTURA with four 10" speakers, Tremolo and Reverberation | 399.50 |
| 510-C | Cover | 15.50 |
| EA-14RVT | ENSIGN with two 10" speakers, Tremolo and Reverberation | 299.50 |
| 200-C | Cover | 11.75 |
| EA-22RVT | MIGHTY MITE small powerful amplifier with one 12" speaker, Tremolo and Reverberation | 267.50 |
| EA-16RVT | LANCER with one 12" speaker, Tremolo and Reverberation | 249.50 |
| 200-C | Cover | 11.75 |
| EA-26RVT | ELECTRA with one 12" speaker, Tremolo and Reverberation | 199.50 |
| 195-C | Cover | 9.75 |
| EA-32RVT | COMET with one 10" speaker, Tremolo and Reverberation | 149.50 |
| 195-C | Cover | 9.75 |
| EA-50T | PACEMAKER with one 10" speaker and Tremolo | 95.00 |
| EA-50 | PACEMAKER with one 10" speaker | 79.50 |
| 195-C | Cover | 9.75 |
| | GADAKART Lightweight amplifier transport aluminum frame—large rubber tread wheels adjustable to all sizes | 30.00 |

## classic guitars—nylon strings

| | | |
|---|---|---|
| EC 300 | BARCELONE, natural top, maple back and rim, authentic mosaic inlay sound hole purfling, fun bracing, French heel | $370.00 |
| EC 200 | ESPANA natural top, maple back and rim, authentic mosaic inlay sound hole purfling, fan bracing, French heel | 245.00 |
| EC 150 | CLASSIC natural top, mahogany back and sides, authentic mosaic inlay sound hole purfling, fan bracing, French heel | 190.00 |
| EC 100 | SEVILLE natural top, mahogany finish | 139.50 |
| 1415-L | Case, hard shell, plush-lined | 53.50 |
| 1317-L | Case, Archcraft | 24.00 |
| 1117-L | Case, chipboard | 14.00 |
| EC 90 | ENTRADA, (petite classic guitar) natural top, mahogany finish | 139.50 |
| 1137-L | Case, Archcraft | 14.00 |
| EC 30 | MADRID high gloss finish, natural top | 129.50 |
| 1415-L | Case, hard shell, plush-lined | 53.50 |
| 1317-L | Case, Archcraft | 24.00 |
| 1117-L | Case, chipboard | 14.00 |

## flat top guitars

| | | |
|---|---|---|
| FT 120 | EXCELLENTE, deluxe flat top | $570.00 |
| 1515-L | Case, hard shell, plush-lined | 60.00 |
| FT 110N | FRONTIER, jumbo, natural top, walnut rim, back and neck, adj. bridge | 290.00 |
| FT 110 | FRONTIER, jumbo, shaded finish, adj. bridge | 290.00 |
| 1515-L | Case, hard shell, plush-lined | 60.00 |
| 1318-L | Case, Archcraft | 26.00 |
| 1118-L | Case, chipboard | 14.50 |
| FT 98 | TROUBADOUR, flat top with classic neck, Frontier body, natural top walnut rim, back and neck | 285.00 |
| 1515-L | Case, hard shell, plush-lined | 60.00 |
| 1318-L | Case, Archcraft | 26.00 |
| 1118-L | Case, chipboard | 14.50 |
| FT 90 | ELDORADO, jumbo, natural top, adj. bridge | 220.00 |
| 1515-L | Case, hard shell, plush-lined | 60.00 |
| 1318-L | Case, Archcraft | 26.00 |
| 1118-L | Case, chipboard | 14.50 |

## flat top guitars (cont.)

| | | |
|---|---|---|
| FT 79N | TEXAN, jumbo, natural finish, adj. bridge | $175.00 |
| FT 79 | TEXAN, jumbo, shaded finish, adj. bridge | 175.00 |
| 1515-L | Case, hard shell, plush-lined | 60.00 |
| 1318-L | Case, Archcraft | 26.00 |
| 1118-L | Case, chipboard | 14.50 |
| FT 45N | CORTEZ, natural top | 140.00 |
| FT 45 | CORTEZ, shaded finish, adj. bridge | 140.00 |
| FT 30 | CABALLERO, light mahogany high-gloss finish | 115.00 |
| FT 28 | CABALLERO TENOR, 4-string light mahogany, high-gloss finish | 115.00 |
| 1415-L | Case, hard shell, plush-lined | 53.50 |
| 1317-L | Case, Archcraft | 24.00 |
| 1117-L | Case, chipboard | 14.00 |

## 12-string flat top guitars

| | | |
|---|---|---|
| FT 112 | BARD, Jumbo 12-string, natural top, adj. pin bridge | $289.50 |
| 1545 | Case, hard shell, plush-lined | 68.00 |
| 1345 | Case, Archcraft | 26.50 |
| FT 85 | SERENADER, 12-string, natural top, adj. pin bridge | 205.00 |
| 1347 | Case, Archcraft | 26.50 |
| 1147 | Case, chipboard | 16.00 |

## 12-string electric guitars

| | | |
|---|---|---|
| E-360TD-12 | RIVIERA-12, thin body, 12 string Royal Tan or shaded finish | $395.00 |
| 1519-L | Case, hard shell, plush lined | 60.00 |
| SB-432-12 | WILSHIRE-12, solid body, 12 string double cutaway, Red Fox or Cherry finish | 295.00 |
| 1727 | Case, hard shell, plush lined | 65.00 |

## 5-string banjos

| | | |
|---|---|---|
| EB 188 | PLANTATION, long neck, open back | $337.00 |
| 1520 | Case, hard shell, plush-lined | 68.00 |
| EB 88 | MINSTREL, flat head, mahogany back | 299.50 |
| 1523 | Case, hard shell, plush-lined | 50.00 |
| 1121 | Case, chipboard | 15.00 |
| EB 44 | CAMPUS, long neck, open back | 205.00 |
| 1123 | Case, Archcraft | 16.00 |

## tenor banjo

| | | |
|---|---|---|
| ETB 77 | TENOR BANJO | $260.00 |
| 1509 | Case, hard shell, plush lined | 54.00 |
| 1120 | Case, chipboard | 15.00 |

## acoustic spanish guitars

| | | |
|---|---|---|
| A 112N | *EMPEROR, full body cutaway, natural finish | $835.00 |
| A 112 | *EMPEROR, full body cutaway, shaded finish | 810.00 |
| 1110 | Case, hard shell, plush-lined | 72.00 |
| A 212N | *DELUXE, full body cutaway, natural finish | 720.00 |
| A 212 | *DELUXE, full body cutaway, shaded finish | 705.00 |
| 1105 | Case, hard shell, plush-lined | 67.50 |
| HR-C | HOWARD ROBERTS CUSTOM Model, full body cutaway, Walnut finish | 550.00 |
| HR-N | HOWARD ROBERTS Model, full body cutaway, Natural top, walnut rims, back and neck | 315.00 |
| HR-S | HOWARD ROBERTS Model, full body cutaway, Sunburst top, walnut rims, back and neck | 295.00 |
| 1515-L | Case, hard shell, plush lined | 60.00 |
| 1303-L | Case, Archcraft | 26.00 |
| A 412N | *TRIUMPH, full body cutaway, natural finish | 357.50 |
| A 412 | *TRIUMPH, full body cutaway, shaded finish | 347.50 |
| 1105 | Case, hard shell, plush-lined | 67.50 |
| A 622 | *ZENITH, full body non-cutaway, shaded finish | 195.00 |
| 1515 | Case, hard shell, plush-lined | 60.00 |
| 1103 | Case, chipboard | 15.00 |
| | Jazz pickup available on A412, A212 and A112 models | 60.00 |

*Special order—120-day delivery

## mandolin

| | | |
|---|---|---|
| EM 66E | VENETIAN MANDOLIN-ELECTRIC carved spruce top, F-holes, nickel plated parts | $245.00 |
| EM 66 | VENETIAN MANDOLIN carved spruce top, F-holes, nickel plated parts | 175.00 |
| 1365 | Case, hard shell, plush-lined | 48.00 |
| 1101 | Case, chipboard | 10.00 |

**Ephiphone Tremotone/Vibrola**

**EPIPHONE TREMOTONE** vibrato available for conventional type and solid body guitars.
Nickel Plating $39.50
Gold Plating 55.00

**VIBROLA** available for solid body guitars.
Nickel Plating $27.50

Effective July 1, 1965. All prices subject to change without notice. To improve the design, quality, and performance of our units and to make use of the best available materials at all times, we reserve the right to change specifications without notice. PRINTED IN U.S.A.

**price list June 22, 1965**

**zone 1**

# guitars amplifiers basses

EPIPHONE, INC., KALAMAZOO, MICHIGAN

**June 22, 1965**
**Catalog Cover and Price list**

## electric spanish guitars

| | | |
|---|---|---|
| E 112T | *EMPEROR, thin body cutaway, shaded finish, 3 humbucking pickups | $1125.00 |
| 1111 | Case, hard shell, plush-lined | 85.00 |
| E 212TNV | SHERATON, thin body double cutaway, natural finish, 2 humbucking pickups and Tremotone vibrato | 770.00 |
| E 212TN | SHERATON, thin body double cutaway, natural finish, 2 humbucking pickups | 720.00 |
| E 212TV | SHERATON, thin body double cutaway, shaded or Cherry finish, 2 humbucking pickups and Tremotone vibrato | 740.00 |
| E 212T | SHERATON, thin body double cutaway, shaded or Cherry finish, 2 humbucking pickups | 690.00 |
| 1519-L | Case, hard shell, plush-lined | 81.00 |
| CaC | AL CAIOLA CUSTOM, thin body double cutaway, 2 humbucking pickups, Tonexpressor, Walnut finish | 650.00 |
| CaS-C | AL CAIOLA STANDARD, thin body double cutaway, 2 pickups, Tonexpressor, Cherry finish | 480.00 |
| CaS | AL CAIOLA STANDARD, thin body double cutaway, 2 pickups, Tonexpressor, shaded finish | 480.00 |
| 1519-L | Case, hard shell, plush-lined | 81.00 |
| 1304-L | Case, Archcraft | 32.00 |
| 1104-L | Case, chipboard | 17.00 |
| E 252N | BROADWAY, rim-2⅛" cutaway, natural finish, 2 humbucking pickups | 555.00 |
| E 252 | BROADWAY, rim-2⅛" cutaway, shaded or Cherry finish, 2 humbucking pickups | 535.00 |
| 1105 | Case, hard shell, plush-lined | 85.00 |
| E-360TDV | RIVIERA, thin body double cutaway, shaded or Cherry finish, 2 humbucking pickups, Tremotone vibrato | 475.00 |
| E 360TD | RIVIERA, thin body double cutaway, shaded or Cherry finish, 2 humbucking pickups | 445.00 |
| 1519-L | Case, hard shell, plush-lined | 81.00 |
| 1304-L | Case, Archcraft | 32.00 |
| 1104-L | Case, chipboard | 17.00 |
| HR-CE | HOWARD ROBERTS Custom Model Walnut Finish with humbucking jazz pickup installed | 725.00 |
| HR-NE | HOWARD ROBERTS Model Natural top, walnut rims, back and neck with humbucking jazz pickup installed | 535.00 |

*Special order—120-day delivery

## electric spanish guitars (cont.)

| | | |
|---|---|---|
| HR-SE | HOWARD ROBERTS Model Shaded top, walnut rims, back and neck with humbucking jazz pickup installed | $515.00 |
| 1515-L | Case, hard shell, plush-lined | 75.00 |
| 1318-L | Case, Archcraft | 33.50 |
| 1103-L | Case, chipboard | 17.00 |
| E 452TDC | SORRENTO, thin body cutaway, Cherry finish, 2 humbucking pickups | 369.50 |
| E 452TD | SORRENTO, thin body cutaway, shaded finish, 2 humbucking pickups | 369.50 |
| E 452TC | SORRENTO, thin body cutaway, Cherry finish, single humbucking pickup | 319.50 |
| E 452T | SORRENTO, thin body cutaway, shaded finish, single humbucking pickup | 319.50 |
| 1519-L | Case, hard shell, plush-lined | 81.00 |
| 1304-L | Case, Archcraft | 32.00 |
| 1104-L | Case, chipboard | 17.00 |
| E 230TDVC | CASINO, thin body double cutaway, Cherry finish, 2 pickups, Tremotone vibrato | 425.00 |
| E 230TDV | CASINO, thin body double cutaway, shaded finish, 2 pickups, Tremotone vibrato | 425.00 |
| E 230TDC | CASINO, thin body double cutaway, Cherry finish 2 pickups | 395.00 |
| E 230TD | CASINO, thin body double cutaway, shaded finish, 2 pickups | 395.00 |
| 1519-L | Case, hard shell, plush-lined | 81.00 |
| 1304-L | Case, Archcraft | 32.00 |
| 1104-L | Case, chipboard | 17.00 |
| E 422T | CENTURY, thin body non-cutaway, shaded finish single pickup | 255.00 |
| 1519-L | Case, hard shell, plush-lined | 81.00 |
| 1304-L | Case, Archcraft | 32.00 |
| 1104-L | Case, chipboard | 17.00 |
| E-444TC | GRANADA, thin body cutaway, built-in pickup, shaded finish | 265.00 |
| E 444T | GRANADA, thin body non-cutaway, built-in pickup, shaded finish | 225.00 |
| 1519-L | Case, hard shell, plush-lined | 81.00 |
| 1304-L | Case, Archcraft | 32.00 |
| 1104-L | Case, chipboard | 17.00 |

## electric spanish guitars, solid body

| | | |
|---|---|---|
| SB 232 | CRESTWOOD DELUXE, solid body double cutaway, cherry red or white finish, three humbucking pickups, Tremotone vibrato | $490.00 |
| 1710 | Case, hard shell, plush-lined | 60.00 |
| SB 332 | CRESTWOOD CUSTOM, solid body double cutaway, Cherry red or white finish, two humbucking pickups, Tremotone vibrato | 365.00 |
| 1710 | Case, hard shell, plush-lined | 60.00 |
| 1115 | Case, chipboard | 17.50 |
| SB 432 | WILSHIRE, solid body double cutaway, Cherry finish, 2 humbucking pickups, Vibrola | 285.00 |
| 1710 | Case, hard shell, plush-lined | 60.00 |
| 1115 | Case, chipboard | 17.50 |
| SB 533 | CORONET, solid body double cutaway, Cherry finish, single pickup, Vibrola | 205.00 |
| 1710 | Case, hard shell, plush-lined | 60.00 |
| 1115 | Case, chipboard | 17.50 |
| SB 722D | OLYMPIC DOUBLE, solid body double cutaway, shaded or Cherry finish, two pickups, Vibrola | 204.50 |
| SB 722 | OLYMPIC, solid body double cutaway, shaded or Cherry finish, single pickup, Vibrola | 182.50 |
| 1115 | Case, chipboard | 17.50 |
| SB 721 | OLYMPIC SPECIAL, solid body double cutaway, shaded finish, single pickup, Vibrola | 169.50 |
| 1154 | Case, chipboard | 16.00 |

## electric bass

| | | |
|---|---|---|
| EB-DL | EMBASSY DELUXE, solid body electric bass, Cherry red, 2 humbucking pickups w/mute | $320.00 |
| 1727 | Case, hard shell, plush-lined | 75.00 |
| EB-S | NEWPORT, solid body electric bass, Cherry finish, single humbucking pickup w/mute | 270.00 |
| 1720 | Case, hard shell, plush-lined | 70.00 |
| 1330 | Case, Archcraft | 31.50 |
| EB-232C | RIVOLI, thin body double cutaway, Cherry finish, w/mute & handrest, single humbucking pickup | 425.00 |
| EB-232 | RIVOLI, thin body double cutaway, shaded finish, w/mute & handrest, single humbucking pickup | 425.00 |
| 1539 | Case, hard shell, plush-lined | 71.50 |
| 1339 | Case, Archcraft | 32.00 |
| 1139 | Case, chipboard | 18.50 |
| | FUZZTONE provides new bass sound—new guitar sound—including battery | 39.95 |

*Custom colors for solid body and bass guitars—$15.00 additional.*

## 12-string electric guitars

| | | |
|---|---|---|
| E-360TD-12C | RIVIERA-12, thin body double cutaway, Cherry finish 2 humbucking pickups | $475.00 |
| E-360TD-12 | RIVIERA-12, thin body double cutaway, Shaded finish, 2 humbucking pickups | 475.00 |
| 1539 | Case, hard shell, plush-lined | 71.50 |
| 1339 | Case, Archcraft | 32.00 |
| 1139 | Case, chipboard | 18.50 |

## amplifiers

| | | |
|---|---|---|
| EA-600RVT | MAXIMA, Solid State—Bass Channel, Guitar Channel—4-10" Heavy duty speakers in two free form cabinets, Reverb, Tremolo, Vibrato | $590.00 |
| 650-C | Set of 3 covers | 22.50 |
| EA-550RVT | SUPERBA—Solid State, 2 channels, 4 inputs, 2 heavy duty 10 inch speakers, Reverb and Tremolo. | 325.00 |
| 550-C | Cover | 9.75 |
| AA-1 | ADD-AN-AMP—Solid State, Self-powered auxiliary speaker-amp. Adds 50 watts to any amplifier. 2-10 inch speakers, 1 input, 1 output, volume control. | 219.50 |
| AA-1-C | Cover | 7.50 |
| EA-300RVT | EMBASSY two 12" speakers, with Tremolo and Reverberation | 469.50 |
| 530-C | Cover | 15.50 |
| EA-72 | CONSTELLATION bass amplifier with one 15" speaker | 415.00 |
| 610-CA | Cover, amp | 6.00 |
| 610-CC | Cover, cabinet | 18.00 |
| EA-71 | CONSTELLATION V bass amplifier with one 15" speaker | 379.00 |
| 710-C | Cover | 16.50 |
| EA-14RVT | ENSIGN with two 10" speakers, Tremolo and Reverberation | 349.50 |
| 214-C | Cover | 11.75 |
| EA-16RVT | REGENT with one 12" speaker, Tremolo and Reverberation | 249.50 |
| 214-C | Cover | 11.75 |
| EA-26RVT | ELECTRA with one 12" speaker, Tremolo and Reverberation | 214.50 |
| 226-C | Cover | 9.75 |
| EA-50T | PACEMAKER with one 10" speaker and Tremolo | 104.50 |
| EA 101 | 10" speaker, Tremolo | 79.50 |
| EA 100 | 10" speaker | 69.50 |
| 101-C | Cover | 2.25 |

## classic guitars—nylon strings

| | | |
|---|---|---|
| EC 300 | BARCELONE natural spruce top, maple back and rim, authentic mosaic inlay sound hole purfling, fan bracing, French heel | $425.00 |
| EC 200 | ESPANA natural spruce top, maple back and rim, authentic mosaic inlay sound hole purfling, fan bracing, French heel | 325.00 |
| EC 150 | CLASSIC natural spruce top, mahogany back and sides, authentic mosaic inlay sound hole purfling, fan bracing, French heel | 245.00 |
| EC 100 | SEVILLE natural spruce top, mahogany finish | 215.00 |
| 1415-L | Case, hard shell, plush-lined | 80.00 |
| 1317-L | Case, Archcraft | 29.00 |
| 1117-L | Case, chipboard | 15.00 |
| EC 30 | MADRID satin finish, spruce top | 165.00 |
| 1415-L | Case, hard shell, plush-lined | 80.00 |
| 1317-L | Case, Archcraft | 29.00 |
| 1117-L | Case, chipboard | 15.00 |

## flat top guitars

| | | |
|---|---|---|
| FT 120 | EXCELLENTE, deluxe flat top | $675.00 |
| 1515-L | Case, hard shell, plush-lined | 75.00 |
| FT 110N | FRONTIER, jumbo, natural top, walnut rim, back and neck, adj. bridge, standard pickguard | 370.00 |
| FT 110 | FRONTIER, jumbo, shaded finish, adj. bridge, large engraved pickguard | 350.00 |
| 1515-L | Case, hard shell, plush-lined | 75.00 |
| 1318-L | Case, Archcraft | 33.50 |
| 1118-L | Case, chipboard | 16.50 |
| FT 90N | ELDORADO, jumbo, natural top, adj. bridge | 295.00 |
| FT 90 | ELDORADO, jumbo, shaded finish, adj. bridge | 275.00 |
| 1515-L | Case, hard shell, plush-lined | 75.00 |
| 1318-L | Case, Archcraft | 33.50 |
| 1118-L | Case, chipboard | 16.50 |
| FT 79N | TEXAN, jumbo, natural finish, adj. bridge | 250.00 |
| FT 79 | TEXAN, jumbo, shaded finish, adj. bridge | 235.00 |
| 1515-L | Case, hard shell, plush-lined | 75.00 |
| 1318-L | Case, Archcraft | 33.50 |
| 1118-L | Case, chipboard | 16.50 |
| FT 45N | CORTEZ, natural top, adj. bridge | 210.00 |
| FT 45 | CORTEZ, shaded finish, adj. bridge | 195.00 |
| FT 30 | CABALLERO, light mahogany satin finish | 149.50 |
| 1415-L | Case, hard shell, plush-lined | 80.00 |
| 1317-L | Case, Archcraft | 29.50 |
| 1117-L | Case, chipboard | 15.00 |

## flat top guitars (cont.)

### folk guitars

| | | |
|---|---|---|
| FT 98 | TROUBADOUR, flat top with classic neck, Frontier body, natural top walnut rim, back and neck | $320.00 |
| 1515-L | Case, hard shell, plush-lined | 75.00 |
| 1318-L | Case, Archcraft | 33.50 |
| 1118-L | Case, chipboard | 16.50 |
| FT 95 | FOLKSTER, flat top natural top, walnut rim and back | 210.00 |
| 1415-L | Case, hard shell, plush-lined | 80.00 |
| 1317-L | Case, archcraft | 29.50 |
| 1117-L | Case, chipboard | 15.00 |

## 12-string flat top guitars

| | | |
|---|---|---|
| FT 112 | BARD, Jumbo 12-string, natural top, adj. bridge | $350.00 |
| 1545 | Case, hard shell, plush-lined | 81.00 |
| 1345 | Case, Archcraft | 33.00 |
| FT 85 | SERENADER, 12-string, natural top, adj. bridge | 265.00 |
| 1347 | Case, Archcraft | 31.50 |
| 1147 | Case, chipboard | 17.00 |

## 5-string banjos

| | | |
|---|---|---|
| EB 88 | MINSTREL, flat head, mahogany back | $375.00 |
| 1523 | Case, hard shell, plush-lined | 62.00 |
| 1121 | Case, chipboard | 18.00 |
| EB 44 | CAMPUS, long neck, open back | 295.00 |
| 1123 | Case, Archcraft | 17.00 |

## tenor banjo

| | | |
|---|---|---|
| ETB 77 | TENOR BANJO | $350.00 |
| 1509 | Case, hard shell, plush-lined | 73.00 |
| 1120 | Case, chipboard | 16.00 |

## mandolin

| | | |
|---|---|---|
| EM 66E | VENETIAN MANDOLIN-ELECTRIC carved spruce top, F-holes | $350.00 |
| EM 66 | VENETIAN MANDOLIN carved spruce top, F-holes | 285.00 |
| 1365 | Case, hard shell, plush-lined | 65.00 |
| 1101 | Case, chipboard | 10.50 |

## acoustic spanish guitars

| | | |
|---|---|---|
| A 112N | *EMPEROR, full body cutaway, natural finish | $950.00 |
| A 112 | *EMPEROR, full body cutaway, shaded finish | 920.00 |
| 1110 | Case, hard shell, plush-lined | 85.00 |
| A 212N | *DELUXE, full body cutaway, natural finish | 850.00 |
| A 212 | *DELUXE, full body cutaway, shaded finish | 820.00 |
| 1105 | Case, hard shell, plush-lined | 85.00 |
| A 412N | *TRIUMPH, full body cutaway, natural finish | 545.00 |
| A 412 | *TRIUMPH, full body cutaway, shaded finish | 515.00 |
| 1105 | Case, hard shell, plush-lined | 85.00 |
| A 622 | *ZENITH, full body non-cutaway, shaded finish | 310.00 |
| 1515-L | Case, hard shell, plush-lined | 75.00 |
| 1103-L | Case, chipboard | 16.50 |
| | Jazz pickup available on A412, A212 and A112 models | 70.00 |

*Special order—120-day delivery

### Epiphone Tremotone/Vibrola

**EPIPHONE TREMOTONE** vibrato available for conventional type and solid body guitars.
Nickel Plating $39.50
Gold Plating 55.00

**VIBROLA** available for solid body guitars.
Nickel Plating $27.50

W. P. Music & Jewelers
5112 W. Irving Park Road
Chicago, Illinois 60641

Effective June 1, 1968. All prices subject to change without notice. To improve the design, quality, and performance of our units and to make use of the best available materials at all times, we reserve the right to change specifications without notice.

681601 PRINTED IN U.S.A.

**Suggested price list June 1, 1968**

W. P. Music & Jewelers
5112 W. Irving Park Road
Chicago, Illinois 60641

EPIPHONE

# guitars amplifiers basses

EPIPHONE GUITARS AND AMPLIFIERS ARE PRODUCTS OF CMI, 7373 N. CICERO, LINCOLNWOOD, ILL. 60646

**June 1, 1968**
**Price List**

Epiphone

# Epiphone Guitars*

## FLATTOP GUITARS

#6732    Natural spruce top, mahogany rims and back, three piece adj. neck, rosewood fingerboard w/dot inlays, adj. bridge, multiple body binding, chrome plated hardware ........ $ 79.50

#802    Durabilt case ................. $ 14.00

#6832    Deluxe model w/natural spruce top, rosewood rims and back, three piece adj. neck, rosewood fingerboard w/block inlays, decorative purfling ring, adj. bridge, chrome plated hardware ................ $105.00

#802    Durabilt case ................. $ 14.00

## JUMBO FLATTOP GUITARS

#6730    Natural spruce top, mahogany rims and back, three piece adj. neck, rosewood fingerboard w/dot inlays, multiple body binding, adj. bridge, chrome plated hardware ......... $ 99.50

#810    Durabilt case ................. $ 15.00

#6830    Deluxe model w/natural spruce top, rosewood rims and back, three piece adj. neck, rosewood fingerboard w/block inlays, decorative purfling rings, adj. bridge, chrome plated hardware ............... $125.00

#810    Durabilt case ................. $ 15.00

## 12 STRING FLATTOP GUITARS

#6735    Sunburst finish spruce top, mahogany rims and back, three piece adj. neck, rosewood fingerboard w/dot inlays, multiple body binding, adj. bridge, chrome plated hardware ... $105.00

#814    Durabilt case ................. $ 16.00

#6834    Deluxe model w/natural spruce top, rosewood rims and back, three piece adj. neck, rosewood fingerboard w/block inlays, decorative purfling ring, adj. bridge, chrome plated hardware ................ $139.50

#814    Durabilt case ................. $ 16.00

## ELECTRIC ACOUSTIC GUITAR

#5102T    Double cutaway, select hardwood top, rims and back, three piece adj. neck, cherry red finish, rosewood fingerboard w/block inlays, multiple body bindings, adj. precision bridge, two pickups, two each volume and tone controls, toggle switch, vibrola, deluxe machine heads, chrome plated hardware ................ $115.00

#805    Durabilt case ................. $ 14.00

## ELECTRIC ACOUSTIC BASS

#5102    Double cutaway, select hardwood top, rims and back, three piece adj. neck, cherry red finish, rosewood fingerboard w/dot inlays, multiple binding, adj. precision bridge, two pickups, two each volume and tone controls, toggle switch, mute, deluxe machine heads, chrome plated hardware ................... $135.00

#819    Durabilt case ................. $ 16.00

## ELECTRIC SOLID BODY GUITAR

#1802T    Double cutaway, cherry red finish, hardwood adj. neck, rosewood fingerboard w/dot inlays, two pickups, toggle switch, tone switch, volume and tone control, vibrola, chrome plated hardware ............... $ 99.50

#809    Durabilt case ................. $ 13.00

## ELECTRIC SOLID BODY BASS

#1820    Double cutaway, cherry red finish, hardwood adj. neck, rosewood fingerboard w/dot inlays, two bass pickups, toggle switch, adj. bridge, foam rubber mute, volume and tone controls, chrome plated hardware .. $115.00

#818    Durabilt case ................. $ 16.00

## CLASSIC GUITARS

#6512    Spruce top, mahogany rims and back, rosewood fingerboard, nickel-silver frets, rosewood bridge, brown celluloid binding, rosewood veneered headpiece, wooden marquetry around sound hole, nickel plated machine heads .......... $ 85.00

#803    Durabilt case ................. $ 14.00

#6514    Spruce top, rosewood rims and back, rosewood fingerboard, nickel-silver frets, rosewood bridge, brown celluloid binding, rosewood veneered headpiece, gold plated machine heads ................... $107.50

#803    Durabilt case ................. $ 14.00

EC-25    Cedar top, rosewood rims and back, ebony fingerboard w/nickel-silver frets, rosewood bridge w/inlaid celluloid decoration, rosewood celluloid bound edges of body, rosewood veneered peghead, wooden marquetry sound hole rings, gold plated machine heads....... $159.50

C-75    Hard-Shell plush case.......... $ 35.00

New revised price list effective Oct. 1, 1970. All prices subject to change without notice. To improve the design, quality and performance of our instruments and to make use of the best available materials at all times, we reserve the right to change specifications without notice.

EPIPHONE product of Chicago Musical Instrument Co. 7373 N. Cicero Ave., Lincolnwood, Ill. 60646

© 1970 U.S.A.

*made in Japan

**October 1, 1970**
**Price List**

## 1971 Catalog

*The first catalog of overseas guitars features:*

*Flat-tops: Martin look, with "belly" below bridge and teardrop pickguard. Bridge adjustable by large screws, strings anchored through bridge with no bridge pins.*

6732: Martin 000 shape (15¼" wide), mahogany back and sides, dot inlay, $79.50

6832: Martin 000 shape (15¼" wide), rosewood back and sides, rectangular inlay, $105

6730: square-shouldered dreadnought shape (16" wide), mahogany back and sides, dot inlay, $99.50

6830: square-shouldered dreadnought shape (16" wide), rosewood back and sides, block inlay, $125

6735: 12-string, square-shouldered dreadnought shape (16" wide), mahogany back and sides, dot inlay, shaded finish, $105

6834: 12-string, square-shouldered dreadnought shape (16" wide), rosewood back and sides, dot inlay, natural finish, $139.50

*Classics*

6512: spruce top, mahogany back and sides, $85

6514: spruce top, rosewood back and sides, $107.50

EC-25: cedar top, rosewood back and sides, $159.50

*Electrics*

5102T: double-cutaway thinline, shape similar to Sheraton, bridge with adjustable saddles, vibrato, block inlay, $115

5120: bass, double-cutaway thinline, 2 pickups, $135

1802: solidbody, Fender Stratocaster shape, 2 pickups, vibrato with large rectangular housing, $99.50

1820: solidbody bass, Fender Stratocaster shape, 2 pickups, $115

# Epiphone Guitars

## FLATTOP GUITARS

**FT-130**   Natural spruce top, mahogany rims and back, three piece adj. neck, rosewood fingerboard w/dot inlays, adj. bridge, multiple body binding, chrome plated hardware................$ 82.50

  **#H-10**   Hardshell (Plush) Case.......$ 37.50

  **#802**   Durabilt Case...................$ 14.00

**FT-132**   Natural spruce top, mahogany rims and back, multiple body binding. Rosewood fingerboard w/dot inlays, laminated mahogany neck. Rosewood bridge. Chrome plated hardware.................................$ 97.50

  **#H-15**   Hardshell (Plush) Case.....$ 35.00

  **#802**   Durabilt Case...................$ 14.00

**FT-135**   Deluxe model w/natural spruce top, rosewood rims and back, three piece adj. neck, rosewood fingerboard w/block inlays, decorative purfling ring, adj. bridge, chrome plated hardware .........................$109.50

  **#H-10**   Hardshell (Plush) Case.......$ 37.50

## JUMBO FLATTOP GUITARS

**FT-145**   Natural spruce top, mahogany rims and back, three piece adj. neck, rosewood fingerboard w/dot inlays, multiple body binding, adj. bridge, chrome plated hardware .................$104.50

  **#H-20**   Hardshell (Plush Case).......$ 40.00

  **#810**   Durabilt case ...................$ 15.00

**FT-150**   Natural spruce top, rosewood rims and back, three piece adj. neck, rosewood fingerboard w/block inlays, decorative purfling rings, adj. bridge, chrome plated hardware ......$129.50

  **#H-20**   Hardshell (Plush) Case.......$ 40.00

**FT-155**   Jumbo Deluxe Model, natural spruce top, w/multiple purfling rings and body binding. Back and rims constructed of unique, highly figured ash. Rosewood fingerboard w/dot inlays ......................................$159.50

  **#H-23**   Hardshell (Plush) Case.......$ 40.00

## 12 STRING FLATTOP GUITARS

**FT-160**   Sunburst finish spruce top, mahogany rims and back, three piece adj. neck, rosewood fingerboard w/dot

\* made in Japan

inlays, multiple body binding, adj. bridge, chrome plated hardware .......$109.50

  **#H-25**   Hardshell (Plush) Case .......$ 45.00

  **#814**   Durabilt case....................$ 16.00

**FT-165**   Deluxe model w/natural spruce top, rosewood rims and back, three piece adj. neck, rosewood fingerboard w/block inlays, decorative purfling ring, adj. bridge, chrome plated hardware ...........................$144.50

  **#H-25**   Hardshell (Plush) Case ......$ 45.00

## ELECTRIC ACOUSTIC GUITAR

**EA-250**   Double cutaway, select hardwood top, rims and back, three piece adj. neck, cherry red finish, rosewood fingerboard w/block inlays, multiple body bindings, adj. precision bridge, two pickups, two each volume and tone controls, toggle switch, vibrola, deluxe machine heads, chrome plated hardware .........................$119.50

  **#H-30**   Hardshell (Plush) Case ......$ 42.50

  **#805**   Durabilt case ...................$ 14.00

## ELECTRIC SOLID BODY GUITAR

**ET-278**   Original Epiphone body design, ebony finish, natural hardwood neck, rosewood fingerboard with dot inlays, two pickups, two volume and tone controls with toggle switch, chrome plated metal parts .........................$159.50

  **#H-43**   Hardshell (Plush) case........$ 42.50

  **#811**   Durabilt case ....................$ 13.00

**ET-270**   Double cutaway, cherry red finish, hardwood adj. neck, rosewood fingerboard w/dot inlays, two pickups, toggle switch, tone switch, volume and tone control, vibrola, chrome plated hardware .........................$109.50

  **#H-40**   Hardshell (Plush) Case......$ 42.50

  **#809**   Durabilt case...................$ 13.00

## ELECTRIC ACOUSTIC BASS

**EA-260**   Double cutaway, select hardwood top, rims and back, three piece adj. neck, cherry red finish, rosewood fingerboard w/dot inlays, multiple binding, adj. precision bridge, two pickups, two each volume and tone controls, toggle switch, mute, deluxe machine heads, chrome plated hardware ................................ $142.50

  **#H-35**   Hardshell (Plush) Case ..... $ 42.50

  **#819**   Durabilt case...................$ 16.00

## ELECTRIC SOLID BODY BASS

**ET-280**   Double cutaway, cherry red finish, hardwood adj. neck, rosewood fingerboard w/dot inlays, two bass pickups, toggle switch, adj. bridge, foam rubber mute, volume and tone controls, chrome plated hardware....$122.50

  **#H-45**   Hardshell (Plush) Case .....$ 42.50

  **#818**   Durabilt case..................$ 16.00

## CLASSIC GUITARS

**EC-20**   Spruce top, matched rosewood back and rims, rosewood fingerboard, nickel silver frets, scrolled gold plated machine heads, ivoroid buttons $ 74.50

  **#804**   Durabilt case ..................$ 14.00

**EC-22**   Spruce top, mahogany rims and back, rosewood fingerboard, nickel-silver frets, rosewood bridge, brown celluloid binding, rosewood veneered headpiece, wooden marquetry around sound hole, nickel plated machine heads ................................$ 89.50

  **#H-50**   Hardshell (Plush) Case.....$ 37.50

  **#803**   Durabilt case..................$ 14.00

**EC-24**   Spruce top, rosewood rims and back, rosewood fingerboard, nickel-silver frets, rosewood bridge, brown celluloid binding, rosewood veneered headpiece, gold plated machine heads ................................$114.50

  **#H-50**   Hardshell (Plush) Case.......$ 37.50

  **#803**   Durabilt case..................$ 14.00

**EC-25**   Cedar top, rosewood rims and back, ebony fingerboard w/nickel-silver frets, rosewood bridge w/inlaid celluloid decoration, rosewood celluloid bound edges of body, rosewood veneered peghead, wooden marquetry sound hole rings, gold plated machine heads ...........................$169.50

  **#H-50**   Hardshell (Plush) case .......$ 37.50

## BANJOS

**EB-98**   A fine quality 5-string banjo, vertical post deluxe machine heads with 5th string peg. Solid rosewood fingerboard with nickel silver frets. Inlaid position markers..................
Mahogany resonator with metal shell. Mahogany neck. 24 tension brackets.$179.50

  **#H-60**   Deluxe Hardshell (Plush) Case.......$ 45.00

New revised price list effective February 1, 1972. All prices subject to change without notice. To improve the design, quality and performance of our instruments and to make use of the best available materials at all times, we reserve the right to change specifications without notice.

**EPIPHONE** product of Chicago Musical Instrument Co. 7373 N. Cicero Ave., Lincolnwood, Ill. 60646

1972 U.S.A. — 841902

**Feb. 1, 1972**
**Price List**

## Epiphone Models
## Price List Specifications

### FLATTOP GUITARS

FT-130   Natural spruce top, mahogany rims and back, three piece adj. neck, rosewood fingerboard w/dot inlays, adj. bridge, multiple body binding, chrome plated hardware . . . . . . . . $ 99.95

   H-10   Hardshell (Plush) Case . . . $ 45.00

   802   Durabilt Case . . . . . . . . . $ 15.50

FT-132   Natural spruce top, mahogany rims and back, multiple body binding. Rosewood fingerboard w/dot inlays, laminated mahogany neck. Rosewood bridge. Chrome plated hardware . . . . . . . . . . . . $124.50

   H-15   Hardshell (Plush) Case . . $ 45.00

   802   Durabilt Case . . . . . . . . . $ 15.50

FT-134   Student model flattop, natural spruce top, mahogany rims and back, special design bracing to strengthen top and augment tonal projection, reinforced adjustable bridge, satin finished neck, individual chrome plated machine heads, shell pickguard . . . . . . . . $129.50

   H-10   Hardshell (Plush) case . . . $ 45.00

   810   Durabilt case . . . . . . . . . $ 15.50

FT-135   Deluxe model w/natural spruce top, rosewood rims and back, three piece adj. neck, rosewood fingerboard w/block inlays, decorative purfling ring, adj. bridge, chrome plated hardware . . . . . . . . . . $139.50

   H-10   Hardshell (Plush) Case . . $ 45.00

### JUMBO FLATTOP GUITARS

FT-145   Natural spruce top, mahogany rims and back, three piece adj. neck, rosewood fingerboard w/dot inlays, multiple body binding, adj. bridge, chrome plated hardware . . . . . . . $132.50

   H-20   Hardshell (Plush) Case . . $ 50.00

   810   Durabilt case . . . . . . . . . $ 16.50

FT-147   Jumbo flattop natural spruce top, highly figured mahogany rims and back, adjustable mahogany neck with French heel design, rosewood fingerboard with dot inlays, adjustable bridge, multiple body binding, chrome plated hardware   $149.50

   H-18   Hardshell (Plush) Case . . $ 50.00

   814   Durabilt case . . . . . . . . . $ 17.50

FT-150   Natural spruce top, rosewood rims and back, three piece adj. neck, rosewood fingerboard w/block inlays, decorative purfling rings, adj. bridge, chrome plated hardware   $154.50

   H-20   Hardshell (Plush) Case . . . $ 50.00

FT-155   Jumbo Deluxe Model, natural spruce top, w/multiple purfling rings and body binding. Back and rims constructed of unique, highly figured ash. Rosewood fingerboard w/dot inlays . . . . . . . . . . . . . . . $199.50

   I-23   Hardshell (Plush) Case . . $ 50.00

### 12 STRING FLATTOP GUITARS

FT-160   Sunburst finish spruce top, mahogany rims and back, three piece adj. neck, rosewood fingerboard w/dot inlays, multiple body binding, adj. bridge, chrome plated hardware . . . . . . . . . . . . . $139.50

   H-25   Hardshell (Plush) Case . . $ 55.00

   814   Durabilt case . . . . . . . . . $ 17.50

FT-165   Deluxe model w/natural spruce top, rosewood rims and back, three piece adj. neck, rosewood fingerboard w/block inlays, decorative purfling ring, adj. bridge, chrome plated hardware . . . . . . . . . . . . . . $179.50

   H-25   Hardshell (Plush) Case . . $ 55.00

### ELECTRIC ACOUSTIC GUITAR

EA-250   Double cutaway, select hardwood top, rims and back, three piece adj. neck, cherry red finish, rosewood fingerboard w/block inlays, multiple body bindings, adj. precision bridge, two pickups, two each

volume and tone controls, toggle switch, vibrola, deluxe machine heads, chrome plated hardware . . $159.50

   H-30   Hardshell (Plush) Case . . $ 50.00

   805   Durabilt case . . . . . . . . . $ 15.50

### ELECTRIC SOLID BODY GUITAR

ET-278   Original Epiphone body design, ebony finish, natural hardwood neck, rosewood fingerboard with dot inlays, two pickups, two volume and tone controls with toggle switch, chrome plated metal parts . . . . . . . . . . . . . . . . . . . . . . $189.50

   H-43   Hardshell (Plush) case . . . $ 50.00

   811   Durabilt case . . . . . . . . . $ 14.50

ET-275   Original Epiphone solid body design, double cutaway, sunburst finish, hardwood adjustable neck, rosewood fingerboard with dot inlays, two pickups, volume and tone controls, pickup selector switch, vibrato tailpiece, chrome plated hardware . . . . . . . . . . . . . . $169.

   H-43   Hardshell (Plush) Case . . $ 50.00

   811   Durabilt case . . . . . . . . . $ 14.50

ET-270   Double cutaway, cherry red finish, hardwood adj. neck, rosewood fingerboard w/dot inlays, two pickups, toggle switch, tone switch, volume and tone control, vibrola, chrome plated hardware . . . . . . . $144.50

   H-40   Hardshell (Plush) Case . . . $ 50.00

   809   Durabilt case . . . . . . . . . $ 14.50

### ELECTRIC ACOUSTIC BASS

EA-260   Double cutaway, select hardwood top, rims and back, three piece adj. neck, cherry red finish, rosewood fingerboard w/dot inlays, multiple binding, adj. precision bridge, two pickups, two each volume and tone controls, toggle switch, mute, deluxe machine heads, chrome plated hardware . . . . . . . . . . . . $184.50

   H-35   Hardshell (Plush) Case . . . $ 50.00

   819   Durabilt case . . . . . . . . . $ 17.50

### ELECTRIC SOLID BODY BASS

ET-285   Electric bass, original Epiphone solid body design, sunburst finish, double cutaway, adjustable hardwood neck, rosewood fingerboard with dot inlays, two powerful pickups, toggle switch, adjustable bridge, foam rubber mute, volume and tone control, chrome plated hardware . . . . . . . . . . . . . . . . . . $189.50

   H-47   Hardshell (Plush) Case . . . $ 50.00

   821   Durabilt case . . . . . . . . . $ 19.00

ET-280   Double cutaway, cherry red finish, hardwood adj. neck, rosewood fingerboard w/dot inlays, two bass pickups, toggle switch, adj. bridge, foam rubber mute, volume and tone controls, chrome plated hardware . . . . . . . . . . . . . . . . $169.50

   H-45   Hardshell (Plush) Case . . . $ 50.00

   818   Durabilt case . . . . . . . . . $ 17.50

### CLASSIC GUITARS

EC-20   Spruce top, mahogany back and rims, rosewood fingerboard, nickel silver frets, scrolled gold plated machine heads, ivoroid buttons . . . . . . $ 99.95

   H-48   Hardshell (Plush) Case . . . $ 47.50

   803   Durabilt case . . . . . . . . . $ 15.50

EC-22   Spruce top, mahogany rims and back, rosewood fingerboard, nickel-silver frets, rosewood bridge, brown celluloid binding, rosewood veneered headpiece, nickel plated machine heads . . . . . . . . . . . . . . . $127.50

   H-50   Hardshell (Plush) Case . . . $ 47.50

   803   Durabilt case . . . . . . . . $ 15.50

EC-23   Student model classic, traditionally finished spruce top, special design bracing to strengthen top and augment tonal projection, student size neck for easy learning . . . . . $124.50

   803   Durabilt case . . . . . . . . . $ 15.50

EC-24   Spruce top, rosewood rims and back, rosewood fingerboard, nickel-silver frets, rosewood bridge, brown

celluloid binding, rosewood veneered headpiece, gold plated machine heads . . . . . . . . . . . . . . . . $144.50

   H-50   Hardshell (Plush) Case . . . $ 47.50

   803   Durabilt case . . . . . . . . . $ 15.50

EC-25   Cedar top, rosewood rims and back, ebony fingerboard w/nickel-silver frets, rosewood bridge w/inlaid celluloid decoration, rosewood celluloid bound edges of body, rosewood veneered peghead, wooden marquetry sound hole rings, gold plated machine heads . . $205.00

   H-51   Hardshell (Plush) Case . . . $ 47.50

### BANJOS

EB-98   A fine quality 5 string banjo, vertical post deluxe machine heads with 5th string peg. Solid rosewood fingerboard with nickel silver frets, inlaid position markers. Mahogany resonator with metal shell. Mahogany neck. 24 tension brackets . . . . . . . . . . . . . . . . . . . . . . $225.00

   H-60   Deluxe Hardshell (Plush) Case . . . . $ 55.00

New revised price list effective May 11, 1973. All prices subject to change without notice. To improve the design, quality and performance of our instruments and to make use of the best available materials at all times, we reserve the right to change specifications without notice.

EPIPHONE product of Chicago Musical Instrument Co. 7373 N. Cicero Ave., Lincolnwood, Ill. 60646

*Epiphone*
## GUITARS

SUGGESTED RETAIL PRICES

Effective May 11, 1973

1973 U. S. A. — 841307RD

May 11, 1973
Price List

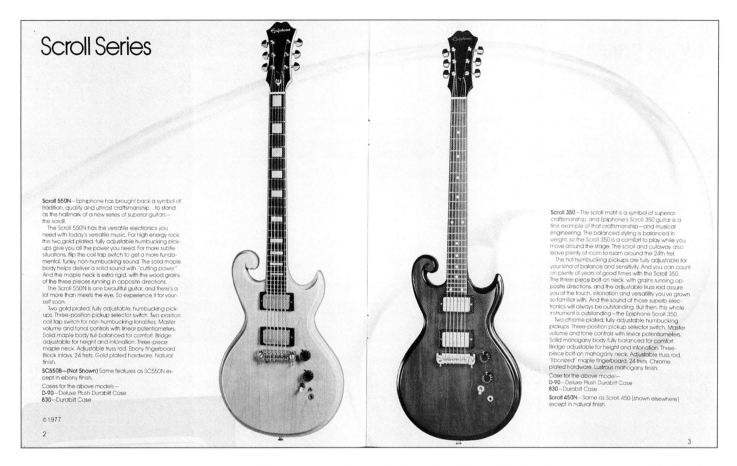

## Scroll Series

**Scroll 550N**—Epiphone has brought back a symbol of tradition, quality and utmost craftsmanship...to stand as the hallmark of a new series of superior guitars—the scroll.

The Scroll 550N has the versatile electronics you need with today's versatile music. For high energy rock, the two gold plated, fully adjustable humbucking pick-ups give you all the power you need. For more subtle situations, flip the coil tap switch to get a more funda-mental, funky, non-humbucking sound. The solid maple body helps deliver a solid sound with "cutting power." And the maple neck is extra rigid, with the wood grains of the three pieces running in opposite directions.

The Scroll 550N is one beautiful guitar, and there's a lot more than meets the eye. So experience it for your-self soon.

Two gold plated, fully adjustable, humbucking pick-ups. Three-position pickup selector switch. Two-position coil tap switch for non-humbucking tonalities. Master volume and tonal controls with linear potentiometers. Solid maple body full balanced for comfort. Bridge adjustable for height and intonation. Three-piece maple neck. Adjustable truss rod. Ebony fingerboard. Block inlays. 24 frets. Gold plated hardware. Natural finish.

**SC550B—(Not Shown)** Same features as SC550N ex-cept in ebony finish.

Cases for the above models—
**D-90**—Deluxe Plush Durabilt Case
**830**—Durabilt Case

©1977

2

**Scroll 350**—The scroll motif is a symbol of superior craftsmanship, and Epiphone's Scroll 350 guitar is a fine example of that craftsmanship—and musical engineering. The balanced styling is balanced in weight, so the Scroll 350 is a comfort to play while you move around the stage. The scroll and cutaway also leave plenty of room to roam around the 24th fret.

The hot humbucking pickups are fully adjustable for your kind of balance and sensitivity. And you can count on plenty of years of good times with the Scroll 350. The three-piece bolt-on neck, with grains running op-posite directions, and the adjustable truss rod assure you of the touch, intonation and versatility you've grown so familiar with. And the sound of those superb elec-tronics will always be outstanding. But then, this whole instrument is outstanding—the Epiphone Scroll 350.

Two chrome plated, fully adjustable humbucking pickups. Three-position pickup selector switch. Master volume and tone controls with linear potentiometers. Solid mahogany body full balanced for comfort. Bridge adjustable for height and intonation. Three-piece bolt-on mahogany neck. Adjustable truss rod. "Ebonized" maple fingerboard. 24 frets. Chrome plated hardware. Lustrous mahogany finish.

Case for the above model—
**D-90**—Deluxe Plush Durabilt Case
**830**—Durabilt Case

**Scroll 450N**—Same as Scroll 450 (shown elsewhere) except in natural finish.

3

## 1976

**Scroll 550N:** natural maple, gold-plated, coil tap, block inlay

**Scroll 550B:** same but in ebony

**Scroll 450:** maple body, mahogany finish, coil tap, chrome-plated, dot inlay

**Scroll 450:** same but with natural finish

**Scroll 350:** natural finish mahogany body, bolt-on neck, no coil tap

**ET-290:** maple body, maple fingerboard, same body shape as 1960s soldbodies, cherry sunburst, gold-plated metal parts, $259.50

**ET-290N:** natural maple, $259.50

**ET-276:** mahogany finish, $199.50

**ET-285:** bass, two pickups, $249.50

**EA-255:** thinline electric, two pickups, gold-plated metal parts, $299.50

**Presentation (PR) 765:** square-shouldered dreadnought, rosewood back and sides, solid top, V-block inlay, vine peghead inlay

**PR-745:** rosewood back and sides, solid top, dot inlay

**PR-725:** mahogany back and sides, laminated top, dot inlay

**FT-550:** square-shouldered dreadnought, three-piece back of maple and jacaranda, block inlay, non-adjustable bridge, $299.50

**FT-350:** rosewood back and sides, non-adjustable bridge, block inlay, $235.50

**FT-200:** The Monticello, embossed eagle on peghead, star fingerboard inlay, non-adjustable bridge, $199.50

**FT-150:** rosewood back and sides, adjustable bridge, block inlay, $225.50

**FT-150BL:** maple back and sides, $225.50

**FT-146:** mahogany back and sides, block inlay, $185.50

**FT-145:** mahogany back and sides, dot inlay, $169.50

**FT-145SB:** same but with sunburst finish, $169.50

**FT-145LH:** left-handed, $179.50

**FT-140:** mahogany back and sides, dot inlay, $145.50

**FT-565:** 12-string, three-piece back of maple and jacaranda, block inlay, $319.50

**FT-165:** 12-string, rosewood back and sides, block inlay, $239.50

**FT-160:** mahogany back and sides, dot inlay, $189.50

**FT-135:** concert (Martin 000) size, rosewood back and sides, block inlay, $199.50

**FT-133:** mahogany back and sides, block inlay, $165.50

**FT-130:** mahogany back and sides, dot inlay, $135.50

**FT-130SB:** same but with sunburst finish, $135.50

**FT-120:** same description as FT-130, $109.50

**FT-570SB:** super jumbo (Gibson J-200) size, block inlay, $275.50

**Bluegrass 440:** mandolin, Florentine style with double body points, oval hole

**Bluegrass 50:** mandolin, A-style (pear-shaped), ƒ-holes, $149.50

**EB-98:** 5-string banjo, dot inlay, $259.50

**EB-90:** 5-string banjo, block inlay, $199.50

**Classic 60:** spruce top, rosewood back and sides, engraved tuners, ornate tailpiece

**EC-25:** cedar top, rosewood back and sides, gold-plated metal parts, $245.50

**EC-20:** spruce top, mahogany back and sides, gold-plated metal parts, $129.50

**EC-15:** spruce top, mahogany back and sides, $99.50

**Nova 390:** rosewood back and sides, "smiling" bridge shape, cloud inlay

**Nova 295:** rosewood back and sides, block inlay

**Nova 245:** 12-string, rosewood back and sides, block inlay

**Nova 180:** mahogany back and sides, dot inlay

## ACOUSTIC GUITARS

| Model | Available Finish | Suggested Retail | Fits Case |
|---|---|---|---|
| *FT-SERIES* | | | |
| FT-120 | N* | $169.95 | 802, D-10 |
| FT-130 | N,SB,MPL** | 189.95 | 802, D-10 |
| FT-140 | N* | 199.95 | 810, D-10 |
| FT-145 | N,SB,MPL** | 219.95 | 810, D-20 |
| FT-150 | N | 269.95 | 810, D-20 |
| FT-160 | N,SB,MPL** | 249.95 | 814, D-25 |
| FT-165 | N | 299.95 | 814, D-25 |
| *PRESENTATION SERIES* | | | |
| PR-725 | N | 299.50 | 822,D-65,H-65 |
| PR-745 | N | 499.50 | 822,D-65,H-65 |
| PR-765 | N | 629.50 | 822,D-65,H-65 |
| *NOVA SERIES* | | | |
| NV-180 | N*** | 299.95 | 822,D-65,H-65 |
| NV-245 | N*** | 399.95 | 822,D-65,H-65 |
| NV-295 | N*** | 399.95 | 822,D-65,H-65 |
| NV-390 | N*** | 499.95 | 822,D-65,H-65 |
| NV-390J | N*** | 499.95 | 822,D-65,H-65 |

## BANJOS AND MANDOLINS

| Model | Available Finish | Suggested Retail | Fits Case |
|---|---|---|---|
| *BANJO SERIES* | | | |
| EB-90 | N*** | $269.95 | D-55,H-60 |
| EB-98 | N*** | 379.95 | D-55,H-60 |
| *MANDOLIN SERIES* | | | |
| BG-50 | SB*** | 199.95 | 815,D-15 |
| BG-440 | SB*** | 419.95 | 815,D-15 |

## CLASSIC GUITARS

| Model | Available Finish | Suggested Retail | Fits Case |
|---|---|---|---|
| EC-15 | N | 159.95 | 803,D-50 |
| CO-60 | N*** | 369.95 | 803,D-50 |

## ELECTRIC GUITARS

| Model | Available Finish | Suggested Retail | Fits Case |
|---|---|---|---|
| *GENESIS SERIES* | | | |
| GN-STD | EB,WR | 299.95 | 832,D-92,H-92 |
| GN-DLX | EB,DS | 349.95 | 832,D-92,H-92 |
| GN-CST | EB,DS | 399.95 | 832,D-92,H-92 |
| *SCROLL SERIES* | | | |
| SC-350 | WAL | 349.50 | 830,D-90,H-90 |
| SC-450 | N,WAL | 399.50 | 830,D-90,H-90 |
| SC-550 | N,EB | 499.50 | 830,D-90,H-90 |
| SCIIB | EB | 399.50 | 831,D-91,H-91 |

## EPI STUDENT GUITARS

| Model | Available Finish | Suggested Retail | Fits Case |
|---|---|---|---|
| *EPI A-SERIES FOLK MODELS* | | | |
| A-10 | N* | $129.95 | 800 |
| A-12 | N | 159.95 | 800 |
| *EPI D-SERIES DREADNOUGHTS* | | | |
| D-10 | N | 149.95 | 810 |
| D-12 | N | 164.95 | 810 |
| D-14 | N | 184.95 | 810 |
| D-16 | N | 199.95 | 810 |
| *EPI C-SERIES CLASSICS* | | | |
| C-10 | N* | 119.95 | 803 |
| C-12 | N | 139.95 | 803 |

## CASES

| | Model | Suggested Retail |
|---|---|---|
| *ECONOMY* | 800 | $18.50 |
| | 802 | 19.00 |
| | 803 | 19.00 |
| | 810 | 22.00 |
| | 814 | 26.00 |
| | 815 | 13.50 |
| | 822 | 24.00 |
| | 830 | 25.50 |
| | 831 | 25.50 |
| | 832 | 22.00 |
| *DURABILT* | D-10 | 27.50 |
| | D-15 | 21.50 |
| | D-20 | 30.50 |
| | D-25 | 31.00 |
| | D-50 | 27.50 |
| | D-55 | 27.00 |
| | D-65 | 33.00 |
| | D-90 | 33.50 |
| | D-91 | 33.00 |
| | D-92 | 29.50 |
| *HARDSHELL* | H-60 | 66.00 |
| | H-65 | 57.00 |
| | H-90 | 67.50 |
| | H-91 | 68.00 |
| | H-92 | 67.50 |

## FINISH ABBREVIATIONS

| | | |
|---|---|---|
| N | = | Natural |
| MPL | = | Maple |
| SB | = | Brown Sunburst |
| DS | = | Dark Sunburst |
| WR | = | Wine Red |
| EB | = | Ebony |
| WAL | = | Walnut |

\*   Sold in two pack only.
\*\*  Add $10.00 to suggested retail price
for figured maple guitars.
\*\*\*Limited availability for 1979.

January 15, 1979
Price List

## ACOUSTIC GUITARS

| Model | Available Finish | Suggested Retail | Fits Case |
|---|---|---|---|
| *FT-SERIES* | | | |
| FT-120 | N* | $169.95 | 802, D-10 |
| FT-130 | N,SB,MPL**+ | 189.95 | 802, D-10 |
| FT-140 | N* | 199.95 | 810, D-10 |
| FT-145 | N,SB,MPL**+ | 219.95 | 810, D-20 |
| FT-150 | N+ | 269.95 | 810, D-20 |
| FT-160 | N,SB,MPL**+ | 249.95 | 814, D-25 |
| FT-165 | N+ | 299.95 | 814, D-25 |
| *PRESENTATION SERIES* | | | |
| PR-725 | N | 299.95 | 822,D-65,H-65 |
| PR-725S | N | 349.95 | 822,D-65,H-65 |
| PR-735 | N | 399.95 | 822,D-65,H-65 |
| PR-735S | N | 449.95 | 822,D-65,H-65 |
| PR-745 | N+ | 499.95 | 822,D-65,H-65 |
| PR-755S | N | 599.95 | 822,D-65,H-65 |
| PR-765 | N+ | 629.95 | 822,D-65,H-65 |
| PR-795AE | N | 499.95 | 822,D-65,H-65 |
| *NOVA SERIES* | | | |
| NV-180 | N+ | 299.95 | 822,D-65,H-65 |
| NV-245 | N+ | 399.95 | 822,D-65,H-65 |
| NV-295 | N+ | 399.95 | 822,D-65,H-65 |
| NV-390 | N+ | 499.95 | 822,D-65,H-65 |
| NV-390J | N+ | 499.95 | 822,D-65,H-65 |

## BANJOS AND MANDOLINS

| Model | Available Finish | Suggested Retail | Fits Case |
|---|---|---|---|
| *BANJO SERIES* | | | |
| EB-90 | N+ | $269.95 | D-55,H-60 |
| EB-98 | N+ | 379.95 | D-55,H-60 |
| MB-100 | N | 399.95 | D-55,H-60 |
| MB-250 | WAL | 599.95 | D-55,H-60 |
| *MANDOLIN SERIES* | | | |
| BG-50 | SB+ | 199.95 | 815,D-15 |
| BG-440 | SB+ | 419.95 | 815,D-15 |
| MM-50 | ASB | 599.95 | 815,D-15 |
| MM-70 | ASB | 699.95 | 815,D-15 |

## CLASSIC GUITARS

| Model | Available Finish | Suggested Retail | Fits Case |
|---|---|---|---|
| EC-15 | N | 159.95 | 803,D-50 |
| CO-60 | N+ | 369.95 | 803,D-50 |

## ELECTRIC GUITARS

| Model | Available Finish | Suggested Retail | Fits Case |
|---|---|---|---|
| *GENESIS SERIES* | | | |
| GN-STD | EB,WR | 299.95 | D-92,H-92 |
| GN-DLX | EB,DS | 349.95 | D-92,H-92 |
| GN-CST | EB,DS | 399.95 | D-92,H-92 |
| *SCROLL SERIES* | | | |
| SC-350 | WAL+ | 349.50 | 830,D-90,H-90 |
| SC-450 | N,WAL+ | 399.50 | 830,D-90,H-90 |
| SC-550 | N,EB+ | 499.50 | 830,D-90,H-90 |
| SCIIB | EB+ | 399.50 | 830,D-90,H-91 |

## EPI STUDENT GUITARS

| Model | Available Finish | Suggested Retail | Fits Case |
|---|---|---|---|
| *EPI A-SERIES FOLK MODELS* | | | |
| A-10 | N* | $129.95 | 800 |
| A-12 | N | 159.95 | 800 |
| *EPI D-SERIES DREADNOUGHTS* | | | |
| D-10 | N | 149.95 | 810 |
| D-12 | N | 164.95 | 810 |
| D-14 | N | 184.95 | 810 |
| D-16 | N | 199.95 | 810 |
| *EPI C-SERIES CLASSICS* | | | |
| C-10 | N* | 119.95 | 803 |
| C-12 | N | 139.95 | 803 |
| *EPI B-SERIES BANJOS* | | | |
| B-10 | WAL | 229.95 | D-55,H-60 |

## CASES

| | Model | Suggested Retail |
|---|---|---|
| ECONOMY | 800 | $18.50 |
| | 802 | 19.00 |
| | 803 | 19.00 |
| | 810 | 22.00 |
| | 814 | 26.00 |
| | 815 | 13.50 |
| | 822 | 24.00 |
| | 830 | 25.50 |
| | 831 | 25.50 |
| DURABILT | D-10 | 27.50 |
| | D-15 | 21.50 |
| | D-20 | 30.50 |
| | D-25 | 31.00 |
| | D-50 | 27.50 |
| | D-55 | 27.00 |
| | D-65 | 33.00 |
| | D-90 | 33.50 |
| | D-91 | 33.00 |
| | D-92 | 29.50 |
| HARDSHELL | H-60 | 66.00 |
| | H-65 | 57.00 |
| | H-90 | 67.50 |
| | H-91 | 68.00 |
| | H-92 | 67.50 |

## FINISH ABBREVIATIONS

| | | |
|---|---|---|
| N | = | Natural |
| MPL | = | Maple |
| SB | = | Brown Sunburst |
| DS | = | Dark Sunburst |
| WR | = | Wine Red |
| EB | = | Ebony |
| WAL | = | Walnut |
| ASB | = | Antique Sunburst |

\* Sold in two pack only.
\*\* Add $10.00 to suggested retail price for figured maple guitars.
+ Limited availability for 1979.

**June 1, 1979**
**Price List**

## ACOUSTIC GUITARS

| Model | Available Finish | Suggested Retail | Fits Case |
|---|---|---|---|
| FT-SERIES* | | | |
| FT-120 | N | $169.95 | 802, D-10 |
| FT-130 | N,SB,MPL**+ | 189.95 | 802, D-10 |
| FT-140 | N | 199.95 | 810, D-20 |
| FT-145 | N,SB,MPL**+ | 219.95 | 810, D-20 |
| FT-150 | N+ | 269.95 | 810, D-20 |
| FT-160 | N,SB,MPL**+ | 249.95 | 814, D-25 |
| FT-165 | N+ | 299.95 | 814, D-25 |
| PRESENTATION SERIES | | | |
| PR-725 | N | 299.95 | 822, D-65, H-65 |
| PR-725S | N | 349.95 | 822, D-65, H-65 |
| PR-735 | N | 399.95 | 822, D-65, H-65 |
| PR-735S | N | 449.95 | 822, D-65, H-65 |
| PR-755S | N | 599.95 | 822, D-65, H-65 |
| PR-795AE | N | 499.95 | 822, D-65, H-65 |

## BANJOS AND MANDOLINS

| Model | Finish | Retail | Case |
|---|---|---|---|
| BANJO SERIES | | | |
| MB-100 | N | 399.95 | D-55, H-60 |
| MB-250 | WAL | 599.95 | D-55, H-60 |
| MANDOLIN SERIES | | | |
| MM-50 | ASB | 599.95 | 815, D-15 |
| MM-70 | ASB | 699.95 | 815, D-15 |

## ELECTRIC GUITARS

| Model | Finish | Retail | Case |
|---|---|---|---|
| GENESIS SERIES | | | |
| GN-STD | EB,WR | 329.95 | D-92, H-92 |
| GN-DLX | EB, DS | 379.95 | D-92, H-92 |
| GN-CST | EB, DS | 429.95 | D-92, H-92 |

## CASES

| | Model | Suggested Retail |
|---|---|---|
| ECONOMY | 800 | $20.00 |
| | 802 | 21.50 |
| | 803 | 21.50 |
| | 810 | 25.00 |
| | 814 | 27.00 |
| | 815 | 15.00 |
| | 822 | 27.00 |
| | 830 | 29.00 |
| | 831 | 25.50 |
| DURABILT | D-10 | 31.00 |
| | D-15 | 25.00 |
| | D-20 | 35.00 |
| | D-25 | 37.00 |
| | D-50 | 30.00 |
| | D-55 | 31.00 |
| | D-65 | 37.00 |
| | D-90 | 39.00 |
| | D-91 | 43.00 |
| | D-92 | 34.00 |
| HARDSHELL | H-60 | 87.00 |
| | H-65 | 87.00 |
| | H-90 | 87.00 |
| | H-91 | 87.00 |
| | H-92 | 87.00 |

## FINISH ABBREVIATIONS

| | | |
|---|---|---|
| N | = | Natural |
| MPL | = | Maple |
| SB | = | Brown Sunburst |
| DS | = | Dark Sunburst |
| WR | = | Wine Red |
| EB | = | Ebony |
| WAL | = | Walnut |
| ASB | = | Antique Sunburst |

\* Sold in two pack only. Mix and match.
\*\* Add $10.00 to suggested retail price for figured maple guitars.
\+ Limited availability for 1980.

**January 7, 1980**
**Price List**

## ACOUSTIC GUITARS

| Model | Available Finish | Suggested Retail | Fits Case |
|-------|------------------|------------------|-----------|
| *FT-SERIES* | | | |
| FT-120 | N,SB+ | $169.95 | 802, D-10 |
| FT-130 | SB+ | 189.95 | 802, D-10 |
| FT-140 | N+ | 199.95 | 810, D-20 |
| FT-145 | N,SB+ | 219.95 | 810, D-20 |
| FT-150 | N+ | 269.95 | 810, D-20 |
| FT-160 | N,SB+ | 249.95 | 814, D-25 |
| FT-165 | N+ | 299.95 | 814, D-25 |
| *PRESENTATION SERIES* | | | |
| PR-600 | N,ASB | 199.95 | 802, D-10 |
| PR-650 | N,ASB | 229.95 | 822, D-65, H-65 |
| PR-650-12 | N,ASB | 259.95 | 814, D-25 |
| PR-715-12 | N,ASB | 299.95 | 814, D-25 |
| PR-725 | N | 299.95 | 822, D-65, H-65 |
| PR-725S | N | 349.95 | 822, D-65, H-65 |
| PR-735 | N | 399.95 | 822, D-65, H-65 |
| PR-735S | N | 449.95 | 822, D-65, H-65 |
| PR-755S | N | 599.95 | 822, D-65, H-65 |
| PR-795AE | N | 499.95 | 822, D-65, H-65 |

## BANJOS AND MANDOLINS

| Model | Finish | Retail | Case |
|-------|--------|--------|------|
| *BANJO SERIES* | | | |
| MB-100 | N | 399.95 | D-55, H-60 |
| MB-250 | WAL | 599.95 | D-55, H-60 |
| *MANDOLIN SERIES* | | | |
| MM-30 | ASB | 219.95 | 815, D-15 |
| MM-50 | ASB | 599.95 | 815, D-15 |
| MM-70 | ASB | 699.95 | 815, D-15 |

## ELECTRIC GUITARS

| Model | Finish | Retail | Case |
|-------|--------|--------|------|
| *GENESIS SERIES* | | | |
| The GN | EB,WR | 279.95 | D-92, H-92 |
| GN-STD | EB,DS | 329.95 | D-92, H-92 |
| GN-DLX | EB,DS | 379.95 | D-92, H-92 |
| GN-CST | EB,DS | 429.95 | D-92, H-92 |
| GN-BA | EB | 349.95 | D-93, H-93 |

## CASES

| | Model | Suggested Retail |
|--|-------|------------------|
| *ECONOMY* | 800 | $20.00 |
| | 802 | 21.50 |
| | 803 | 21.50 |
| | 810 | 25.00 |
| | 814 | 27.00 |
| | 815 | 15.00 |
| | 822 | 27.00 |
| | 830 | 29.00 |
| | 831 | 25.50 |
| *DURABILT* | D-10 | 31.00 |
| | D-15 | 25.00 |
| | D-20 | 35.00 |
| | D-25 | 37.00 |
| | D-50 | 30.00 |
| | D-55 | 31.00 |
| | D-65 | 37.00 |
| | D-90 | 39.00 |
| | D-91 | 43.00 |
| | D-92 | 34.00 |
| | D-93 | 44.00 |
| *HARDSHELL* | H-60 | 87.00 |
| | H-65 | 87.00 |
| | H-90 | 87.00 |
| | H-91 | 87.00 |
| | H-92 | 87.00 |
| | H-93 | 87.00 |

## FINISH ABBREVIATIONS

N = Natural
SB = Brown Sunburst
DS = Dark Sunburst
WR = Wine Red
EB = Ebony
WAL = Walnut
ASB = Antique Sunburst

+ Limited availability for 1980.

**July 1, 1980**
**Price List**

*Sheraton - 699.95*
*♡ 129.50*

## ACOUSTIC GUITARS

| Model | Available Finish | Suggested Retail | Fits Case |
|---|---|---|---|
| PR-600 | N,ASB,ACS | $224.95 | 802, D-10 |
| PR-650 | N,ASB,ACS | 249.95 | 822, D-65, H65 |
| PR-650-12 | N,ASB,ACS | 279.95 | 814, D-25 |
| PR-715 | N,ASB,ACS | 279.95 | 822, D-65, H-65 |
| PR-715-12 | N,ASB,ACS | 319.95 | 814, D-25 |
| PR-725 | N,ASB,ACS | 329.95 | 822, D-65, H-65 |
| PR-725S | N,ASB,ACS | 374.95 | 822, D-65, H-65 |
| PR-735 | N,ASB,ACS | 424.95 | 822, D-65, H-65 |
| PR-735S | N,ASB,ACS | 474.95 | 822, D-65, H-65 |
| PR-755S | N,ASB,ACS | 629.95 | 822, D-65, H-65 |

## MASTERBUILT BANJOS & MANDOLINS

| | | | |
|---|---|---|---|
| MB-100 | N | 459.95 | D-55, H-60 |
| MB-250 | WAL | 629.95 | D-55, H-60 |
| MM-30 | ASB | 229.95 | D-15 |
| MM-50 | ASB | 649.95 | D-16 |
| MM-70 | ASB | 769.95 | D-16 |

## CASES

| | Model | Suggested Retail |
|---|---|---|
| Economy | 802 | $26.00 |
| | 814 | 32.00 |
| | 822 | 34.00 |
| Durabilt | D-10 | 36.00 |
| | D-15 | 31.50 |
| | D-16 | 31.00 |
| | D-25 | 42.00 |
| | D-65 | 44.00 |
| Hardshell | H-60 | 90.00 |
| | H-65 | 90.00 |

## FINISH ABBREVIATIONS

N = Natural   W = Walnut
ASB = Antique Sunburst
ACS = Antique Cherry Sunburst

P.O. Box 10087 • Nashville, TN 37210

0000 RD©1981 Norlin                    Printed in U.S.A.

## SUGGESTED RETAIL PRICE LIST
### EFFECTIVE MAY 15, 1981

May 15, 1981
Price List

## American Series

Spirit single pickup
Available in EB..................475.00
      VWB finish additional.......24.00
Spirit double pickup
Available in EB..................525.00
      VWB finish additional.......24.00
Special single pickup
Available in EB..................475.00
      CH ASB finish additional....24.00
Special double pickup
Available in EB..................525.00
      CH ASB finish additional....24.00
Fits Epiphone Protector Case........74.50

## COLOR CODES

EB—EBONY
VWB—VINTAGE WINE BURST
CH—CHERRY
ASB—ANTIQUE SUNBURST

### Gibson

A DIVISION OF NORLIN INDUSTRIES
P.O. BOX 100087, NASHVILLE, TN 37210

833100RD        Printed in U.S.A.

**June 1, 1982**
**Price List**

# Epiphone ®

## PRICE LIST
### Effective September 1, 1982

### ACOUSTIC GUITARS

| Model | Available Finish | Suggested Retail | Case |
|---|---|---|---|
| PR-600 | N,ASB,ACS | $249.95 | 802, D-10 |
| PR-650 | N,ASB,ACS | 279.95 | 822, D-65, H-65 |
| PR-650-12 | N,ASB,ACS | 299.95 | 814, D-25 |
| PR-715 | N,ASB,ACS | 299.95 | 822, D-65, H-65 |
| PR-715-12 | N,ASB,ACS | 319.95 | 814, D-25 |
| PR-725 | N,ASB,ACS | 329.95 | 822, D-65, H-65 |
| PR-725S | N,ASB,ACS | 374.95 | 822, D-65, H-65 |
| PR-735 | N,ASB,ACS | 424.95 | 822, D-65, H-65 |
| PR-735S | N,ASB,ACS | 474.95 | 822, D-65, H-65 |
| PR-755S | N,ASB,ACS | 629.95 | 822, D-65, H-65 |
| PR-795AE | N,ASB,ACS | 624.95 | 822, D-65, H-65 |

### THIN LINE ELECTRICS

| Model | Available Finish | Suggested Retail | Case |
|---|---|---|---|
| Emperor F | ASB | $989.95 | 600 |
| Emperor (T) | ASB | 899.95 | 603 |
| Sheraton | ASB/WR | 699.95 | 519 |
| Riviera | ASB/WR | 629.95 | 519 |
| Casino | ASB/WR | 579.95 | 519 |

### MASTERBUILT BANJOS & MANDOLINS

| Model | Available Finish | Suggested Retail | Case |
|---|---|---|---|
| MB-100 | N | $459.95 | D-55, H-60 |
| MB-250 | WAL | 629.95 | D-55, H-60 |
| MM-30 | ASB | 229.95 | D-15 |
| MM-50 | ASB | 649.95 | D-16 |
| MM-70 | ASB | 769.95 | D-16 |

### CASES

| | Model | Suggested Retail |
|---|---|---|
| Economy | 802 | $26.00 |
| | 814 | 32.00 |
| | 822 | 34.00 |
| Durabilt | D-10 | 36.00 |
| | D-15 | 31.50 |
| | D-16 | 31.00 |
| | D-25 | 42.00 |
| | D-65 | 44.00 |
| Hardshell | H-60 | 90.00 |
| | H-65 | 90.00 |
| Gibson | 600 | 129.50 |
| | 603 | 119.50 |
| | 519 | 129.50 |
| | 440 | 129.50 |

### FINISH CODE

N = Natural
W = Walnut
ASB = Antique Sunburst
ACS = Antique Cherry Sunburst
WR = Wine Red

Products listed herein may be limited or discontinued and prices for the products may be changed without notice. To improve the design, quality and performance of our instruments and to make use of the best available materials at all times, we reserve the right to change specifications without notice.

**Gibson ®**

A Division of Norlin Industries
P.O. Box 100087, Nashville, TN 37210

834117

**September 1, 1982**
**Catalog "Card" and Price List**

134

# Epiphone®

## PRICE LIST
### Effective January 1, 1983

### ACOUSTIC GUITARS

| Model | Available Finish | Suggested Retail | Case |
|---|---|---|---|
| PR-600 | ASB,ACS | $249.95 | 802, D-10 |
| PR-650 | ASB,ACS | 279.95 | 822, D-65, H-65 |
| PR-650-12 | ASB,ACS | 299.95 | 814, D-25 |
| PR-715 | ASB,ACS | 299.95 | 822, D-65, H-65 |
| PR-715-12 | ASB,ACS | 319.95 | 814, D-25 |
| PR-725 | ASB,ACS | 329.95 | 822, D-65, H-65 |
| PR-725S | ASB,ACS | 374.95 | 822, D-65, H-65 |
| PR-735 | ASB,ACS | 424.95 | 822, D-65, H-65 |
| PR-735S | ASB,ACS | 474.95 | 822, D-65, H-65 |
| PR-755S | ASB,ACS | 629.95 | 822, D-65, H-65 |
| PR-795AE | ASB,ACS | 624.95 | 822, D-65, H-65 |

Optional NAT .................. additional $20.00

### THIN LINE ELECTRICS

| Model | Available Finish | Suggested Retail | Case |
|---|---|---|---|
| Emperor F | ASB | $999.95 | 600 |
| Emperor (T) | ASB | 909.95 | 603 |
| Sheraton | ASB/WR | 729.95 | 519 |
| Riviera | ASB/WR | 659.95 | 519 |
| Casino | ASB/WR | 599.95 | 519 |

### MASTERBUILT
### BANJOS & MANDOLINS

| Model | Available Finish | Suggested Retail | Case |
|---|---|---|---|
| MB-100 | N | $479.00 | D-55, H-60 |
| MB-250 | WAL | 649.00 | D-55, H-60 |
| MM-30 | ASB | 249.00 | D-15 |
| MM-50 | ASB | 669.00 | D-16 |
| MM-70 | ASB | 789.00 | D-16 |

### CASES

| | Model | Suggested Retail |
|---|---|---|
| Economy | 802 | $ 26.00 |
| | 814 | 32.00 |
| | 822 | 34.00 |
| Durabilt | D-10 | 36.00 |
| | D-15 | 31.50 |
| | D-16 | 31.00 |
| | D-25 | 42.00 |
| | D-65 | 44.00 |
| Hardshell | H-60 | 90.00 |
| | H-65 | 90.00 |
| Gibson | 600 | 129.50 |
| | 603 | 119.50 |
| | 519 | 129.50 |
| | 440 | 129.50 |

### FINISH CODE

| | | |
|---|---|---|
| N | = | Natural |
| W | = | Walnut |
| ASB | = | Antique Sunburst |
| ACB | = | Antique Cherry Sunburst |
| WR | = | Wine Red |

Products listed herein may be limited or discontinued and prices for the products may be changed without notice. To improve the design, quality and performance of our instruments and to make use of the best available materials at all times, we reserve the right to change specifications without notice.

## Gibson®
### A Division of Norlin Industries
### P.O. Box 100087, Nashville, TN 37210

834117

**January 1, 1983**
**Price List**

## 1986 Price List

*The first price list from the Juszkiewicz/Berryman regime offers all models with vibrola and the following options (with up-charge): chrome hardware with standard vibrola (base), chrome hardware with Bennder vibrola ($30), black hardware with standard vibrola ($20), black Bennder vibrola ($50), chrome Kahler vibrola ($80), black Kahler vibrola ($100).*

| Model | Base price |
| --- | --- |
| V-2 | $239 |
| Explorer | $239 |
| S-200 | $249 |
| S-300 | $249 |
| S-400 | $249 |
| S-500 | $259 |
| S-600 | $269 |

## 1989

*Electrics*

Pro: Stratocaster shape sculpted body, scimitar peghead, dots on edge of fingerboard, 1 humbucker, 1 single coil, Floyd Rose tremolo

435i: 2 single coils, 1 humbucker, Bennder tremolo

635i: 2 single coils, 1 humbucker, Floyd Rose tremolo

935i: 1 humbucker, 1 single coil, Floyd Rose tremolo, set neck

T-310: Telecaster body

Flying V

S-310: Stratocaster body type

G-310: SG body, dot inlay, 2 humbuckers

G-400: SG body, dot inlay, 2 humbuckers, set neck

Les Paul Custom

Les Paul Standard

Accu Bass: P-Bass style

Rock Bass: Jazz Bass style

Power Bass: split P-Bass style pickup, straight Jazz Bass style pickup

Country Gentleman II: *f*-hole archtop, cutaway, half-moon inlays

Emperor: rounded cutaway, wedge-block abalone inlay, vine peghead inlay

Howard Roberts Fusion II: pointed cutaway, 2 humbuckers

Howard Roberts Fusion III: 2 single coils, 1 humbucker

Sheraton II: double cutaway wedge block inlay, vine peghead inlay

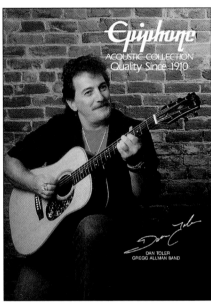

DAN TOLER
GREGG ALLMAN BAND

*Acoustics*

PR 715: dreadnought, dot inlay, herringbone trim

SQ 160: Everly Brothers style

PR 350: dreadnought, snowflake inlay

PR 350 Ebony: black finish

PR 350-12: 12-string

PR 350S: solid top

MB 250: 5-string banjo

MM 30: A-style mandolin

C 50 classic: rosewood body, ebony fingerboard

C 40 classic: rosewood body, rosewood fingerboard

C 30 classic: mahogany body

# WE KNOW GUITARS...

Price List Effective 3/1/92
*supercedes all previous price lists*
F.O.B. CMI Nashville Warehouse

| Family Code | Model/Case | Finish | Hardware | Suggested Retail | Case Price |
|---|---|---|---|---|---|
| **CLASSICAL GUITARS** | | | | | |
| EC25 | C-25/E800 | NS | CH | 219.00 | 33.00 |
| EC40 | C-40/E800 | NA | GH | 259.00 | 33.00 |
| | | | | | |
| **ACOUSTIC GUITARS** | | | | | |
| EA20 | PR-200/E822 | NS | CH | 239.00 | 33.00 |
| EA35 | PR-350/E822 | NA | CH | 309.00 | 33.00 |
| EA35 | PR-350/E822 | EB | CH | 319.00 | 33.00 |
| EA05 | PR-350S/E822 | NA | CH | 374.00 | 33.00 |
| EAOL | PR-350SL/E822 | NA | CH | 384.00 | 33.00 |
| EA3T | PR-350-12/E822 | NA | CH | 354.00 | 33.00 |
| EAQ1 | SQ-180/E822 | EB | CH | 354.00 | 33.00 |
| EA72 | PR-720S/E822 | AS | GH | 439.00 | 33.00 |
| EAJ2 | EJ-200/E822 | BK,NA,VS | GH | 569.00 | 33.00 |
| | | | | | |
| **ACOUSTIC-ELECTRIC GUITARS** | | | | | |
| EE35 | PR-350-E/E822 | NA | CH | 409.00 | 33.00 |
| EE3T | PR-350-12E/E822 | NA | CH | 469.00 | 33.00 |
| EEP5 | PR-5-E/E822 | NA | GH | 529.00 | 33.00 |
| EEP5 | PR-5-E/E822 | EB,VS | GH | 549.00 | 33.00 |
| | | | | | |
| **BLUEGRASS** | | | | | |
| EF30 | MM-30 Mandolin/ED15 | AS | CH | 319.00 | 28.00 |
| EFB2 | MB-250 Banjo/EH60 | MR | CH | 699.00 | 77.00 |
| | | | | | |
| **ORVILLE SERIES GUITARS** | | | | | |
| EO1E | EO-1 Acoustic-Electric/E800 | NA,VS | CH | 499.00 | 33.00 |
| EO2E | EO-2 Acoustic-Electric/E800 | BB,EB | CH | 509.00 | 33.00 |
| EO7S | PR-775S Acoustic/E822 | AN | CH | 499.00 | 33.00 |
| EO7T | PR-775-12 Acoustic/E822 | AN | CH | 499.00 | 33.00 |
| EOC7 | C70-CE Classical-Electric/E800 | AN | GH | 499.00 | 33.00 |
| | | | | | |
| **THINLINE ELECTRIC GUITARS** | | | | | |
| ETS2 | Sheraton/E519 | EB,NA,PW,VS | GH | 649.00 | 112.00 |
| ETE2 | Emperor/EEMCS | NA,VS | GH | 729.00 | 110.00 |
| | | | | | |
| **SOLID BODY ELECTRIC GUITARS** | | | | | |
| EGS1 | S-310/ESCS | BM,NY,PW,RM,SG,SM | CT | 289.00 | 74.00 |
| EGT1 | T-310/ETCS | EB,FC,RE | CH | 319.00 | 74.00 |
| EGG1 | G-310/EGCS | AW,EB,RE | CH | 339.00 | 74.00 |
| EGG4 | G-400/EGCS | CH | CH | 449.00 | 74.00 |
| EGV1 | Flying V/EVCS | AW,EB,RE | CH | 449.00 | 85.00 |
| EGM1 | EM-1/Gigbag | CH,EB,FB,PW,VS | GT | 449.00 | 47.00 |

**March 1, 1992**
**Price List—front**

| Family Code | Model/Case | Finish | Hardware | Suggested Retail | Case Price |
|---|---|---|---|---|---|
| EGM2 | EM-2/Gigbag | BM,BU,PW,RM | GF | 549.00 | 47.00 |
| ENS- | LP Standard/ENLPCS | HB,HS | CH | 629.00 | 85.00 |
| ENC- | LP Custom/ENLPCS | AW,EB | GH | 729.00 | 85.00 |
| * | Epiphone Gigbag Option | | | | 47.00 |

### BASS GUITARS

| Family Code | Model/Case | Finish | Hardware | Suggested Retail | Case Price |
|---|---|---|---|---|---|
| EBAC | Accu Bass/ERCS | EB/PW | CH | 369.00 | 94.00 |
| EBRO | Rock Bass/ERCS | EB/PW | CH | 379.00 | 94.00 |
| EBPO | Power Bass/ERCS | EB/PW | BH | 419.00 | 94.00 |
| EBM4 | EBM-4/Gigbag | CH,EB,FB,PW,VS | GH | 579.00 | 49.00 |
| EBM5 | EBM-5/Gigbag | CH,EB,FB,PW,VS | GH | 619.00 | 49.00 |

## MADE IN U.S.A. EPIPHONE GUITARS

| Family Code | Model/Case | Finish | Hardware | Suggested Retail | Case Price |
|---|---|---|---|---|---|
| EUPR | EPI Pro I/8383 | AW,CR,EB | FR | 599.00(A) | 125.00 |
| * | EPI Gigbag Option | | | | 47.00 |
| EUC- | EPI Coronet w/ Active Electronics | BG,CB,CP,CR | GH | 899.00(A) | incl. gigbag |
| EUC- | EPI Coronet w/ Active Electronics | BG,CB,CP,CR | FR | 999.00(A) | incl. gigbag |

## ALL EPIPHONE GUITARS CARRY A 3 YEAR WARRANTY
## SEE YOUR WARRANTY CARD FOR DETAILS

### EPIPHONE FINISH CODES

| | | | | |
|---|---|---|---|---|
| AN | Antique Natural | HB | Honey Burst |
| AS | Antique Sunburst | HS | Heritage Cherry Sunburst |
| AW | Alpine White | MR | Red Brown Mahogany |
| BB | Brown Burst | NA | Natural |
| BG | Bullion Gold | NS | Natural Satin |
| BK | Black Burst | NY | Nuclear Yellow |
| BM | Black Metallic | PW | Pearl White |
| CB | Candy Apple Blue | RE | Red |
| CH | Cherry | RM | Red Metallic |
| CP | Candy Apple Purple | SA | Satin Amber |
| CR | Candy Apple Red | SG | Seafoam Green |
| EB | Ebony | SM | Silver Metallic |
| FB | Frost Blue | VS | Vintage Sunburst |
| FC | French Cream | RM | Red Metal Flake |

### HARDWARE CODES

| | |
|---|---|
| BH | Black Hardware |
| CH | Chrome Hardware |
| CT | Chrome Tremolo |
| FR | Floyd Rose Licensed Tremolo System |
| GF | Gold Floyd Rose Licensed Tremolo System |
| GH | Gold Hardware |
| GT | Gold Tremelo |

**March 1, 1992**
**Price List—back**

## EPIPHONE...WE KNOW GUITARS.

| Family Code | Model/Case | Finish | H/W | US Sug. Retail | Case Price |
|---|---|---|---|---|---|
| **SOLID BODY ELECTRIC COLLECTION** | | | | | |
| EGS1 | S-310*/ESCS | BM,NY,PW,RM,SG,SM | CT | $299 | $74 |
| EGT1 | T-310/ETCS | EB,FC,RE | CH | $329 | $74 |
| EGG1 | G-310*/EGCS | AW,EB,RE | CH | $349 | $74 |
| EGG4 | G-400/EGCS | CH | CH | $449 | $74 |
| EGV1 | Flying V/EVCS | AW,EB,RE | CH | $469 | $85 |
| EGM1 | EM-1/Gigbag | CH,EB,FB,PW,VS | GT | $449 | $47 |
| EGM2 | EM-2/Gigbag | BM,BU,PW,RM | GF | $549 | $47 |
| EXP1 | Explorer/EEXP | AW,EB,RE | CH | $449 | $85 |
| EES1 | Stiletto/ENLPCS | AW,EB,FB, RM,SM | CH | $499 | $85 |
| ENB- | LP-100 Standard/ENLPCS | EB,PW,RE | CH | $399 | $85 |
| ENB- | LP-100* Standard/ENLPCS | AS,HS,VS | CH | $449 | $85 |
| ENS- | LP* Standard/ENLPCS | HB,HS | CH | $629 | $85 |
| ENC- | LP Custom/ENLPCS | AW,EB | GH | $729 | $85 |
| **THINLINE ELECTRIC** | | | | | |
| ETS2 | Sheraton II/E519 | EB,NA,PW,VS | GH | $679 | $112 |
| ETE2 | Emperor II/EEMCS | NA,VS | GH | $749 | $110 |
| **IMPERIAL COLLECTION** *(Made in Japan)* | | | | | |
| EIHR | Howard Roberts 1960's/EEMCS | WA,WR | GH | $1599 (A) | $110 |
| EIEM | Emperor 1930's/CS30 | AN,VS | GH | $2749 (A) | $175 |
| EIZE | Zephyr/CS93 | AN,VS | GH | $1999 (A) | $175 |
| **NASHVILLE USA COLLECTION** *(Made in USA)* | | | | | |
| EUPR | Pro I/8383 | AW,CR,EB | FR | $599 (A) | $125 |
| EUC- | Coronet w/Active Elec/GIGBAG | BG,CB,CP,CR | GH | $899 (A) | incl. gig |
| EUC- | Coronet w/Active Elec/GIGBAG | BG,CB,CP,CR | BC | $999 (A) | incl. gig |
| ENS1 | Sheraton**/E519 | EB,HS,NA,VS | GH | $999 (A) | $112 |
| ENR- | Riviera**/E519 | CH,NA,VS | CH | $899 (A) | $112 |
| **BASS COLLECTION** | | | | | |
| EBAC | Accu Bass/ERCS | EB,PW | CH | $389 | $94 |
| EBRO | Rock Bass/ERCS | EB,PW | CH | $399 | $94 |
| EBPO | Power Bass*/ERCS | EB,PW | BH | $449 | $94 |
| EBM4 | EBM-4/Basgig | CH,EB,FB,PW,VS | GH | $599 | $49 |
| EBM5 | EBM-5/Basgig | CH,EB,FB,PW,VS | GH | $649 | $49 |
| **BLUEGRASS COLLECTION** | | | | | |
| EFD1 | MD-30 Dobro/E822 | NA | CH | $649 | $33 |
| EF30 | MM-30 Mandolin/ED15 | AS | CH | $369 | $28 |
| EF50 | MM-50 Mandolin "/"-style/ED50 | VS | GH | $799 | $77 |
| EFB1 | MB-200 Banjo/EH60 | MR | CH | $669 | $77 |
| EFB2 | MB-250 Banjo/EH60 | MR | CH | $959 | $77 |

**April 1, 1993**
**Price List—front**

| Family Code | Model/Case | Finish | H/W | US Sug. Retail | Case Price |
|---|---|---|---|---|---|
| **ACOUSTIC COLLECTION** | | | | | |
| EA20 | PR-200/E822 | NS | CH | $269 | $33 |
| EA20 | PR-200/E822 | EB,NA,VS | CH | $279 | $33 |
| EA35 | PR-350/E822 | NA | CH | $329 | $33 |
| EA35 | PR-350/E822 | EB,VS | CH | $339 | $33 |
| EA3T | PR-350-12/E822 | NA | CH | $399 | $33 |
| EA05 | PR-350S/E822 | NA | CH | $419 | $33 |
| EAOL | PR-350SL/E822 | NA | CH | $429 | $33 |
| ER35 | PR-350RW/E822 | NA | CH | $449 | $33 |
| EA3C | PR-350C/E822 | NA | CH | $449 | $33 |
| EA3C | PR-350C/E822 | EB,VS | CH | $459 | $33 |
| EAQ1 | SQ-180/E822 | EB | CH | $399 | $33 |
| EA72 | PR-720S/E822 | SA | GH | $479 | $33 |
| EAJ2 | EJ-200/E822 | BK,NA,VS | GH | $599 | $33 |
| EAJT | EJ-212/E822 | BK,NA,VS | GH | $649 | $33 |
| **MONTANA USA COLLECTION** *(Made in USA - limited availability)* | | | | | |
| EM10 | EM-10 Acoustic Dreadnought | NS,SV | CH | $599 (A) | $99 |
| EM20 | EM-20 Acoustic Dreadnought | NS,SV | CH | $799 (A) | $99 |
| EMAE30 | EMAE-30 Acoustic-Electric | NS,SV | CH | $999 (A) | $99 |
| **ACOUSTIC-ELECTRIC COLLECTION** | | | | | |
| EE35 | PR-350-E/E822 | NA | CH | $469 | $33 |
| EE35 | PR-350-E/E822 | EB,VS | CH | $479 | $33 |
| EE3T | PR-350-12E/E822 | NA | CH | $529 | $33 |
| EER3 | PR-350RW-E/E822 | NA | CH | $529 | $33 |
| EE3C | PR-350C-E/E822 | NA | CH | $519 | $33 |
| EE3C | PR-350C-E/E822 | EB,VS | CH | $529 | $33 |
| EEP5 | PR-5-E/E822 | NA | GH | $579 | $33 |
| EEP5 | PR-5-E/E822 | EB,VS | GH | $589 | $33 |
| EEP6 | PR-6-E/E822 | HS,RD,TA,TS | GH | $649 | $33 |
| EPP6 | PR-6-E Deluxe(Silky Oak)/E822 | HS,RD,TA,TS | GH | $659 | $33 |
| EEP7 | PR-7-E (Birdseye)/E822 | NA,OS,RD | GH | $699 | $33 |
| **ORVILLE COLLECTION** | | | | | |
| EO1E | EO-1 Acoustic-Electric/E800 | NA,VS | CH | $529 | $33 |
| EO2E | EO-2 Acoustic-Electric/E800 | BB,EB | GH | $569 | $33 |
| EO7S | PR-775S Acoustic/E822 | AN | GH | $549 | $33 |
| EO7E | PR-775S-E Acoustic-Electric | AN | GH | $679 | $33 |
| EOTE | PR-775-12 Acoustic | AN | GH | $549 | $33 |
| EOTE | PR-775-12E Acoustic-Electric | AN | GH | $659 | $33 |
| EO7C | PR-775SC Acoustic Cut/E822 | AN | GH | $569 | $33 |
| EO77 | PR-775SC-E Acous-Elec/E822 | AN | GH | $679 | $33 |
| EOC7 | C70-CE Classical-Electric/E800 | AN | GH | $549 | $33 |
| **CLASSICAL COLLECTION** | | | | | |
| EC25 | C-25/E800 | NS | CH | $269 | $33 |
| EC40 | C-40/E800 | NA | GH | $299 | $33 |
| **ACCESSORIES** | | | | | |
| EPIGIG | Epiphone Guitar Gigbag | | | $47 | |
| BASGIG | Epiphone Bass Gigbag | | | $49 | |

*(\*Available in Left-Handed Version for additional $25 retail; \*\*Available in Left-Handed version for addtional $200 retail.)*

# Epiphone ®
### Quality Since 1910
## The Mark Of A Great Guitarist.
1818 Elm Hill Pike Nashville, TN USA 37210  Phone: 1-800-444-2766
*A Division of Gibson Guitar Corp.*

**U.S.A. SUGGESTED**
## RETAIL PRICE
**Effective May 15, 1994**
*(supercedes all other prices)*

| | MODEL | MODEL CODE | COLOR | H/W | U.S. SUG. RETAIL | MODEL CODE | U.S. SUG. RETAIL |
|---|---|---|---|---|---|---|---|
| | **CLASSICAL COLLECTION** | | | | | | |
| | C-25 | EC25 | NS | CH | $299 | E800 | $35 |
| | C-40 | EC40 | NA | GH | $349 | E800 | $35 |
| | C70-CE | EOC7 | AN | GH | $749 | EPR6 | $109 |
| | **ACOUSTIC COLLECTION** | | | | | | |
| | PR-200 | EA20 | NS | CH | $299 | E822 | $36 |
| | PR-200 | EA20 | EB, NA, VS | CH | $309 | E822 | $36 |
| | PR-350 | EA35 | NA | CH | $369 | E822 | $36 |
| | PR-350 | EA35 | EB, VS | CH | $379 | E822 | $36 |
| | PR-350-12 | EA3T | NA | CH | $449 | E822 | $36 |
| NEW! | PR-350M | EM35 | NS | GH | $369 | E822 | $36 |
| | PR-350RW | ER35 | NA | CH | $529 | E822 | $36 |
| | PR-350C | EA3C | NA | CH | $449 | E822 | $36 |
| | PR-350C | EA3C | EB, VS | CH | $459 | E822 | $36 |
| | PR-350S | EA05 | NA | CH | $489 | E822 | $36 |
| NEW! | PR-350S | EA05 | EB, VS | CH | $499 | E822 | $36 |
| | PR-350S LEFT-HANDED | EA0L | NA | CH | $514 | E822 | $36 |
| | PR-720S | EA72 | SA | GH | $499 | EDREAD | $109 |
| | PR-775S | EO7S | AN, NA | GH | $749 | EDREAD | $109 |
| | PR-775-12 | EO7T | AN, NA | GH | $749 | EDREAD | $109 |
| | PR-775-SC | EO7C | AN, NA | GH | $799 | EDREAD | $109 |
| | PR-800S | EA80 | NA | GH | $699 | EDREAD | $109 |
| | SQ-180 | EAQ1 | EB | CH | $479 | EDREAD | $109 |
| NEW! | EJ-200 | EAJ2 | BK, NA, VS | GH | $729 | EJUMBO | $125 |
| NEW! | EJ-212 | EAJT | BK, NA, VS | GH | $799 | EJUMBO | $125 |
| NEW! | BLUESMASTER | EABM | EB, NA, VS | CH | $729 | EBLCS | $110 |
| NEW! | HUMMINGBIRD | EAHB | CH | CH | $729 | EDREAD | $109 |
| | **ACOUSTIC/ELECTRIC COLLECTION** | | | | | | |
| NEW! | PR-200-E | EE20 | EB, NA, VS | CH | $369 | E822 | $36 |
| | PR-350-E | EE35 | NA | CH | $519 | E822 | $36 |
| | PR-350-E | EE35 | EB, VS | CH | $529 | E822 | $36 |
| | PR350-12E | EE3T | NA | CH | $589 | E822 | $36 |
| NEW! | PR350M-E | EME5 | NS | GH | $489 | E822 | $36 |
| | PR-350RW-E | EER3 | NA | CH | $659 | E822 | $36 |
| | PR-350C-E | EE3C | NA | CH | $579 | E822 | $36 |
| | PR-350C-E | EE3C | EB, VS | CH | $589 | E822 | $36 |
| | PR-775-SE | EO7E | AN, NA | GH | $879 | EDREAD | $109 |
| | PR-775-12E | EOTE | AN, NA | GH | $879 | EDREAD | $109 |
| | PR-775-SCE | EO77 | AN, NA | GH | $929 | EDREAD | $109 |
| | PR-800S-E | EE80 | NA | GH | $799 | EDREAD | $109 |
| NEW! | JEFF BAXTER MODEL | EAJB | BR, NA | GH | $749 | EBAXCS | $110 |
| | PR5-E | EEP5 | NA | GH | $659 | EPR5 | $109 |
| NEW! | PR5-E LEFT-HANDED | EEP5L | NA | GH | $684 | EPR5 | $109 |
| | PR5-E | EEP5 | EB, VS, WH | GH | $669 | EPR5 | $109 |
| NEW! | PR5-E ARTIST | EEA5 | HS, NA, VS | GH | $749 | EPR5 | $109 |
| NEW! | PR6-E | EEP6 | HS, RD, TA, TS | CH | $729 | EPR6 | $109 |
| | PR6-E DELUXE | EPP6 | HS, RD, TA, TS | CH | $729 | EPR6 | $109 |
| | PR7-E | EEP7 | HS, NA, OS,TB, VC | GH | $779 | EPR5 | $109 |
| | **CHET ATKINS COLLECTION** | | | | | | |
| NEW! | CHET ATKINS STANDARD | ECSS | EB, HS, NA | GH | $749 | ECACS | $119 |
| NEW! | CHET ATKINS CUSTOM | ECSF | HS, NA | GH | $799 | ECACS | $119 |
| NEW! | CHET ATKINS DELUXE | ECBE | HS, NA | GH | $849 | ECACS | $119 |
| NEW! | CHET ATKINS CEC | ECCE | AN | GH | $749 | ECACS | $119 |
| | **ORVILLE COLLECTION** | | | | | | |
| | EO-1 | EO1E | NA, VS | CH | $679 | E800 | $35 |
| | EO-2 | EO2E | EB | GH | $749 | EPR6 | $109 |
| | **BLUEGRASS COLLECTION** | | | | | | |
| | MM-30 | EF30 | AS | CH | $429 | ED15 | $32 |
| | MM-50 | EF50 | VS | GH | $919 | ED50 | $119 |
| | MB-200 | EFB1 | MR | CH | $749 | EH60 | $109 |
| | MB-250 | EFB2 | MR | CH | $1,049 | EH60 | $109 |
| | MD-30 | EFD1 | NA | CH | $749 | EDREAD | $109 |
| | **ARCHTOP COLLECTION** | | | | | | |
| NEW! | RIVIERA | ETRI | CH, EB, NA, VC | CH | $849 | E519 | $112 |
| NEW! | CASINO | ETCA | CH, EB, NA, VC | CH | $829 | E519 | $112 |
| NEW! | SORRENTO | ETSO | AS, CH, EB, OR, VC | CH | $849 | E519 | $112 |
| | SHERATON II | ETS2 | EB, NA, PW, VS | GH | $849 | E519 | $112 |
| | EMPEROR II | ETE2 | HS, NA, VS | GH | $929 | EEMCS | $110 |
| NEW! | EMPEROR REGENT | ETEM | AS, NA, VC | GH | $1,129 | EERCS | $110 |
| | **IMPERIAL COLLECTION** | | *Made in Japan* | | | | |
| | EMPEROR RE-ISSUE | EIEM | AN, VS | GH | $3,199 | ESUPERIV | $175 |
| | H. ROBERTS RE-ISSUE | EIHR | WA, WR | GH | $1,999 | EEMCS | $110 |
| | ZEPHYR RE-ISSUE | EIZE | AN, VS | GH | $2,299 | EZEPH | $175 |

**May 15, 1994**
**Price List—front**

# Epiphone ®
### Quality Since 1910

## The Mark Of A Great Guitarist.

1818 Elm Hill Pike Nashville, TN USA 37210 Phone: 1-800-444-2766
*A Division of Gibson Guitar Corp.*

**U.S.A. SUGGESTED**
# RETAIL PRICE
**Effective May 15, 1994**
*(supercedes all other prices)*

| | MODEL | MODEL CODE | COLOR | H/W | U.S. SUG. RETAIL | MODEL CODE | U.S. SUG. RETAIL |
|---|---|---|---|---|---|---|---|
| | **ELECTRIC COLLECTION** | | | | | | |
| | S-310 | EGS1 | BM, NY, PW, RM, SG, SM, TS, VW | CT | $349 | ESCS | $99 |
| | S-310 LEFT-HANDED | EGS1L | BM | CT | $374 | ESCS | $99 |
| NEW! | S-310 CUSTOM | EGS1 | NM | CT | $489 | ESTWEED | $149 |
| | T-310 | EGT1 | EB, FC, RE, VW | CH | $389 | EGCS | $99 |
| NEW! | T-310 CUSTOM | EGT1 | NM | CH | $489 | ETTWEED | $159 |
| | G-310 | EGG1 | AW, EB, RE | CH | $429 | EGCS | $99 |
| | G-310 LEFT-HANDED | EGG1L | EB | CH | $454 | EGCS | $99 |
| | G-400 | EGG4 | CH | CH | $549 | EGCS | $99 |
| | LP-100 | ENB- | EB, RE, PW | CH | $479 | ENLPCS | $99 |
| | LP-100 | ENB- | AS, HS, VS | CH | $529 | ENLPCS | $99 |
| | LP-100 LEFT-HANDED | ENBL | HS | CH | $554 | ENLPCS | $99 |
| | STILETTO | EES1 | AW, EB, FB, RM, SM | CH | $599 | ENLPCS | $99 |
| | FLYING-V | EGV1 | AW, EB, RE | CH | $549 | EVCS | $119 |
| | EXPLORER | EXP1 | AW, EB, RE | CT | $549 | EEXP | $119 |
| | EM-1 | EGM1 | CH, EB, FB, PW, VS | GT | $529 | XEGIG | $39 |
| | EM-2 | EGM2 | BM, BU, PW, RM | GF | $649 | XEGIG | $39 |
| | **LES PAUL COLLECTION** | | | | | | |
| NEW! | LES PAUL SPECIAL | ELPS | CH, EB, TV | CH | $749 | ENLPCS | $99 |
| NEW! | LES PAUL STD GOLDTOP | ENS- | MG | CH | $879 | ENLPCS | $99 |
| NEW! | LES PAUL CLASSIC B'EYE | ENSB | AM, HS, NA | CH | $829 | ENLPCS | $99 |
| | LES PAUL STANDARD | ENS- | HB, HS | CH | $779 | ENLPCS | $99 |
| | LES PAUL STD LEFT-HAND | ENSL | HS | CH | $789 | ENLPCS | $99 |
| | LES PAUL CUSTOM | ENC- | AW, EB | GH | $899 | ENLPCS | $99 |
| | **BASS COLLECTION** | | | | | | |
| NEW! | EL CAPITAN | EBEC | EB, NA, VS | CH | $949 | EABCS | $135 |
| | ACCU BASS | EBAC | EB, PW | CH | $449 | ERCS | $119 |
| NEW! | ACCU BASS LEFT-HANDED | EBACL | EB | CH | $474 | ERCS | $119 |
| | ROCK BASS | EBRO | EB, PW | CH | $469 | ERCS | $119 |
| | POWER BASS | EBPO | EB, PW | BH | $519 | ERCS | $119 |
| | POWER BASS LEFT-HAND | EBPOL | EB | BH | $544 | ERCS | $119 |
| NEW! | RIVOLI BASS | EBRI | CH, EB, NA, VC | CH | $929 | ERVCS | $110 |
| NEW! | EXPERT BASS (6 STRING) | EBEX | NM | BH | $1,299 | BASGIG | $65 |
| | EBM-4 | EBM4 | CH, EB, FB, PW, VS | GH | $689 | BASGIG | $65 |
| NEW! | EBM-4 CUSTOM | EBM4 | NM | GH | $799 | BASGIG | $65 |
| | EBM-5 | EBM5 | CH, EB, FB, PW, VS | GH | $749 | XBGIG | $42 |
| NEW! | EBM-5 CUSTOM | EBM5 | NM | GH | $849 | XBGIG | $42 |
| | **EPI ACCESSORIES** | | | | | | |
| NEW! | Acoustic Gigbag | XAGIG | Black re-inforced nylon/oxford with 5mm padding and pocket. | | | XAGIG | $39 |
| NEW! | Classical Gigbag | XCGIG | Black re-inforced nylon/oxford with 5mm padding and pocket. | | | XCGIG | $39 |
| NEW! | Acoustic Starter Kit | EASK | Includes strap, pitchpipe, stringwinder, polish, cloth and picks. | | | EASK | $30 |
| NEW! | Electric Starter Kit | EESK | Includes strap, pitchpipe, stringwinder, cord and picks. | | | EASK | $30 |
| NEW! | Epi T-shirt | E-TSHIRT | Lt. Grey with two color logo front & back. Specify S,M,L, or XL. | | | E-TSHIRT | $15 |
| NEW! | Epi Ball Cap | E-BLCAP | High-quality ball cap with Epi logo on front & back. | | | E-BLCAP | $18 |

*For more great Epiphone accessories including Epiphone Strings - contact Gibson Strings & Accessories at 1-800-544-2766!*

## ALL EPIPHONE INSTRUMENTS CARRY A 10-YEAR LIMITED WARRANTY.
*See warranty card for details.*

### COLOR CODES

| | | | | |
|---|---|---|---|---|
| AM | Amber | | OR | Orange |
| AN | Antique Natural | | OS | Orange Sunburst |
| AS | Antique Sunburst | | PW | Pearl White |
| AW | Alpine White | | RD | Translucent Red |
| BK | Black | | RE | Red |
| BM | Black Metallic | | RM | Red Metallic |
| BR | Brown | | SA | Satin Amber |
| CH | Cherry | | SG | Seafoam Green |
| EB | Ebony | | SM | Silver Metallic |
| FB | Frost Blue | | TA | Translucent Amber |
| FC | French Cream | | TB | Translucent Black |
| HB | Honey Burst | | TS | Tobacco Sunburst |
| HS | Heritage Cherry Sunburst | | TV | "TV" Yellow |
| MG | Metallic Gold | | VC | Vintage Cherry Sunburst |
| MR | Red Brown Mahogany | | VS | Vintage Sunburst |
| NA | Natural | | VW | Vintage White |
| NM | Natural Matte | | WA | Walnut |
| NS | Natural Satin | | WH | White |
| NY | Nuclear Yellow | | WR | Wine Red |

### HARDWARE CODES

| | |
|---|---|
| BH | Black Hardware |
| CH | Chrome Hardware |
| CT | Chrome Tremelo |
| GF | Gold Floyd Rose |
| | Licensed Tremelo |
| GH | Gold Hardware |
| GT | Gold Tremelo |

*In order to continually improve the design, quality, and performance of our instruments and to make use of the best available materials at all times, Epiphone reserves the right to change specifications and prices without notice.*

**May 15, 1994**
**Price List—back**

# EPIPHONE SPECIFICATIONS

| Model | Pickups | Hrdwr | Scale | Nut Width | Neck Joint | Neck Material | FB / Inlay | Binding | Body Matl. | Top | Also Available |
|---|---|---|---|---|---|---|---|---|---|---|---|
| **ARCHTOP COLLECTION** | | | | | | | | | | | |
| Emperor Regent | OBL Floating Mini-HB | Gold | 25.5" | 1.68" | Set | 3-pc Maple | RW / Block & Tri | B / N / H | Lam. Maple | Select Spruce | |
| Joe Pass Emperor II | 2 Humbuckers | Gold | 24.75" | 1.68 | Set | Maple | RW / Block | B / N / H | Lam. Maple | Lam. Maple | |
| Sheraton II | 2 Humbuckers | Gold | 24.75" | 1.68" | Set | Maple | RW / Block | B / N / H | Lam. Maple | Lam. Maple | |
| Riviera | 2 Humbuckers | Chrome | 24.75" | 1.68" | Set | Mahogany | RW / Parallelgrm | B / N | Lam. Maple | Lam. Maple | |
| Casino | 2 P-90s | Chrome | 24.75" | 1.68" | Set | Mahogany | RW / Parallelgrm | B / N | Lam. Maple | Lam. Spruce | |
| Sorrento | 2 P-90s | Chrome | 24.75" | 1.68" | Set | Mahogany | RW / Dot | B / N | Lam. Maple | Lam. Spruce | |
| **LES PAUL COLLECTION** | | | | | | | | | | | |
| LP-100 Studio | 2 Humbuckers | Chrome | 24.75" | 1.68" | Bolt | Mahogany | RW / Dot | | Alder / Mahogany | Alder / Maple | |
| L P Special Dbl Cut | 2 P-90s | Chrome | 24.75" | 1.68" | Set | Mahogany | RW / Dot | | Mahogany | Mahogany | |
| L P Studio Standard | 2 Humbuckers | Chrome | 24.75" | 1.68" | Bolt | Mahogany | RW / Dot | B / N | Mahogany | Flame Maple | |
| Les Paul Standard | 2 Humbuckers | Chrome | 24.75" | 1.68" | Set | Mahogany | RW / Trapezoid | B / N | Mahogany | Flame Maple | |
| Les Paul Classic | 2 Humbuckers | Chrome | 24.75" | 1.68" | Set | Mahogany | RW / Trapezoid | B / N | Mahogany | Birdseye Maple | |
| Les Paul Goldtop | 2 Humbuckers | Chrome | 24.75" | 1.68" | Set | Mahogany | RW / Trapezoid | B / N | Mahogany | Maple | |
| Les Paul Custom | 2 Humbuckers | Gold | 24.75" | 1.68" | Set | Mahogany | RW / Block | B / N / H | Mahogany / Alder | Maple / Alder | |
| **SOLID BODY COLLECTION** | | | | | | | | | | | |
| S-310 | 3 Single | Chrome | 25.5" | 1.68" | Bolt | Maple | Maple / Dot | | Alder | | |
| S-310 Custom | 3 Single | Chrome | 25.5" | 1.68" | Bolt | Maple | Maple / Dot | | Ash | | |
| T-310 | 2 Single | Chrome | 25."5 | 1.68" | Bolt | Maple | Maple / Dot | | Alder | | |
| T-310 Custom | 2 Single | Chrome | 25."5 | 1.68" | Bolt | Maple | Maple / Dot | | Ash | | |
| G-310 | 2 Humbuckers | Chrome | 24.75" | 1.68" | Bolt | Mahogany | RW / Dot | | Alder | | |
| G-400 | 2 Humbuckers | Chrome | 24.75" | 1.68" | Set | Mahogany | RW / Dot | | Mahogany | | |
| Flying V | 2 Humbuckers | Chrome | 24.75" | 1.68" | Set | Mahogany | RW / Dot | | Alder | | |
| Explorer | 2 Humbuckers | Chrome | 24.75" | 1.68" | Set | Mahogany | RW / Dot | | Alder | | |
| **PERFORMANCE COLLECTION - (OBL EQUIPPED ELECTRICS)** | | | | | | | | | | | |
| Coronet | 1 OBL SC-1 / 1 OBL HBB-1 | Chrome | 24.75" | 1.68" | Bolt | Maple | RW / Block | N | Maple | | |
| Nighthawk SP3 | 2 OBL HB / 1 OBL SC-1 | Gold | 25.5" | 1.68" | Bolt | Mahogany | RW / Dot | B / N | Mahogany / Alder | | |
| Nighthawk ST3 | 2 OBL HB / 1 OBL SC-1 | Gold | 25.5" | 1.68" | Bolt | Mahogany | RW / Split Parall | B / N | Mahogany | Flame Maple | |
| PRO-1 | 1 OBL SC-1 / 1 OBL HBB-1 | Black | 25.5" | 1.68" | Bolt | Maple | RW / M-III | | Alder | | |
| PRO-2 | 2 OBL Humbuckers | Black | 25.5" | 1.68" | Bolt | Maple | RW / M-III | | Alder | | |
| Del Rey | 2 OBL Humbuckers | Gold | 24.75" | 1.68" | Bolt | Mahogany | RW / Dot | B | Mahogany | Flame Maple | |
| Firebird | 2 OBL Mini-HBs | Chrome | 24.75" | 1.68" | Bolt | Mahogany | RW / Dot | | Mahogany / Alder | | |
| **BASS COLLECTION** | | | | | | | | | | | |
| Accu-Bass | 1 Split HB | Chrome | 34" | 1.65" | Bolt | Maple | RW / Dot | | Maple / Alder | | |
| Accu-Bass Custom | 1 Split HB | Chrome | 34" | 1.65" | Bolt | Maple | RW / Dot | | Ash | | |
| Power Bass | Split HB / Single | Black | 34" | 1.65" | Bolt | Maple | RW / Dot | | Maple | | |
| Rock Bass | 2 Single | Chrome | 34" | 1.65" | Bolt | Maple | RW / Dot | | Maple | | |
| EBM-4 | Split HB / Single | Gold | 34" | 1.65" | Bolt | Maple | RW / Dot | | Alder | | 5-String - EBM-5 |
| EBM-5 Custom | Split HB / Single | Gold | 34" | 1.73" | Bolt | Maple | RW / Dot | | Ash | Ash | 4-String - EBM-4 Custom |
| Les Paul Bass | 2 EMG Humbuckers | Black | 34" | 1.65" | Bolt | Maple | RW / Trapezoid | | Maple | Flame Maple | |
| Thunderbird-5 | Spilt HB / Single | Chrome | 34" | 1.73 | Bolt | Maple | RW / Dot | | Alder | | 4-String - T Bird 4 |
| Expert | 2 Singles | Black | 34" | 2.05 | N-Thru | 3-pc Maple | RW / Dot | | Ash | | |
| **ACOUSTIC & SEMI ACOUSTIC BASS COLLECTION** | | | | | | | | | | | |
| Viola Bass | 2 Mini HBs | Chrome | 30.5" | 1.65" | Set | Maple | RW / Dot | B / H | Lam. Maple | Flame Maple | |
| Rivoli Bass | 1 Humbucker | Chrome | 30.5" | 1.65" | Set | Maple | RW / Dot | B | Lam. Maple | Lam. Maple | |
| El Capitan | Piezo / Para-EQ Standard | Chrome | 34" | 1.65" | Set | Maple | RW / Dot | B / N / H | Maple | Maple | |
| El Capitan-5 Cutaway | Piezo / Para-EQ Standard | Chrome | 34" | 1.73" | Set | Maple | RW / Dot | B / N / H | Maple | Maple | 4 String - El Capitan-4 Cut |
| **NUEVO COLLECTION** | | | | | | | | | | | |
| El Diablo | Piezo / Para-EQ Standard | Chrome | 25.5" | 1.68" | Set | Mahogany | RW / Dot | B | Resophonic FRP | Spruce | |
| El Rio | Piezo / Para-EQ Standard | Gold | 25.5" | 1.68" | Set | Mahogany | RW / Split Diamond | B / N | Resophonic FRP | Flame Maple | |
| EL Nino | | Chrome | 22" | 1.625" | Set | Mahogany | RW / Dot | B / N | Resophonic FRP | Spruce | |
| **ACOUSTIC COLLECTION** | | | | | | | | | | | |
| PR-200 | | Chrome | 25.5" | 1.68" | Set | Mahogany | RW / Dot | B | Mahogany | Spruce / Cedar | Piezo- PR-200E |
| PR-350S | | Chrome | 25.5" | 1.68" | Set | Mahogany | RW / Split Diamond | B | Mahogany | Solid Spruce | Piezo/Para-EQ- PR-350E<br>Select Spruce Top-PR-350 |
| PR-350-12 | | Chrome | 25.5" | 1.68" | Set | Mahogany | RW / Split Diamond | B | Mahogany | Select Spruce | Piezo/Para-EQ- PR-350-12E |
| PR-350C | | Chrome | 25.5" | 1.68" | Set | Mahogany | RW / Split Diamond | B | Mahogany | Select Spruce | Piezo/Para-EQ- PR-350CE |
| PR-350M | | Gold | 25.5" | 1.68" | Set | Mahogany | RW / Dot | B | Mahogany | Select Mahogany | Piezo/Para-EQ- PR-350ME |
| **PERFORMANCE COLLECTION - (ACOUSTIC & ACOUSTIC ELECTRICS)** | | | | | | | | | | | |
| PR-5-E | Piezo / Para-EQ Standard | Gold | 25.5" | 1.68" | Set | Mahogany | RW / Split Diamond | B / N | Mahogany | Select Spruce | |
| PR-5-E Artist | Piezo / Para-EQ Standard | Gold | 25.5" | 1.68" | Set | Mahogany | RW / Split Diamond | B / N | Mahogany | Flame Maple | |
| PR-6-E | Piezo / Para-EQ Standard | Gold | 25." | 1.68" | Set | Mahogany | RW / Dot | B / N / H | Flame Maple | Flame Maple | |
| PR-7-E | Piezo / Para-EQ Standard | Gold | 25.5" | 1.68" | Set | Mahogany | RW / Split Diamond | B / N | Birdseye Maple | Birdseye Maple | |
| SQ-180 | | Chrome | 24.75 | 1.68" | Set | Mahogany | RW / Stars | B / N | Maple | Select Spruce | |
| Bluesmaster | | Chrome | 24.75" | 1.75" | Set | Mahogany | RW / Dot | B / N / H | Mahogany | Solid Spruce | |
| Hummingbird | | Chrome | 24.75" | 1.68" | Set | Mahogany | RW / Split Parall | B / N | Mahogany | Solid Spruce | |
| EJ-200 | | Gold | 25" | 1.68" | Set | Maple | RW / Crown | B / N / H | Maple | Select Spruce | 12-String - EJ-212 |
| EJ-200CE | Piezo / Para-EQ Standard | Gold | 25" | 1.68" | Set | Maple | RW / Crown | B / N / H | Maple | Select Spruce | |
| PR-775S | | Gold | 25." | 1.68" | Set | Mahogany | RW / Block & Tri | B / N / H | Rosewood | Solid Spruce | Piezo/Para-EQ- PR-775SE |
| PR-775S-C | | Gold | 25." | 1.68" | Set | Mahogany | RW / Block & Tri | B / N / H | Rosewood | Solid Spruce | Piezo/Para-EQ- PR-775SCE |
| PR-800S | | Gold | 25.5" | 1.68" | Set | Mahogany | RW / Split Diamond | B / N / H | Rosewood | Solid Spruce | Piezo/Para-EQ- PR-800SE |
| Jeff "Skunk" Baxter | Piezo / Para-EQ Standard | Gold | 25.5" | 1.68" | Set | Mahogany | RW / Split Diamond | B / N / H | Mahogany | Select Spruce | |
| **CHET ATKINS COLLECTION** | | | | | | | | | | | |
| Chet Atkins SST Custom | Piezo / 1 Tone; 1 Volume | Gold | 24.75" | 1.68" | Set | Mahogany | RW / Dot | B | Mahogany | Flame Maple | Standard -Spruce Top<br>Deluxe - Birdseye Maple Top |
| Chet Atkins CEC | Piezo / 1 Tone; 1 Volume | Gold | 25.5" | 2.0" | Set | Mahogany | RW /None | B | Mahogany | Select Spruce | |
| **ORVILLE COLLECTION** | | | | | | | | | | | |
| EO-1 | Piezo / Para-EQ Standard | Chrome | 25" | 1.68" | Set | Mahogany | RW / Dot | B / N / H | Mahogany | Select Spruce | |
| EO-2 | Piezo / Para-EQ Standard | Gold | 25" | 1.68" | Set | Mahogany | RW / Dot | B / N / H | Mahogany | Select Spruce | |
| **CLASSICAL COLLECTION** | | | | | | | | | | | |
| C-25 | | Chrome | 25.5" | 2.0" | Set | Mahogany | RW / None | B | Mahogany | Select Spruce | |
| C-40 | | Gold | 25.5" | 2.0" | Set | Mahogany | RW / None | B | Mahogany | Select Cedar | |
| C-70 CE | Piezo / Para-EQ Standard | Gold | 25" | 2.0" | Set | Mahogany | RW / None | B | Rosewood | Select Spruce | |
| **BLUGRASS COLLECTION** | | | | | | | | | | | |
| MM-30 | | Chrome | 14" | 1.06" | Set | Maple | RW / Dot | B / N | Maple | Solid Spruce | Shadow Piezo - MM-30E |
| MM-50 | | Gold | 14" | 1.06" | Set | Maple | RW / Dot | B / N | Maple | Solid Spruce | Shadow Piezo - MM-50E |
| MD-30 | | Chrome | 25.5" | 1.68" | Set | Mohgy/ Round | RW / Split Diamond | B | Mahogany | Spruce / Chrome | Raised Nut Optional |
| MB-200 | | Chrome | 26.25" | 1.25" | Bolt | Mahogany | RW / Dot | B / N | Mahogany | US Remo Head | |
| MB-250 | | Chrome | 26.25" | 1.25" | Bolt | Mahohany | RW / Heart | B / N | Maple | US Remo Head | |

**1995 Spec List**

# Serial Numbers

## New York-made, 1930–57

*Guitars, 1930–57, number on label.*

| Number | Year |
|---|---|
| 1000–3000, electrics only | 1937–38 |
| 4000–5000, electrics only | 1939–41 |
| 5000, acoustics | 1932 |
| 6000 | 1933 |
| 7000 | 1934 |
| 8000–9000 | 1935 |
| 10000 | 1930–32, 1936 |
| 11000 | 1937 |
| 12000 | 1938 |
| 13000 | 1939–40 |
| 14000–15000 | 1941–42 |
| 16000–18000 | 1943 |
| 19000 | 1944 |
| 51000–52000 | 1944 |
| 52000–54000 | 1945 |
| 54000–55000 | 1946 |
| 56000 | 1947 |
| 57000 | 1948 |
| 58000 | 1949 |
| 59000 | 1950 |
| 60000–63000 | 1951 |
| 64000 | 1952 |
| 64000–66000 | 1953 |
| 68000 | 1954 |
| 69000 | 1955–57 |
| 75000–85000 | 1948–49 |

## Gibson-made in Kalamazoo, 1958–69

*Hollowbodies, 1958–60, number on label inside guitar.*

| Number | Year |
|---|---|
| A-1000 | c. 1958 |
| A-2000 | c. 1959 |
| A-3000–4000 | c. 1960–early 1961 |

*Solidbodies, 1958–60, number inked onto back of headstock.*

| First digit | Year |
|---|---|
| 8 | 1958 |
| 9 | 1959 |
| 0 | 1960 |

*All models, 1960–69, number pressed into back of headstock.*

| Number | Year |
|---|---|
| 100–41199 | 1961 |
| 41200–61180 | 1962 |
| 61450–64222 | 1963 |
| 64240–70501 | 1964 |
| 71180–95846 | 1962 |
| 95849–99999 | 1963 |
| 000001–099999 | 1967 |
| 100000–106099 | 1963 or 1967 |
| 106100–108999 | 1963 |
| 109000–109999 | 1963 or 1967 |
| 110000–111549 | 1963 |
| 111550–115799 | 1963 or 1967 |
| 115800–118299 | 1963 |
| 118300–120999 | 1963 or 1967 |
| 121000–139999 | 1963 |
| 140000–140100 | 1963 or 1967 |
| 140101–144304 | 1963 |
| 144305–144380 | 1963 or 1964 |
| 144381–145000 | 1963 |
| 147001–149891 | 1963 or 1964 |
| 149892–152989 | 1963 |
| 152990–174222 | 1964 |
| 174223–179098 | 1964 or 1965 |
| 179099–199999 | 1964 |
| 200000–250199 | 1964 |
| 250540–290998 | 1965 |
| 300000–305999 | 1965 |
| 306000–306099 | 1965 or 1967 |
| 307000–307984 | 1965 |
| 309653–310999 | 1965 or 1967 |
| 311000–320149 | 1965 |
| 320150–320699 | 1967 |
| 320700–325999 | 1967 |
| 325000–326999 | 1965 or 1966 |
| 327000–329999 | 1965 |
| 330000–330999 | 1965 or 1967 or 1968 |
| 331000–346119 | 1965 |
| 346120–347099 | 1965 or 1966 |
| 348000–349100 | 1966 |
| 349101–368639 | 1965 |
| 368640–369890 | 1966 |
| 370000–370999 | 1967 |
| 380000–380999 | 1966–68 |
| 381000–385309 | 1966 |
| 390000–390998 | 1967 |
| 400001–400999 | 1965–68 |
| 401000–408699 | 1966 |
| 408800–409250 | 1966 or 1967 |
| 420000–438922 | 1966 |
| 500000–500999 | 1965–66 or 1968–69 |
| 501009–501600 | 1965 |
| 501601–501702 | 1968 |
| 501703–502706 | 1965 or 1968 |
| 503010–503109 | 1968 |
| 503405–520955 | 1965 or 1968 |
| 520956–530056 | 1968 |
| 530061–530850 | 1966 or 1968 or 1969 |
| 530851–530993 | 1968 or 1969 |
| 530994–539999 | 1969 |
| 540000–540795 | 1966 or 1969 |
| 540796–545009 | 1969 |
| 555000–556909 | 1966 |
| 558012–567400 | 1969 |
| 570099–570755 | 1966 |
| 580000–580999 | 1969 |
| 600000–600999 | 1966–69 |
| 601000–606090 | 1969 |
| 700000–700799 | 1966 or 1967 |
| 750000–750999 | 1968 or 1969 |
| 800000–800999 | 1966–69 |
| 801000–812838 | 1966 or 1969 |
| 812900–819999 | 1969 |
| 820000–820087 | 1966 or 1969 |
| 820088–823830 | 1966 |
| 824000–824999 | 1969 |
| 828002–847488 | 1966 or 1969 |
| 847499–858999 | 1966 or 1969 |
| 859001–895038 | 1967 |
| 895039–896999 | 1968 |
| 897000–898999 | 1967 or 1969 |
| 899000–972864 | 1968 |

## Japanese-made, 1970–83

*Numbers are unreliable during this period. Instruments can be roughly dated by their appearance in catalogs.*

## Korean-made, 1984–85

*The following series appear on guitars in 1984 and 1985. They may also appear on guitars from other years.*

| Number | Year | Type |
|---|---|---|
| K84000 | 1984 | flat-tops |
| K85000 | 1985 | flat-tops |
| 0800000 | 1985 | flat-tops |
| 0810000 | 1985 | flat-tops |
| 0910000 | 1985 | flat-tops |
| 1000 | 1985 | solidbodies |
| 4000000 | 1985 | electric hollowbodies |
| 4100000 | 1985 | electric hollowbodies |
| 5060000 | 1985 | solidbodies |
| 5080000 | 1985 | solidbodies |
| 5090000 | 1985 | electric hollowbodies |
| 5100000 | 1985 | solidbodies |

## American-made, 1990s

*Epiphones made in Gibson's Nashville or Montana factories follow standard Gibson serial number systems. The number will consist of eight digits. Except in 1994, the configuration is:*

YDDDYNNN
   YY is the year.
   DDD is the day of the year (001 to 366).
   NNN is the instrument's ranking for that day. Montana begins numbering at 101 each day; Nashville begins at 501.

*In 1994 and only in the Nashville plant, serial numbers have this configuration:*

YYNNNNNN
   YY is year (94).
   NNNNNN is the instrument's ranking for the entire year.

## Korean-made, 1993 onward

*The number following the initial letter denotes the year of manufacture.*

Example: S4061234 or S94061234
   S = manufacturer code
   4 or 94 = year (1994)
   06 = month (June)
   1234 = instrument ranking
Example: R95E1234
   95 = year

# *Acknowledgments*

One person with a box of old papers can organize a chronology of facts and call it a history, but it takes real people—many of them—to bring a story alive. The Epiphone story could not have been told without their kind help.

The flavor of the Epiphone family came from family members themselves. Epi's sister Elly Retsas offered her memories. Her daughter and son-in-law, Diane and Dom Cagianese, shared their knowledge, photographs, and hospitality. And their son Robert Cagianese contributed, among other things, his family's continuing passion for guitars.

The photographs from Frank Driggs' collection are a book unto themselves, and they put faces on the many musicians who have played Epiphones.

Thanks to the memories of guitar greats Tony Mottola, Al Caiola, Les Paul, and Harry Volpe, we get a taste of the atmosphere in the years when the guitar was an exciting new and emerging force in music.

Nick Skopelitis and Jimmy Archey of the Gibson/Epiphone office in New York located the many collectors and musicians who graciously allowed their Epiphones to be beautifully photographed by Anthony Stroppa. Michael Wright tapped his collection of 1970s Epi literature.

Author Jim Fisch filled in many facts from his own detailed research of pre-Gibson Epiphone history. And John Stoltzfus' memories painted the sad picture of Epiphone's last days as a family business.

Ted McCarty, John Huis, and Andy Nelson provided valuable insight into Epiphone's rebirth as a division of CMI/Gibson.

The Norlin years, from 1970 to 1985, were a dark age of information until Stan Rendell, Nort Stevens, Bruce Bolen, Bob Lynch, and Bill Nothdorft shed the light of their experiences on this era.

Tim Shaw provided an insider's view of Epiphone's emergence as a force in the international guitar market.

Even the most recent history would be obscure without the candid observations of David Berryman, Henry Juszkiewicz, and Jim Rosenberg.

Many heartfelt thanks to these and all the people who made the Epiphone story.

# INDEX